Thomas Rawson Birks

Supernatural Revelation

Or, first principles of moral theology

Thomas Rawson Birks

Supernatural Revelation
Or, first principles of moral theology

ISBN/EAN: 9783337418809

Printed in Europe, USA, Canada, Australia, Japan

Cover: Foto ©Lupo / pixelio.de

More available books at **www.hansebooks.com**

WORKS BY THE SAME AUTHOR.

1. FIRST PRINCIPLES OF MORAL SCIENCE; A First Course of Lectures delivered in the University of Cambridge. Crown 8vo. 8s. 6d.

2. MODERN UTILITARIANISM; or The Systems of Paley, Bentham, and Mill, examined and compared. Crown 8vo. 6s. 6d.

3. MODERN PHYSICAL FATALISM, and the Doctrine of Evolution, including an Examination of Mr Herbert Spencer's First Principles. Crown 8vo. 6s.

4. THE DIFFICULTIES OF BELIEF in connection with the Creation and the Fall, Redemption and Judgment. Second Edition, enlarged. Crown 8vo. 5s.

5. AN ESSAY ON THE RIGHT ESTIMATION OF MSS. EVIDENCE in the Text of the New Testament. Crown 8vo. 3s. 6d.

6. COMMENTARY ON THE BOOK OF ISAIAH. Second Edition, revised. 8vo. 12s. 6d.

MACMILLAN AND CO.

7. THE BIBLE AND MODERN THOUGHT.

8. THE EXODUS OF ISRAEL.

9. HORÆ APOSTOLICÆ.

RELIGIOUS TRACT SOCIETY.

10. THE WAYS OF GOD.

11. THE TREASURES OF WISDOM.

SEELEY, JACKSON & HALLIDAY.

12. SCRIPTURE DOCTRINE OF CREATION.

SOCIETY FOR PROMOTING CHRISTIAN KNOWLEDGE.

13. THE SACRAMENTS, SCIENCE AND PRAYER.

CHRISTIAN BOOK SOCIETY.

FIRST PRINCIPLES OF MORAL THEOLOGY.

BY THE

REV. T. R. BIRKS,

PROFESSOR OF MORAL THEOLOGY, CAMBRIDGE.

London:

MACMILLAN AND CO.

1879

[*The Right of Translation is reserved.*]

Cambridge:
PRINTED BY C. J. CLAY, M.A.
AT THE UNIVERSITY PRESS.

PREFACE.

FOR forty-two years I have had the great privilege
of unfolding and maintaining the great truths of the
word of God both by speech and writing, as a clergyman
of the English Church. For the future I expect to be
restricted chiefly to the second means alone. The obligation to maintain and unfold Christian truth through
the press is thus increased; especially since I hold the
office of Professor of Moral Theology and Moral Philosophy in the University of Bacon, Newton, and Milton.
Attacks have been made and are still in progress on
Christianity and on all the foundations of our Christian
empire, by three allied systems of error—Ultramontan-
ism, Agnosticism, or Secularism, and the Liberationism,
which would banish the name of Christ from the whole
world of politics. At such a time, I would earnestly
counsel the younger clergy, and the moral instructors
of the next generation, lay or clerical, to lay to heart
the charge of St Paul, just before his martyrdom, to
Timothy, his son and companion in the faith. That

caution applies with equal force to the varieties of
unbelieving thought in our days, as to the Gnosticism
of the first century. "O Timothy, keep that which is
committed to thy trust, avoiding profane and vain babblings, and oppositions of science falsely so called, which
some professing have erred concerning the faith."

What "babblings" can be more "profane and vain"
than those of Positivism with its "new Supreme Being;"
or of Agnosticism, which places an algebraical x, THE
UNKNOWABLE, on the throne of the universe? What
can be more falsely named science than the audacious
conjectures which have been of late repeatedly dignified
with the name of scientific theories? Such as the constant generation of the unlike from the unlike, through
infinite ages of geological time, before there existed
a single man who could witness this prodigious inversion of the countless experiences of all real science for
the last six thousand years?

One great duty of Cambridge at this crisis, is in
the study of nature to abide stedfastly by the inductive principles of the philosophy of Bacon and Newton,
so well carried out by many Cambridge students of
these later times. But this implies the further duty to
refrain from that unbridled license of imagination in
scientific subjects, which leads many to dignify plausible
or even unplausible conjectures with the name of science.
Conjectures in science have a great use, but this depends
on our never confounding them with proved facts.

Their magnitude to the senses of casual observers, like
that of the tails of comets, is sometimes in inverse propor-

tion to their solid mass. Yet even when their solid substance is small and almost evanescent, it is often possible that by their means, when carefully examined, weighty scientific conclusions may be attained.

A second great duty is to apply this same principle of careful and inductive search to the study of the sacred Scriptures. The word of God will else be overlaid with ambiguities, uncertainties, and partial misconceptions, human traditions, distortions and corruptions of its genuine meaning, which not only obscure its heavenly brightness, but are liable to become a great encouragement to the assaults of open unbelief.

There is scarcely any revealed limit to the apprehension of the beauty, truth and harmony of the Holy Scriptures which may be attained by those who study them with prayer, humility and perseverance, not as if they were isolated and accidental compositions, but as one comprehensive whole. The neglect of such study by too many Christians, is one great cause of the many controversies by which the church has been disfigured, and its peace and unity disturbed. There is a promise in the word of God, not only of the increase of natural knowledge in the last days, but of the increase of spiritual knowledge also. In the great day of the Lord, "at eventide there will be light." "Then shall we know if we follow on to know the Lord." "The path of the just is as a shining light, that shineth more and more unto the perfect day."

May the University of Cambridge, by this double work, the inductive study of all nature, and the induc-

viii

tive and persevering study of all Scripture, fulfil in fuller and still fuller measure its true office and calling, as a seminary both of sound learning and religious education.

The present work, while endeavouring to clear away some of the mists of unbelieving philosophy, is intended, if life be spared, to be followed by others, in which I would attempt, in reliance on the promised help of the Holy Spirit, to unfold some of the manifold harmonies of truth in the sacred Scriptures, the "lively oracles" of the Living God.

CAMBRIDGE,
    February, 1879.

CONTENTS.

CHAPTER I.

INTRODUCTORY. THE SCEPTICAL STARTING-POINT.

CHAPTER II.

THE AUTHOR'S STATEMENT OF THE OBJECT OF HIS WORK.

CHAPTER III.

PROTESTANT FAITH IN CONTRAST WITH FREE-THINKING.

CHAPTER IV.

REASON AND SUPERNATURAL REVELATION.

CHAPTER V.

REASON AND THE CHRISTIAN REVELATION.

CHAPTER VI.

The Perfection of Nature, and Four Mock Deities of Scepticism.

CHAPTER VII.

Mr Spencer's Three Theories of the Universe.

CHAPTER VIII.

Nature without Man or God.

CHAPTER XII.

THE THREEFOLD INCONSTANCY OF TERRESTRIAL NATURE.

CHAPTER XIII.

THE WITNESS OF ALL NATURE TO THE BEING AND PERFECTIONS OF GOD.

CHAPTER XIV.

THE CENTRIFUGAL AND CENTRIPETAL TENDENCIES OF MODERN SCIENCE.

CHAPTER XV.

THREE HEADLESS PHILOSOPHIES.

CHAPTER XVI.

THE FOUR MAXIMS OF MODERN NATURE-WORSHIP.

CHAPTER XVII.

THE ATTEMPT TO REVIVE HUME'S ARGUMENT.

CHAPTER XVIII.

THE LAW OF GOD, AND THE CREATED UNIVERSE.

CHAPTER XXIII.

THE ANTAGONISM BETWEEN CHRISTIAN FAITH AND SCIENCE "FALSELY SO CALLED" IN THE LAST DAYS.

CHAPTER XXIV.

THE REVELATION IN THE OLD AND NEW TESTAMENTS ONE HARMONIOUS WHOLE.

ERRATA.

Page 17, line 4, *for* centripetal *read* centrifugal
 ,, 94, ,, 8, ,, more ,, some

SUPERNATURAL REVELATION,

OR

FIRST PRINCIPLES OF MORAL THEOLOGY.

INTRODUCTORY CHAPTER.

THE SCEPTICAL STARTING-POINT.

THE anonymous work named "Supernatural Religion" has attained sudden notoriety within the last few years, and flashed like a lurid meteor across the theological firmament. It is a formal challenge to all believers in the old and everlasting Gospel to give a reason of the faith that is in them. The writer complains that Dr Lightfoot and Dr Westcott have not touched his main thesis and central argument, but have turned aside to a secondary issue as to the Ignatian Epistles. I intend, in this work, to take up the main issue alone, though if life be spared I shall hope to resume, with the added light of thirty years' further study, the subject treated in "Horae Evangelicae," and to place in a still clearer light the concurrence of external and internal evidence for the truth, authenticity, and Divine authority of the four Gospels.

B. 1.

For thirty years I have been mainly engaged, in
more than twelve works, in labouring to vindicate the
truth and authority of the Scriptures and the Gospel
of Christ, against several of the persevering attacks to
which they have been exposed, both from open unbelievers and halting or timorous half-believers, whose
groundless surrenders of the truth of God are sometimes more dangerous than the assaults of its open
opposers.   The works against which I have especially
contended are (1) Strauss's " Life of Jesus," with its
mythical theory of the Gospels.   (2) The assault on
the authenticity of the Books of Moses by Bishop
Colenso and the German critics whom he has followed.
(3) The " Seven Essays and Reviews," with their
varied attacks on the fundamentals of Christianity.
(4) The " First Principles," of Mr. Herbert Spencer,
and the Bampton Lectures on " The Limits of Religious
Thought," with their common theory which makes all
genuine revelation strictly impossible.   (5) In my " Commentary on Isaiah," I have replied to the attack of
Dr Davidson and the German sceptical critics on the
authenticity of that Book.

The present century, following close on the short-
lived infidel outbreak of the French Revolution, has been
marked through its whole course by a series of earnest
attacks on revealed religion, and the very foundations
of morality and religious faith, by a series of writers
of reputation and ability.   Besides an immense mass
of loose and popular writing in the cause of scepticism,
there have been many leading schools of unbelieving
thought, each with a multitude of attached and credulous
followers, but distinct from, and even opposed to each
other, agreeing in little else than a rejection of the
Bible, and the Gospel of Christ, and faith in the God
of the Bible, whom some of them style " the wrathful

Jehovah of the Old Testament." An exhaustive list would be impossible, for the varied forms of unbelief, like the heads of a Hydra, are intertwined with each other, and agree in little else than a common antipathy to the truth of God's Word. The following are some of the chief divisions of the embattled array. (1) The destructive criticism of Germany, aimed against the authenticity and truth of the Old Testament Scriptures, beginning with Strauss's "Life of Jesus," and the work of Renan, followed in our country by the writings of Bishop Colenso, and a multitude of similar works. (2) The assaults on the historical truth and authenticity of the Gospels, forming the mythical School of modern German criticism. (3) The Positive Philosophy of M. Comte, with its double rejection of Metaphysics and Theology, as superstitions of the infancy and youth of mankind, and its fictitious law of human progress culminating in the rejection of the living God, as a dream of superstition, to be replaced by a new religion, and a "new Supreme Being," the worship of Collective Humanity; a kind of earnest of the last manifestation of that "Man of Sin" who will "seat himself in the temple of God," averring that he is God. (4) A fourth variety of unbelief is the agnostic philosophy of Mr Spencer, summed up in this one statement; that Pantheism, Atheism and Theism—meaning by the last faith in a personal God—are three equally futile attempts to solve the great problem of the universe, with the added axiom that the unknown cause of the universe is, and must ever remain, completely inscrutable. (5) This Cimmerian creed of midnight darkness receives a further supplement. Its author propounds to us a new Trinity of Matter, Force, and Motion, each alike indestructible. This supplement of the agnostic theory is an apotheosis of solar force, embodying itself in the

monstrous paradox that force and motion are indestructible, but that the sun, which is their great source,
is being steadily exhausted by his own activity, and his
diffusion of light and heat, so that all motion is con-
stantly tending to equilibration and rest, and the universe, under its new Divinity, tending steadily to the
reign of Omnipresent Death. (6) A sixth form of
unbelief is the elastic materialism of Dr Tyndall in
his Belfast Address, who thinks that modern science
binds fast all nature in the bonds of fate, and that
matter contains in itself the promise and potency of
every kind of life. (7) A seventh is what may be
called the negative materialism of Mr Mill, and his
sensational philosophy; he denies that matter exists at
all, but allows us to speak of minds as if they did exist,
though strict philosophy would lead to the nihilism
which denies both mind and matter, and replaces both
by "permanent possibilities of sensation." (8) The
doctrine of Evolution, and Natural Selection, as held
by Mr Darwin and his disciples, which fills up by conjecture the intervals between a hundred thousand existing or extinct species of plants and animals by a thousand times the number, or ten thousand thousand
intermediate varieties or types of being, which must
have existed if the theory be true, and have passed
utterly away without leaving a trace of their existence
either among the fossils or the actual flora and fauna.
This gigantic mass of conjecture, when supplemented
by the doctrine of natural selection, or survival of the
fittest, or by millions of millions of acts of choice where
there is no one to choose, and the survival of millions
of millions of organisms, on the ground of their superior
fitness to accomplish some wholly unconceived end or
purpose of the great scheme of the universe; this
pyramid of pure conjecture, of telescopic magnitude,

resting on a microscopic apex of ascertained and certain fact, is gravely propounded even by some Divines, as the latest revelation of God to man, to which all our other beliefs, whether drawn from the Bible or genuine science, must be made subordinate.   (9) The direct and simple Atheism or Monism of Professor Haeckel is another variety.   (10) A tenth, and perhaps least remote from Christian faith, is the new Manicheism of Mr Mill in his posthumous Essays; a kind of half-way house in a progress from the outer darkness of utter atheism to the dubious light on the verge and outskirts of morality and religion.   In various works I have examined at length several of these main varieties of sceptical thought, and shewn the great amount of error and self-contradiction which they contain.   I shall now confine myself to two of the latest; the anti-super-naturalism of "Supernatural Religion;" and Mr Mill's posthumous Essays: the parting contribution to this great inquiry of one of the ablest and, as I think, the most candid and truth-seeking of the leaders of modern scepticism, whose early training makes regret and pity almost forbid indignation even at those con-clusions which are most abhorrent to the instincts of Christian faith.

The danger to the faith from these many forms of modern sceptical thought is somewhat lessened by their internal strife and antagonism.   The hosts of unbelief resemble the camp of Agramant in Ariosto, when discord had been sent by the archangel to hinder their threatened attack on the Christian host by stirring up strife among the Moorish paladins, and succeeded so well that a mortal feud ensued between each separate pair of the Paynim leaders, and these were followed by secondary quarrels which pair should have the first turn in the bloody tournament by which their strife was to be decided.   There is here the same kind of conflict, but one still more strange, for each school of infidel philosophy includes some essential contradiction, by which it is at hopeless variance with itself, and a lateral feud by which it is in hopeless rivalry with each of its neighbours.   How refreshing it is to escape from this dark and dreary chaos of human error and contradiction, to the sacred confines of those true sayings of God, where chaos first retires, and the ceaseless strife of human error and falsehood is replaced by the dawning of light from the eternal source and fountain of light.

The work I now propose to examine has a direct bearing on the aim and purpose of the Knightbridge Professorship.   During the six years I have held that office, I have published three volumes directly on Moral Science, but none hitherto on Moral Theology.   The work in question contains a thousand pages devoted to the task of proving supernatural revelation impossible or incredible, and Christianity, in claiming to convey a message from God to sinful men, a gigantic fraud wholly unworthy the faith of rational beings.   No more audacious Goliath has ever stood forth to challenge and defy the armies of the living God.   One hundred pages are occupied with an attempt to prove that the claim of Christianity is to be a supernatural revelation founded on miraculous evidence, and itself miraculous, but that all miracles are impossible and incredible; a hundred pages more are employed in defaming the Apostles and first Christians, as a set of credulous simpletons steeped to the neck in Jewish prejudices, credulity and childish superstition.

This accusation against the witnesses chosen before by God for the transmission of His message, is supported by laying to their charge all the follies and fables in the rabbinical writings, and in the forgeries of the

Apocryphal Books, wholly overlooking the charge which St Paul has given against "giving heed to Jewish fables." Tit. i. 13, 14. The other eight hundred pages are spent in an attempt to prove that the four Gospels themselves have no evidence of their existence before the end of the second century, and are therefore forgeries by unknown parties, which gained acceptance afterwards in the church without any solid reason, as the writings of two of the Apostles, and two companions of the Apostles. The manner of dealing with the mass of evidence, in the three first centuries, of their public acceptance by all the churches of Christ as inspired Scripture, is the very same by which some geologists suppose that our present continents are being carted away, grain by grain, by sub-aerial denudation, till they may come to be buried at length in the depth of the ocean ; but on this part of the subject I do not now enter. The first hundred pages alone, on which the whole argument rests, will afford ample materials for inquiry, analysis and refutation. The writer complains that his critics have dealt only with a side issue, but had he really been seeking for truth, as he professes, he would have found in Dr Westcott's "Gospel of the Resurrection" much truth that bears directly on the main issue, and a virtual reply to the greater part of his argument.

THE DUTY OF INQUIRY.

In a work where the unbelief is so deep and all-pervading it is needful to pause at the outset, and dig down to find if possible some first principle from which our reasoning may proceed, that we may not fight in utter darkness. Such a principle I find in the caustic

censure of the Introduction, on the inconsistent half-
faith of many Christians, who strive

"with thoughtless dexterity to eliminate from Christianity every supernatural element which does not quite accord with current opinion;
...they ignore the fact that, in so doing, ecclesiastical Christianity
has been altogether abandoned." "This tendency is fostered with
profoundly illogical zeal by many distinguished men within the church
itself, who endeavour to arrest for a moment the pursuing wolves of
doubt and unbelief by practically throwing to them, scrap by scrap,
the very doctrines which constitute the claims of Christianity to be
regarded as a Divine revelation...They abandon some of the most
central doctrines of Christianity, and try to spiritualize or dilute the
rest into a form which does not shock their reason; yet they cling to
the delusion that they still retain the consolation and hope of truths
which, if not divinely revealed, are mere speculation regarding matters
beyond reason. They have in fact as little warrant to abandon the
one part as they have to retain the other; they build their house on the
sand, and the waves which have already carried away so much may any
day engulph the rest." S. R. Introduction, pp. xcii. xciii.

These remarks are clear, forcible and true, like a streak
of morning light in contrast to the thick moral darkness which marks the rest of the book, from its beginning to its close. If Christianity is a message from
God to men, guaranteed by works of supernatural power
and prophecies of superhuman wisdom, it is plainly
foolish to concede that we are at liberty to choose out
scraps and fragments of the message at our own pleasure,
and can retain our faith in those which fall in with our
wishes or tastes, while we reject all the rest. This arbitrary separation into two parts of a message which
has been attested as a whole, exposes those who practise
it to the charge of irrational superstition in what they
retain, on evidence which the very separation would
prove worthless, or else of profaneness and unbelief as
to the parts which they reject.

The one positive principle here implied is the duty

of adequate inquiry into the truth of any statement of serious importance before believing it.

"This," the writer says, "is universally admitted in theory, but in practice no duty is more universally neglected, especially in regard to religion." He continues, "Neglect of examination can never advance truth, as the severest scrutiny can never retard it. Belief without discrimination can only foster ignorance and superstition. It is in this conviction that the following enquiry into the reality of divine revelation was originally undertaken, and that others should enter upon it. . If truth acquired do not compensate for every illusion dispelled, the path is thorny indeed, but must be faithfully trodden." Pp. xci. xcviii.

Here then, amidst abysses of sceptical thought, we have something like a first principle—man is a moral being; he has duties and obligations he is bound to fulfil: one of these is to search after truth; another implied duty is to reject all detected falsehood. There is a person whom the writer calls "the great teacher," and who calls himself "The Truth." Now the aim of the work, pursued through a thousand pages, is to prove that this "great teacher" ought rather to be styled by the opposite name, which He applies to the great source of all evil, "the father of lies;" inasmuch as by false claims to a nature He did not possess, and to a commission He had not received, He has been really the parent and author of the most extensive and prevalent fraud on the credulity of mankind, which has ever been practised since the beginning of time, when we take into account the number of those who have been thus deceived, and their intellectual eminence; so that the history of mankind for 1800 years will have been turned into a gigantic mass of credulity, deception and falsehood. Thus the duty of inquiry after truth in the abstract is made the starting-point for the most extensive and thoroughgoing rejection of concrete truth, and the most complete reversal, in reality, of the duty which is professedly the

mainspring of the whole inquiry, which it is possible to
conceive. Let us examine this first principle a little
more closely. Is this duty of inquiry one without any
limit? The duty of seeking for unknown truth must
imply the prior duty of holding fast some truth already
known; but the duty of searching for unknown truth
and holding fast known truth both involve the same
condition, a power to discriminate between truth and
falsehood; both in the case of known and unknown truth,
the duty to hold fast and to acquire implies two things,
a faculty of discernment by which we may distinguish
truth from falsehood, and a capacity of growth, by
which we may enlarge the sphere of our knowledge,
and contract the range of our ignorance. Thus, the
first principle, when developed, implies three great
germinant principles—(1) That man is a moral creature,
subject to a law of duty, and bound to use aright the
faculties of discernment and investigation that God has
given. (2) That he is a knowing or intelligent creature,
who is capable of discriminating truth from falsehood.
(3) That he is a creature capable of indefinite progress,
of adding to his treasury of known truth, and of
detecting falsehood and separating it as dross from the
truth with which it had been mingled. What are the
conditions then under which the duty of inquiring after
truth in religion can alone take effect? The truths to
be inquired into are the existence, the character and
attributes of the first Great Cause, the vast scheme of
universal Providence, and our own place in connection
with it, whether of hope of good to come, or fear of
future evil, or of duties and obligations towards God,
our fellow-men and ourselves.

There can be no duty in the case of one who is blind
to attempt to trace out all the mazy pathways and
jungles of that infinite forest—the universe. The duty

of inquiry can belong only to a moral being who has not put out the eyes of his own soul, or had them blinded by sensuality and vice, who has some firm standing for his feet upon clear and definite truth, and something like a pathway open before him in which progress is possible.   These conditions are all expressly taught us by "the great Teacher" who is the Truth. "The light of the body is the eye : if thine eye be single, thy whole body shall be full of light." "While ye have light, walk in the light, that ye may be children of light." "He that walketh in darkness knoweth not whither he goeth."

REAL AND FICTITIOUS INQUIRY AFTER TRUTH.

The duty of inquiry or search after religious truth, or truth of any kind, is one of three connected duties which cannot be sundered from each other. (1) The first is the duty to retain and hold fast truth already known. (2) The second is to discriminate that truth from adherent falsehood, to reject all that is false and untrue, as well as to retain the true. (3) The third is to seek for the knowledge of truths before unknown. The first is the protection against indefinite instability and change, in which the master passion is the love of novelty and not the love of truth ; the second is the protection against indefinite credulity, building up a heterogeneous compound of truth and falsehood ; the third is the antidote to moral and intellectual stagnation. Wherever there is life there must be growth ; the only condition under which truth which we have, can be retained as a real possession, is that of seeking to add to it by the accession of further truth. "The well-spring of wisdom is as a flowing brook," and he who holds partial truth without seeking to add to it, changes the flowing brook into a stagnant marsh, liable to be covered with a thick slime of superstitious folly, and to breed by its stagnation a moral pestilence. Whately says : " It makes all the difference in the world whether we place truth in the first place or in the second place ;" but our author, in quoting this caution, has committed the very fault against which it warns us.

Sir William Hamilton has said (after Lessing), that if any one offered him truth with one hand, and inquiry after truth with the other, he would prefer the second. By this one remark he forfeits his claim to the title of a philosopher, and proclaims himself a mere philo-athlete : a lover of intellectual exercise rather than a lover of truth and wisdom. It is not surprising that such a starting-point should lead to no better issue than St Paul has described in his last Epistle, of those who are "ever learning and never able to come to a knowledge of the truth," and whom Cowper has pithily described as " Dropping buckets into empty wells, and growing old in drawing nothing up." What are the three prominent features of this famous writer, I cannot call him a philosopher after his own confession, though he has had a large school of admiring disciples ? The first is a malignant attack on the moral character of the leading heroes of the great Reformation, which brought upon him the keen and indignant rebuke of Archdeacon Hare. The second is a persistent and bitter depreciation of Cambridge University, the parent and nurse of the greatest intellectual names of modern times. The third is a like depreciation of mathematical study, the only field of thought where pure, certain, and demonstrable truth is widely accessible to men, without the help of Divine revelation, and their previous extrication, at least in part, from the deflecting power of moral evil within.

What have been the practical fruits of this preference of the intellectual hunting-field to truth itself, of this contempt for the chosen instruments of the Spirit of God in the great work of extricating the church from its Babylonian captivity to superstition, and of the University of Bacon, Newton, Barrow, Hooker, Joseph Mede, Thomas More and Cudworth? this contempt of that one field of thought where even in a world in which the higher regions of truth have all been obscured and clouded by the prevalence of moral evil, clear and certain truth has been and is still attained through successive generations of mankind, from Euclid onward, till it has become a stately and imposing structure, the basis of all concrete physical science and also an earnest and pledge that truth and assured certainty are attainable when sought in due order, and under the needful moral conditions, in the higher fields of Ethical Science, Theology, and that Knowledge of the Most Holy, which is the truest and highest wisdom? What have been the practical fruits of this pretentious "philosophy of the unconditioned[1]?" The only results I know of are first, a principle which makes all real revelation of Himself by the true God to finite creatures strictly impossible, and fixes a great gulf across which no ray of real light can pass between the most Holy God and the whole world of His creatures; secondly, an exposition of one word in the inscription on the Athenian altar, which contradicts the whole passage where it occurs and the discourse of St Paul himself, based upon it. A third result is a tissue of contradictions with regard to the Absolute, the Infinite and the Unknowable, made up of the wildest chimeras that ever passed through the brain of man. That the Unknowable may be defined as a genus containing two species, the Absolute and the Infinite; that all the Know-

[1] See "Scripture Doctrine of Creation."

able lies as a mean between them; that reason teaches
that one of these two extremes must exist, and leaves it
uncertain which, so that one of the two must be a synonym
for the only true God, and the other denote an impossible
mental fiction; but that which of the two is a name of
a worthless and impossible fiction, and which a synonym
of the God of glory, the great and eternal Jehovah, must
remain for ever unknown. A fourth and last result,
is the logical invention of the quantification of the
predicate. The author's contempt for mathematics has
here avenged itself by leading him to corrupt his own
favourite science, with a strange addition, which would
put every process of reasoning into masquerade, en-
cumbering every statement of known truth with an
added alternative of something wholly unknown. The
real process of reasoning is thus confused and obscured.
Thus, if I say 'All philosophers are wise'—this known
truth has for its shadowy attendant this alternative, either
' Philosophers are the only wise beings'—or, ' There are
some other wise beings besides them.' Or again, the
truth 'All men are mortal'—has the attendant shadow,
either, ' Men are the only mortal existences,' or, ' There
are some other mortal things besides.' The "quantification of the predicate" requires us, in all our reasoning,
to cut the living child in two, and suspend the two
halves on the horns of this dilemma. A more retrogade
step from clear reasoning into confusion and mental
darkness, was never taken than in Sir W. Hamilton's
pseudo-mathematical improvement on the Logic of
Aristotle. While such have been the negative results
of Sir W. Hamilton's preference of intellectual gym-
nastics to truth itself, what fruits have accrued from
the study he loads with contempt in the University
which he has followed with persistent calumny? It
has extended the boundaries of the Solar system nearly

to twice its former range, by the conjoint labours of
two of its Professors, one in the way of direct observation, and the other of mathematical reasoning and
analysis : the triumph is shared indeed with Berlin and
Paris, two other great centres of mathematical study and
experimental science. It has solved, by another mathe-
matician, the mysterious problem of the rings of Saturn,
near the former verge of the system. It has provided
at the head of our national Observatory, one who by
his double skill as an analyst and a practical observer,
has kept our country in the van of modern progress
in physical science, and to whom has been committed,
by European consent, the treatment of the latest transit
observations, to obtain from them the most probable esti-
mates of the actual magnitudes and distances of the Sun
and all the constituents of the Solar system. It has
popularized by him the results of the mathematical
reasoning of another eminent French analyst, and by
one of its own Professors has added to them fresh discoveries, thus perfecting our knowledge of that agent
which forms the first step in the Divine record of
creation, and which is now becoming an instrument of
unexpected discoveries with regard to the motions,
the changes, and chemical constituents of the most distant
stars and of the mighty Sun himself. Such opposite
results naturally follow from the two opposite principles:
the love and pursuit of truth itself, and a professed
preference for mere intellectual gladiatorship. In that
arena the swordsman of to-day often falls by his own
weapon, and oftener still is the Retiarius of the morrow,
and falls at last ignominiously entangled in the meshes
of his own or his rival's metaphysical abstractions. In
the present case, the misfortune is that the Scotch
gladiator has found disciples among English divines,
who have striven to fling the net of these abstractions

over the whole range of Christian theology. Sir W.
Hamilton, though himself personally a Christian believer,
has thus, through his English disciple, provided a logical
pedestal for the most comprehensive and audacious
system of antichristian speculation which our age has
witnessed.

Inquiry after truth has two different forms, which
bear a close analogy to the Newtonian doctrine of central forces, and the exploded Cartesian theory of vortices
or celestial whirlpools. The first of these explains the
planetary motions by central forces tending towards the
Sun, and the other by centrifugal forces in imaginary
revolving whirlpools of unformed matter, tending to carry
planets outward to the farthest verge of the system;
so, when with a small stock of known truth we begin
an inquiry after all that is unknown, there are two
opposite ways in which that inquiry may be carried on.
The first is to begin with what we know, the certainties
already attained; to dwell upon them in thought till
their light becomes clearer and more distinct; to develope their internal relations from the centre outward till
at the further edge they may begin to win a little on the
surrounding darkness, and the "sacred influence of light
shoots into the bosom of dim night a glimmering dawn."
For light is like life and has a generative power, "that
which maketh manifest is light." Partial truth carefully
and reverently studied tends, however slowly, to enlarge
its own domain. The kingdom of light and knowledge
is like that of a civilized empire, which, surrounded
by the kingdom of darkness, like a host of barbarous
and ever-conflicting tribes, by its unity and compacted
strength tends, even without any sinful ambition, to enlarge its own borders and annex some outlying districts
to its domain. There is an opposite course which may

be pursued under the deceptive title of inquiry into religious truth. It is that which neglects the modicum of
moral and religious truth already known, because it is
so small, and plunges itself at once with a centripetal
instinct into the vast and shoreless regions of the unknown. Such is the course pursued by the author of
" Supernatural Religion." His knowledge at the outset,
the definite truth firmly and clearly held, is so small as
to approach to utter nescience. The few grains of truth
which he admits are nowhere plainly stated, but have
to be culled out with care from indirect and accidental
admissions. On the other hand, he launches at once
into the deepest abysses and mysteries of God's Providence, and of the statements of Scripture, and the super-
structures of theological systems, and the whole range
of Talmudical literature, the apocryphal forgeries of the
first and second centuries, and the patristic literature of
the three first centuries. A slighter skiff and more
feebly manned never undertook to cross the Atlantic
Ocean: it is no wonder that the result should be an
entire shipwreck of what little faith he ever possessed.
But the effect is more mournful still, a deliberate and
prolonged effort to extinguish God's own lighthouse,
the one Pharos lighted by Him who is " the dayspring
from on high...to give light to those who are sitting
in darkness," to the myriads of voyagers across the
dark and troublous waves of this mortal life, and to
guide their steps to a haven of peace and light. The
guilt of one single murder, which shortens the span
of one little life, seems trivial compared with the guilt
of this prolonged effort, under the pretext of fulfilling
the duty of religious inquiry, to reverse and annul the
greatest gift of Divine goodness to a dark and sin-
disordered world; and, after the true Light has dawned,
to shut up the present and all future generations of man-

kind in Stygian darkness for evermore. Before any
statement of what little truth he does hold or believe,
he plunges at once into an attempted summary of the
contents of the Bible and of the Christian faith, made
up by selecting those elements which he thinks the most
unreasonable and incredible, and completing them with
gross misrepresentations of his own, and proceeds to
build up a kind of panoply of darkness from the in-
accurate statements or the conflicting views with regard
to the truths of revelation, and the evidence upon which
it rests, of a dozen divines of four or five diverging
types of thought or schools of theology.   It is not surprising, in such a mode of inquiry, that instead of light
winning upon the darkness, moral and intellectual confusion win upon the scanty modicum of known or recognized truth with which the voyage of discovery began.
To call such a process a fulfilment of the duty of
adequate inquiry into the truth of supernatural religion
is to confound opposites.   It is rather like what I have
called elsewhere—"a dip into chaos in order to guess
out the nature of the coming world."

There are three elements which seem to make up the
modicum of faith or unbelief with which the anonymous
author sets out on his inquiry.   He combines the features of the ancient Jewish Sadducee and the modern
Gentile agnostic or negative atheist.   To these two
first principles of his negative creed he adds a third,
the predicted doctrine of the scoffers of the last times,
the unalterable and necessary constancy of the laws or
forces of Nature, as incapable of any interruption from
any source whatever.   He does not believe in angel,
demon or spirit of any kind, or in a resurrection, or a
life to come, or in a Personal God, or in anything but

the unalterable continuance of things seen and temporal, the world as limited by the experience of men between the cradle and the grave for the last 2000 years ; the Non-existence of God and the Omnipotence of Death. With such a starting-point he can hardly be left in deeper darkness at the end of his crusade against Christianity than he was in at its commencement. His creed as a Sadducee may be seen in the 150 pages, chh. III.—VI., which he devotes to the task of defaming the Apostles and the first Christians as wholly incompetent witnesses to the leading facts of the Gospel history. His proof of this incompetence of the Apostles as witnesses is, in one word, that they were not Sadducees, and did believe in the resurrection of the dead, and in the existence of angels and demons. He ascribes to them, on this negative ground, all the superstitions which he can find in the Book of Tobit, the Book of Enoch, and the Jewish Talmud and Targums, and completes the list with various theories with regard to the stars, demons, and magic, to be found in the writings of the Fathers. The Apostles and first disciples are credited at once, because they were not Sadducees, with the whole farrago of Jewish fables and superstitions in these apocryphal books or Targums. On this sole ground, that the Apostles were not Sadducees, and did believe that the resurrection of the dead was possible by the power of God, he sets them down as witnesses wholly incompetent to report whether they had seen, and conversed and eaten and drunk with the Lord forty days after His crucifixion. Because they had more faith in the express words of the Lord of glory, and in their own experience when they returned from their first mission, " Lord, even the spirits are subject unto us through Thy name," than in the creed of the ancient or modern Sadducee, we are told there is every reason for

2—2

"Concluding with certainty that their ignorance of natural laws, their proneness to superstition, their love of the marvellous, and their extreme religious excitement" would make them utterly untrustworthy, "and peculiarly liable to incorrectness in their observation of phenomena, and to error in the inferences drawn from them." P. 92.

He quotes from Dean Milman and the elder Lightfoot to prove that "the nation of the Jews were given to magical arts beyond measure, and to an easiness of believing all manner of delusions, and that it is disputable whether the nation were more mad with superstition in matters of religion, or with superstition in curious arts." The whole mass of opinions in the Talmud, in later Christian forgeries like the Book of Enoch, and the writings of the early Fathers, the fable of the Phœnix, and the remarks of Lactantius on the Antipodes, are shoaled together to convict the Apostles and first disciples of gross superstition and extreme credulity, though there is no proof or sign whatever of their sharing in those superstitious follies, and they have even given us an express warning against them. The author, while he charges the whole Christian Church and Christ Himself, his own future Judge, with gross superstition, because of their belief in angels, spirits and demons, seems not aware that in that very act he convicts himself of the worst extreme of presumption. His little knowledge, being limited to the experience of a few hundred years on the surface of one little planet, he dogmatizes with regard to the whole range of the universe as if he were omniscient, and treats what lies beyond the petty range of his own experience as if it were non-existent, and as if to believe anything on the very highest authority, beyond that limit, were gross and culpable credulity.

The writer's spiritual parentage is not that of the old Jewish Sadducee alone, but of a modern Gentile

Agnostic. He borrows from modern Christian divines these maxims—that the Being of God as a personal conscious Agent is a pure assumption without any evidence, and that nature bears no witness to the existence of an Omnipotent Supreme Being, and thus that the whole evidence of revelation is a vicious circle left suspended in space, revelation resting on miracles, and miracles resting on revelation. For this view he quotes Dr Mozley's Bampton Lectures. He says that Butler, Paley and all other Divines have equally been obliged to commence with the same assumption. He praises the candour of Dr Mozley, for honestly admitting the difficulty of the case. He adds that the

"Conception of the Deity proposed by theologians must be pronounced irrational and derogatory to the wisdom and perfections which we recognize in the invariable course of nature."

He adopts the doctrine from Dean Mansel and Sir W. Hamilton that

"The class of phenomena which requires that kind of cause we denominate a Deity is exclusively given in the phenomena of mind, and that the phenomena of matter taken by themselves do not warrant any inference as to the existence of a God."

He adds from Spinoza that

"Miracles, as contrary to the order of nature, should rather lead us to doubt the existence of God."

His final conclusion is that

"Both the supernatural religion and its supernatural evidence labour in common under the fatal disability of being antecedently incredible."

He borrows further from Dr Irons the rule that

"We are not bound to believe in any miracle related in the Old Testament which has not been confirmed by the direct reference to it of Jesus. The doctor abandons altogether the popular theory that the Bible and the doctrines supposed to be derived from it can be established by literary evidence; thus cutting away all solid ground, he attempts to stand upon nothing in the shape of the *vague feeling*

that the records are supernatural." "His admissions," the writer
continues, "as to the insufficiency of the evidence are creditable to
his honesty as a scholar, but his conclusion is simply lame and impotent!" "This he denies to be an admission to which he is reluc-
tantly driven, and explains it as a vindication of the only possible
grounds on which revelation can rest." Pp. 65, 66. The writer adds
the comment, "After shewing revelation to be wholly unsupported
by anything worthy of the name of evidence, he affirms the religion
and the book to be supernatural because he *feels* they are so. No
one who does not feel as he does receives much help from the theory
of Dr Irons."

With such lamentable surrenders of the cause of Christ,
the Gospel, and the Bible, on the part of their professed
champions and defenders, can it be surprising that infidelity should advance with rapid and gigantic strides?
This Agnostic theory, borrowed from the Hamiltonian
metaphysics, then taken up by Dean Mansel, and transferred from both to the pages of Herbert Spencer, to
form an adequate logical basis for a massive pyramid
of utter unbelief, is then made the ground of a system
of thought the most antithetic to the whole range of
religion, natural and revealed, which has ever appeared.
And accepted in patches, and shreds, even by many who
have shrunk from the doctrine of utter darkness to
which it logically tends, it has spread like a thick and
blighting fog over the whole range of Christian theology.

The thesis of "Supernatural Religion" as a whole may
be summed up in these four propositions. (1) That Christianity as a supernatural revelation consists of a series of
doctrines which are antecedently incredible, and contrary
to reason. He gives a summary of them in four pages to
prove this indictment. (2) That the miracles or supernatural facts by which it is alleged to be proved are themselves unreal and impossible, and of such antecedent in-
credibility as hardly any conceivable amount of evidence
could overcome. (3) That the Apostles and the first

Christians are among the most incompetent of witnesses, as belonging to an age and nation peculiarly credulous, ignorant of natural laws and steeped in the grossest superstition.   (4) That in the New Testament we have not even the testimony of these incompetent witnesses ; that the Gospels are unauthentic memoirs, of the existence of which before the close of the second century there is no evidence whatever; so that they are probably forgeries of about that date by unknown parties, who contrived to foist them off and get them accepted by the whole Church as the writings of four eye-witnesses, two of them Apostles, and the two others companions of the Apostles.   The 900 pages, in which these latter propositions are unfolded, would require a lifetime, to analyse, dissect and refute the multifarious mass of error and misrepresentation of which they consist.   In the " Horæ Evangelicæ " I have discussed the same subject. If life be spared I shall hope to discuss it more fully, and to vindicate afresh the authenticity, the consistency, the historical reality, the internal harmonies, the cumulative evidences of truth and wisdom, and the divine authority of the four Gospels.   In the present work I can deal only with the hundred pages of the Book which unfold the two first propositions.   I have already refuted by anticipation all the main elements of the writer's argument in more than a hundred pages of discussion of the same subject in the " Bible and Modern Thought," and in a supplement to " Paley's Evidences."   But the forms and the combinations under which falsehood may be presented are endless, and whatever there is of novelty in the writer's reasoning is due chiefly, to the confusion of thought or baseless concessions of Christian Divines, whose words he presses into the service of his own sceptical argument.

The first condition for the genuine fulfilment of the

duty of inquiry into religious truth is to hold fast all
truth already known and received.   But the present
writer seems precluded from satisfying this condition of
the duty he recognizes, by the fact that he does not
seem at the outset to accept any religious or moral truth
whatever.   His first principles are thus described by
Him whom he styles "the great Teacher," or the
Apostles whom He commissioned to proclaim His message to the world.   The first is the doctrine of the
Sadducees, "who say that there is no resurrection,
neither angel nor spirit;" on which Christ gives the
brief comment, " Ye do err, not knowing the Scriptures,
nor the power of God."   The next is the Agnostic creed,
that the existence of God is a mere assumption, resting
on no evidence whatever.   This is briefly described by
the Psalmist, " The fool hath said in his heart, There is
no God ; the Lord looked down from heaven to see if
there were any that did understand and seek God,"...
" Have all the workers of iniquity no knowledge......they
call not upon the Lord."   The same appeal is repeated
in another form, " Understand, ye brutish among the
people ; ye fools, when will ye be wise ? He that planted
the ear, shall He not hear ; He that formed the eye, shall
He not see ?   He that teacheth man knowledge, shall
not He know ?" Ps. xciv.   The great Apostle of the
Gentiles teaches the same truth in a more direct and
dogmatic form.   " The wrath of God is revealed from
heaven against the ungodliness of men who hold down
(or stifle) the truth in unrighteousness: for the invisible
things of God," he says, " from the creation of the world
are clearly seen, being understood by the things that are
made, even His eternal power and Godhead, so that they
are without excuse."   He goes on to denounce the gross
folly as well as the guilt of their unbelief.   " When they
knew God they glorified Him not as God, neither were

thankful; but became vain in their imaginations and
their foolish heart was darkened." He then states the
solemn judgment that ensued on their folly. "Even as
they did not like to retain God in their knowledge, God
gave them over to an undiscerning mind." The same
Apostle, as God's ambassador, gives further this solemn
prophecy, that the Lord Jesus will hereafter "be revealed
from heaven with His mighty angels, in flaming fire tak-
ing vengeance upon them that know not God." Such is
the real character, and the predicted issue of two of the
main principles of unbelief with which the writer begins
his inquiry. His third main principle, the unalterable
constancy of the course of physical change deduced from
experience, free from all intervention of a Supreme Lawgiver, has also been the subject of an express prediction
by another Apostle. "Knowing this first, that there shall
come in the last days scoffers......saying, Where is the
promise of His coming? for since the fathers fell asleep
all things continue as they were from the beginning of
the creation." "This they willingly are ignorant of,
that by the word of God the heavens were of old......
but the heavens and the earth which are now, by the
same word are kept in store, reserved unto fire against
a day of judgment and perdition of ungodly men." He
then cautions the Church long beforehand, "Beloved,
beware lest ye also, being led away by the delusion of
the wicked, fall from your own stedfastness;" and his
further charge is a full antithesis to the Agnostic theory,
"Grow in grace and in the knowledge of our Lord and
Saviour Jesus Christ."

The old maxim of philosophy, "*Ex nihilo nihil
fit,*" finds a fresh illustration in the present work. The
starting-point being an absolute blank, a state of utter
religious nescience, there seems no nucleus of truth to
which accessions may be made, by accretions, as in all

inquiry after truth which is real and genuine. The long inquiry of a thousand pages begins with bare negations, and ends exactly where it began. The whole is a dreary waste of darkness and confusion. The only ray of light I can detect in the work from first to last is the implied admission at the outset that man is a moral being, and lies under a moral obligation to search after truth not yet attained, implying of course the two closely related duties, to hold fast and walk in the light of truth already known, and to reject and put away all falsehood either already accepted, or that solicits his acceptance in the course of that inquiry. But this first implied truth remains like an unsprung seed, without any attempt to trace out its related truths or ulterior consequences. Thus at page 41 he says, that he will pass over Dr Mozley's reference to the laws of *moral* being as "involving questions too intricate for treatment and alien from the argument." Had the author held fast this one truth, he would have been kept from the contemptuous disparagement of the statements he afterwards quotes from Archbishop Trench, Professor Mozley, and Dr Heurtley, as to the moral world higher than the physical, and a region of moral laws higher than physical sequence and uniformity, which lies at the basis of the whole inquiry ; but neglecting to unfold and develope the little morsel of truth he does recognize, and clinging with passive credulity to the giant falsehoods with which he starts, he wanders on through a thousand pages of almost unmitigated darkness and delusion.

CHAPTER II.

The Author's Statement of the Object of his Work.

"There can be no more urgent problem for humanity to solve than the question: Is Christianity a supernatural Divine Revelation or not? To this we may demand a clear and decisive answer. The evidence must be of no uncertain character which can warrant our abandoning the guidance of Reason, and blindly accepting doctrines which, if not supernatural truths, must be rejected by the human intellect as monstrous delusions. We propose in this work to seek a conclusive answer to this momentous question."..."To no earnest mind can such inquiry be otherwise than a serious and often a painful task, but, dismissing preconceived ideas and preferences derived from habit and education, and seeking only the Truth, and holding it, whatever it may be, to be the only object worthy of desire, or capable of satisfying a rational mind, the quest cannot but end in peace and satisfaction...the path is thorny indeed, although it must still be faithfully trodden." Pp. xci—xcviii.

The Author in commencing his work of a thousand pages, of which the object is to prove Christianity a mere illusion, opposed to reason and devoid of all evidence, has to meet at the outset a very grave objection. The faith which he so describes is held at the present day by about two hundred millions of men, including the most civilized, developed, and powerful nations. One hundred millions at least, including the foremost empire of the world, have held the same faith, in one form or other, throughout fifteen centuries of past time. The moral presumption that all these have not accepted a very unreasonable creed without any evidence worthy of the name, is plainly extreme. The author endeavours to remove this insuperable prejudice against his conclusions by the assumption that all these accepted it without thought, inquiry, or serious reflection, under the bias of their birth and education alone. It is certainly true of a very large proportion, that their faith has been accepted as a whole, without any separate inquiry into the reasonableness of each part, or the evidence upon which that particular part reposes. Let us consider the question more in detail. Three-fourths of the whole number belong to the Greek or the Latin Churches, or main sects separated from them, or those members of the Anglican Church who have renounced the name of Protestants. Now all of these have formally renounced the principle of free inquiry, or the exercise of private judgment on each part of the faith, and have replaced it by that of deference to Church authority. They differ only as to the particular authority to which this deference is due. Their testimony then, however large the amount of it, has little weight to confirm particular doctrines or fragments of the faith, which they have only received in gross along with the rest. But it by no means follows that their authority has no moral weight whatever. The case may be compared to that of miners in the gold field, when they lay aside certain nuggets among their stores, because they are convinced from their appearance they contain so much gold that they will more than repay the toil of a later analysis. When the sceptic dilates on what he thinks the unreasonableness and lack of evidence of many parts of the Christian religion, and thinks that if tried by pure reason alone, they must be held to be monstrous delusions, he does not observe that in proportion as he darkens the colours of his indictment, he increases the force of the moral presumption in favour of those main truths and elements of the faith, the importance of which, and the evidence with which they commend themselves both to the reason and the conscience, have made hundreds of millions, including the most intelligent of the human race, through successive generations, willing to receive the whole mingled mass, rather than weaken their hold on those great fundamental verities. What are those doctrines the importance of which, their moral attractiveness, or the strong presumption in favour of their truth, has made this immense multitude of human beings cling to Christianity as a whole, in spite of all the objections or difficulties which may seem to press against certain parts of the composite message? They are mainly these. (1) The existence of God, the conscious, intelligent, and benevolent Author of the Universe. (2) Divine Providence. That the world is not the sport of chance, nor subject to blind fate, but governed and guided by a powerful and good Intelligence. (3) The beauty and excellency of the moral character of Christ, and of some of the leading precepts of the Gospel. (4) The doctrine of Immortality, or a life after death, the happiness or unhappiness of which is closely connected with the conduct of men in the present life. (5) The doctrine of Divine mercy, or a message of grace and forgiveness to man as guilty and sinful, and proffered terms of restoration to the Divine favour. (6) The doctrine of judgment to come, in which God will bring every work into judgment, whether it be good or evil. (7) The doctrine that the whole course of Providence is so ordered that in the fulness of time there will be a glorious issue worthy of the ·All-wise God, of whom are all things, and to whom are all things. The preciousness and excellence of these truths outweighing doubts, difficulties and perplexities as to other elements included in the Scriptures, or in the various forms of ecclesiastical Christianity, can alone account for the tenacity with which the Christian faith has been

held and retained by hundreds of millions of intelligent
men through successive generations.   The more the
sceptic exaggerates the accessory difficulties of the
Creed, and depreciates the direct evidence in its favour,
the more does he confirm, in spite of himself, the
preciousness and immense importance of these central
truths, which have led millions on millions, even of those
who have neglected a minute analysis, to lay it up among
their choicest treasures.

There are from thirty to fifty millions of Christians
however, who, instead of accepting the principle of implicit faith as a duty, and rejecting inquiry as a sin,
hold the very reverse.   This is the nominal creed of
all Protestants, but probably of these there are not
more than one in ten whose practice corresponds with
their theory, and who really submit every part of
the faith to a serious personal inquiry.   In the others,
either worldliness or religious indifference, or intellectual
torpor, or the passive acceptance of some ecclesiastical
creed, or current of religious thought, in the midst
of which they have been trained, transfers them really
to the large class whose faith is an implicit faith in
Christian doctrine as a whole, in one or other of its
many corporate forms, and not the result in detail,
of personal investigation and inquiry.   The other
nine-tenths, in common with all the Christians of
the Greek and Roman churches, contribute a general
evidence of the preciousness and importance of those
great central truths of the Bible, for the sake of which
they are willing, at least in outward profession, to believe
all the rest.   But there are left some millions at least
in every age, from Constantine until now, who hold
it a duty, in questions of such supreme importance,
to search and inquire for themselves, and to receive
nothing into the citadel of their understanding, which

they do not believe in their inmost hearts to be sustained by sufficient and reasonable evidence, whether that of natural reason or of supernatural revelation. Against these, we have to place the negative presumption from some hundreds of thousands of sceptics, who profess after inquiry to have discovered the emptiness of the claims of Christianity to be a supernatural message from God, and convince themselves that there is no evidence of reason, even in favour of what are called the doctrines of natural religion. The author, in his Introduction, after dismissing as worthless the moral presumption from the faith of hundreds of millions of Christians through successive generations as simply "due to preconceived ideas, and preferences derived from habit and education," and complaining of the "general eclipse of faith," and blaming the uneasy position of so many Christians in these days, who profess to retain their faith in the Gospel as a supernatural message, and "still clip and prune its doctrines down to the standard of human reason," adds,

"The mass of intelligent men in England are halting between two opinions, standing in what seems to us the most unsatisfactory position conceivable : they abandon, in deference to the current of popular opinion, some of the most central doctrines of Christianity, and try to spiritualize or dilute the rest into a form which does not shock their reason."

He claims for his own work, that it is the result of

"Many years of inquiry, undertaken for the regulation of personal belief, and as a contribution towards the establishment of truth in the minds of others who are seeking for it ... Seeking only the truth and holding it, whatever it may be, as the only object worthy of desire."

The same is the frequent profession of " Free-thinkers," who are accustomed to claim a thousandfold weight for their own conclusions, as conducted without bias and with an honest search for truth alone. Now what are the signs of this freedom from bias in the present case? The author begins his task as a Sadducee, who believes neither resurrection to be possible, nor angel or spirit to exist, that a Supernatural Revelation from God is either impossible or incredible, and that the works of Nature furnish no presumption whatever for the existence of God as a personal and conscious Intelligence. To these he adds the further doctrine that the course of Nature, as known by the experience of the last thousand years is fixed, necessary and invariable; can never have suffered a change or interruption in past time, nor suffer such an interruption in the eternity to come. With these doctrines he starts, and only adds to them at the close, the high probability that the ‾Apostles were credulous and superstitious simpletons, wholly unworthy of credit, if we were quite sure that we had the actual words of their testimony; and that the Gospels are most probably forgeries of four unknown writers, about the close of the second century, and therefore almost wholly worthless as historical testimony to the sayings and works of the Lord Jesus. Here then, there is not the slightest trace of that unbiassed inquiry, "dismissing preconceived ideas," the want of which the writer imputes to hundreds of millions of Christian men, as depriving their faith of all moral weight. The only spark of truth recognized, that man is a moral being, who has a duty to fulfil, remains wholly undeveloped through a thousand pages, and when once forced upon his notice by a quotation from Dr Mozley, he coolly passes over it, as involving "questions too intricate for treatment, and alien from the argument." The falsehoods with which he sets out, remain undisturbed and unquestioned from first to last: as if they were self-evident and unquestionable truths.

The duty of searching after unknown truth can only be satisfied under two conditions; first, to have some small amount of known and certain truth from which to start, and next, to proceed from this centre to develope and unfold what is already known, so as to reclaim some part from the outer darkness beyond. The author wholly fails to satisfy both these conditions; his starting-point is a triad of untested falsehoods which remain in undisturbed supremacy to the end of the work. He plunges at once into the region of darkness, the wide range of talmudical and patristical superstitions, and the varied forgeries as well as genuine writings of the three first centuries, and a chaos of the critical speculations of the modern Sadducees of Germany. Thus, professing to "seek only the truth, and hold it, as the only object worthy of desire," he proceeds to answer the question of Pilate, "What is truth?" very much as Pilate himself answered it, when he gave up the Lord of glory, who is Himself the Truth, to be exposed to the scorn and hate of the Jewish rabble on the cross, between two malefactors. He comes practically to the conclusion that the "great Teacher" Himself, and the Apostles who were His ambassadors to the world, were either most culpable impostors, or amongst the most blind, superstitious, credulous and unreasoning of men, who never once caught a glimpse of the three doctrines which are the alpha and omega of his own inquiry. By calling this an unbiassed search for truth only, he brings himself under that solemn sentence of the prophet, "Woe unto them that call evil good and good evil, that put darkness for light and light for darkness."

CHAPTER III.

THE name Protestant has been rejected by many in our days on the ground that it expresses a mere negation. This is a great and grievous error. Protestantism is simply submission to that Divine command, "Prove all things—hold fast that which is good." It is opposed alike to two extremes, an implicit and traditional faith which rests only on Church authority, which swallows blindly whatever ecclesiastical teachers put into its mouth, neglecting the spirit of Christ's command, "Call no man your father upon the earth, neither be ye called master, for one is your master, even Christ." The other extreme is that free handling of religious and moral truth, of which the "Essays and Reviews" were a specimen, which does not "hold fast that which is good," or recognize any clear definite principles of truth to be first believed, and work out from these to the region beyond, but counts it the condition of free inquiry to have the mind like a sheet of blank paper, ready to receive any inscription whatever that may be traced upon it. Honest inquiry implies a capacity in those by whom it is made to apprehend the force of evidence, and to discriminate between truth and falsehood. It does not imply a state of entire equilibrium and strict indifference. Even among philosophers and metaphysicians, since their speculations began, there has

never been a case of pure, abstract, colourless indifference to the truth or falsehood of Christianity ; the words
of Christ make no exception for philosophers or sceptics
any more than for Divines.   " He that is not for me is
against me, and he that gathereth not with me, scattereth
abroad."   Neutrality is here strictly impossible.   He
who begins an inquiry with no bias in favour of the
Gospel, will certainly have a strong bias against it.
The first requisite of honest inquiry is to take stock of
our actual convictions, to sift them in turn, to hold fast
those which are good, and to reject those, however long
we may have held them, and whatever authorities we
may quote in their favour, which inquiry discovers to
have no sure evidence or firm foundation.   The genuine
Protestant is he who acts on this principle, and obeys
this Divine command.   The same inquiry which may
relax his hold on more disputable and doubtful parts
of his actual faith, will be sure to strengthen and
confirm it on those parts which are true and sound.
Truth shines by a light of its own, only that light is
obscured and clouded as soon as it is mingled with falsehood.   The Christian acts as a disciple of Him who is
the Truth, in retaining every particle of truth, moral,
religious, or natural, which he already holds, and in
rejecting detected falsehood of every kind.   In this work
he is aided by a threefold promise, " If any man be willing to do the will of God, he shall know of the doctrine
whether it be true."   " If thine eye be single, thy whole
body shall be full of light."   (2) " Then shall we know
if we follow on to know the Lord."   (3) " To him that
hath shall be given, and he shall have more abundance ;"
and " he that seeketh shall find."   To be able to discern
and retain old truth, and to add to it fresh truth, is the
promise of Christ to every faithful disciple, " Every
scribe instructed unto the kingdom of heaven, is like

unto a householder who bringeth forth out of his treasure
things new and old," and the parting command of the
Apostle is, "Grow in grace and in the knowledge of the
Lord and Saviour Jesus Christ." The revealed description of the Scriptures is this, "The words of the Lord
are pure words, as silver tried in a furnace of earth,
purified seven times." "Thy word is very pure," and
"every one of Thy righteous judgments endureth for
ever." No bound is set to the growing light and
increasing knowledge of the Name and Character of
God, of the excellency of His word, and the grandeur
and wisdom of His counsels of Redemption and
Providence, which the Christian may gain by the persevering study of those Divine oracles, which are the
most precious gift of God the Holy Ghost to the successive generations of mankind. We have no right to
expect indeed that all doubts and darkness shall disappear until the coming Day-star shall arise. The light
shines here in a dark place, but to those who study and
reverently search into the Scriptures of truth, it will
continue to shine more and more, until at length the
"day shall dawn and the Day-star arise in their hearts."
My own experience for forty years has been, that growing study has more and more convinced me of the
perfect truthfulness of those canonical Scriptures which
are called in the Articles, "God's word written;" in the
Ordination Service, "God's most holy word;" which
many, even amongst the defenders of the faith, in the
present day, are making it a part of their new creed to
lower to the level reached by the words of all good
and honest men, that is, a mixture of Divine truth
and human falsehood, in which the first predominates.
But Dr Westcott's "Introduction to the Gospels" and
Bp Ellicott's "Lectures on the Life of Christ" and
Bp Wordsworth's "Commentary on the New Testament"

are some out of many faithful testimonies which still remain to the doctrine of the entire truthfulness of the Gospels and the Canonical Scriptures. My own experience has been at every step, while unlearning some secondary misinterpretations, or faulty human inferences attaching themselves to, and obscuring the great truths of Revelation, that fresh harmonies of truth have been discovered lying either just below the surface, or deeper in the mines of Scripture, for the solution of doubts and difficulties which had once been perplexing. Thus year by year a more harmonious apprehension of the great truths and doctrines revealed, has been attained, and a clearer conviction of the authenticity, and manifold historical relations, of those lively oracles in which they are revealed. The opposite experience of the author of "Supernatural Religion" setting out in the deep shadows of a modern sceptical philosophy, to end in a darkness where even the few remaining stars seem to be blotted out, impresses me with a feeling of profound pity, not unmixed with indignation.

CHAPTER IV.

REASON AND SUPERNATURAL REVELATION.

THE author in his first chapter constructs an apparent puzzle by combining three different statements of Christian divines, with regard to the relation between reason and the contents of a Divine Revelation. (1) He quotes from Dr Mozley, Dean Mansel, Dr Heurtley, Paley, Bp Butler, and J. H. Newman to shew that miracles and prophecy are the natural and necessary credentials of a Supernatural Revelation. This truth, confirmed by the testimony of the Holy Spirit on the day of Pentecost, and the preaching of the Apostles, is only contravened (so far as I know) by the Bampton Lecturer of 1877, who strives to refute Dr Mozley's true statement on this head. Again, he quotes Archbishop Trench, Dr Mozley, and Dr Newman, and the express words of Scripture to shew that there may be false as well as true miracles, or Satanic as well as Divine; so that miraculous evidence alone would not suffice to guarantee a message as really Divine. He quotes several authors to establish a third principle, that the proper subject of supernatural revelation is to impart truths beyond the range of human reason, which the human intellect could not otherwise have discovered; that " no one would maintain a system discoverable by reason to have been supernaturally communicated." The only truths proper to such a revelation are by the hypothesis "beyond our reason." Thus any appeal to reason, or the moral sense, to confirm the divine origin of a message which signs and wonders are insufficient to prove, he infers to be precluded and impossible; for internal evidence

"is itself an appeal to reason, but human reason cannot, in the nature of the case, prove that which by the very hypothesis lies beyond human reason." Therefore it follows "that no doctrine which lies beyond reason, and requires the attestation of miracles, can possibly afford that indication of the source and reality of miracles which is necessary to endow them with evidential value."

He quotes both Newman and Mozley to shew that they recognize the difficulty and do not remove it. He says further, that

"to argue, as some theologians do, that the ambiguity of their testimony is deliberately intended as a trial of our faith, is absurd, for reason being unable to judge of the nature either of supernatural fact or doctrine, it would be mere folly and injustice to submit to such a test, being wholly incapable of sustaining it." Pp. 3—17.

Here, two clear and certain truths of Scripture, confirmed by a general consent of Christian divines, are joined with a statement so ambiguous, as without fuller explication, to involve the whole subject in hopeless confusion. Let us analyze this statement, that supernatural Revelation, in its own nature, is solely of truths undiscoverable by reason and outside its range. In what sense is our knowledge of the course of nature, and of common things, due to a process of reasoning? how far is it due to the evidence of our senses, personal experience, and human testimony? Our knowledge of no one being or circumstance around us is due to pure reason alone; for this would require us to know it and learn it as a corollary and consequence from our own knowledge à priori of the scheme of the universe. What are the means by which we attain our limited knowledge of the course of nature? First, direct consciousness with regard to our own existence, thoughts, and actions; next, direct observation with regard to the existence and actings, or position and changes, of a certain number of human beings, plants and animals, and material objects immediately around us; thirdly, the extension of this knowledge by the credible testimony of competent witnesses to a larger range of men, animals, plants, and places which we have never seen or visited; fourthly, the extension of this from the present living generation to two or three past generations, with the same varieties of immediate, indirect, and more remote testimony. This sixfold variety of evidence is completed, and enlarged further, by written records of various kinds, by which evidence of more remote events may be transmitted and preserved from utter oblivion. Our knowledge, then, of the world around us, and of the course of nature, is simply the summation of these various particulars, of which only a small part is obtained from inward consciousness and from personal experience, and nearly the whole from direct or indirect testimony of our fellow men, either of the present or of past generations. The chief office of reason is to sum up the information thus gained with regard to each material object, plant, animal and human being, or each particular part of the earth's surface accessible to the foot of man. Besides this knowledge of individual beings, or places, or successive changes, there are a few further conclusions which reason is able to deduce from comparison of these with each other. None of these of course can have a higher evidence of reason than the elements of which they are composed. This loose classification gives birth to maxims which are called "laws of nature" in a loose and popular sense, such as these: That water will extinguish flame; that water may be evaporated by fire and disappear; that it may be frozen by cold and turned to ice; that solid

lumps of any kind of matter will fall to the ground if not
supported; that a piece of gold is heavier than an equal
bulk of lead, or iron, and that an iron axe if not sustained
will sink in water. Another large class of such laws
depend on the two great sets of changes, the succession
of light and darkness, of day and night, and the circuit
of the seasons, summer, autumn, winter and spring. All
these so-called laws of nature are a summation of specific
facts derived from the experience, direct and indirect,
of ourselves and our fellow men. This experience excludes of course all future time, and all past time except
about two thousand years, and even within these limits
it is inferential, constructive and liable to many illusions,
except for one century alone, that is, the furthest range of
the living generation of mankind. It is confined also in
place to the surface of our own planet, and to a depth
of one or two miles below that surface, with some scanty
information, derived from transient experiences alone,
with regard to the whole range of the visible universe
beyond. These individual men, plants, and animals,
coming within the range of observation by their birth
and successive generation, pass out of the range of
human observation by death and dissolution, at the other
limit. Thus the whole range of our experimental knowledge is shut in between the cradle and the grave. The
problem then of reason under a scheme of natural religion, apart from supernatural revelation, is to construct
a consistent and satisfactory theory to account for the
facts of human experience as a whole. The first and
simplest, that the universe has been created by a self-
existent Being, of perfect wisdom and goodness, is met
at once by the difficulty that the work of production is
everywhere followed by death and dissolution; that the
generations of mankind appear and disappear like a
passing dream, and that not only the benefits, pleasures,

and enjoyments of life, but strife, discord, conflict, violence, wrong and crime, with their fruits of suffering, bloodshed, and desolation, go on in almost undiminished current as far back as human experience extends. Hence reason is forced to make an uneasy choice amongst seven or eight different alternatives. The first is that of pure Monotheism, the dominion of a good and wise Creator, leaving unexplained the long and fearful prevalence of moral evil and physical suffering. (2) The second is a theory of despair, which gives up the problem as inscrutable, and denies that there is any evidence at all for a good Creator distinct from the universe, in consequence of the dark and fearful prevalence of moral and physical evil. (3) The third is a doctrine of confusion, which denies any contrast between the self-existent Creator and the totality of existent things, which makes God and the universe the same, an immense total including all conceivable contrasts and disparities of Being, the Pan of old heathen mythology, fitly symbolized by a hideous and misshapen Satyr. (4) A fourth is Fetichism or Polytheism, which recognizes some supernatural power concealed behind, or included in, each natural object, or class of natural objects, which sacrifices unity, but retains diversity, and indulges the deep instinct of mystery, by peopling each class of objects with its own divinities, nymphs of the woods, of the rivers, and of the mountains, the gnomes of the ocean depth, and sportive, fairy-like denizens of the upper air or ether. (5) Fifthly, the Manichean doctrine, which cuts the knot reason fails to untie, by assuming two rival or balanced powers of Good and Evil, contending long for the mastery through successive ages. This may assume various forms, from that which recognizes a strict equality and co-eternity of these two powers, through many stages of subordination of the destructive Siva or

Demon, to the good and beneficent Power.   Two other
hypotheses may be included : (6) The sixth, which
recognizes the strict and unlimited Omnipotence of the
Creator, but ascribes to Him a very imperfect and
limited goodness, with some predominence only of a
benevolent over a malevolent disposition.   (7) A seventh
variety is that which recognizes a Creator of pure and
perfect benevolence, but of limited and imperfect power,
who is thwarted and defeated in His kindly intentions
either by rival and malignant powers, or by the intract-
able nature of the materials and the beings with which
He has to deal.   To these seven, we may add a last,
and perhaps the worst: the doctrine of simple Fate ;
blind, dark, fatal necessity.   The difficulty then, of this
grand problem, proposed to the reason of man, is no
result of Christianity or the special revelations of the
Bible.   The Bible has certainly not created the difficulties of the problem ; the only reasonable charge that
can be brought against it, is that it has failed to remove
them, and throw full light upon the darkness.

What are the conclusions of natural reason in the
case of two of the most eminent of unbelieving philosophers of our own day ? One pronounces that Atheism,
Deism and Pantheism are three equally untenable
attempts to explain the great mystery of being, and
that the power which the universe manifests (he should
have said, conceals), is utterly inscrutable by us, and
must ever so remain.   The other comes to a conclusion
which is in appearance a new kind of Manicheanism, but
is really a closer approach to the teaching of the Bible
than it is in appearance, summed up in these words :

" The belief of Christians is not more absurd or immoral than the
belief of Deists who acknowledge an Omnipotent Creator ; the morality
of the Gospels is far higher and better than that which shews itself in
the order of nature, and what is morally objectionable in the Christian

theory of the world, is objectionable only when taken in conjunction with the doctrine of an Omnipotent God, at least as understood by the majority of Christians[1]."

What then is the express claim of Christianity, as a Supernatural Revelation? Is it simply and absolutely to solve that great problem, which has proved able to baffle, through successive ages, all the unassisted efforts of human reason, starting from the limited data of past experience? Its claim is of a wholly different kind. It is to supply us with fresh facts attested by firm and distinct *à posteriori* evidence, like all the facts which form the stock of our previous knowledge, but intimately connected with this great mystery of the origin and destinies of the universe, and of the whole human race, and of each individual man, and throwing clear and distinct light upon the darkness. These facts all centre in the appearance of a fresh Person within the sphere of human observation; a Person wholly unique in the world's history, by the admission of the most eminent unbelievers who reject the Christian view of His nature; concerning Whom, when we combine all the elements as to the facts of His personal history on earth, and the later results that have flowed from it, the only conclusions consistent with any shew of reason, are, either that He was a Prophet singled out and commissioned by the unseen Creator, for the fuller exposition of His nature and purposes to men; or that He is One who shares in the Divine nature and prerogatives of the invisible God whom He came to reveal. The words and acts of such a Person are supernatural only in this sense, that they lie outside the very narrow and limited bounds of the previous experiences of individual men in their brief earthly lifetime. Instead

[1] Mill's "Posthumous Essays," p. 214.

of lying outside the domain of Reason itself, they are those added experiences which raise man out of darkness into a region of dawning light.   To confound those fetters by which the faculty of Reason in men in general is crippled and confined, in the usual conditions of their earthly life, with the glorious faculty itself, so that the gracious act of God, by which He removes the fetters, and calls reason to exercise itself on a wider range of facts, should be mistaken for its extinction, is a strange and prodigious error.   He who has come near to us, and revealed Himself to the children of men in the Gospels, in the thirty-three years of an earthly lifetime, and in the glorious records of His sayings, and His works of Divine power, is Himself the Word, the Reason, the Truth, the "true Light which lighteth every man that cometh into the world."   All reason in others is only like a spark derived from this glorious "Sun of Righteousness."   The first rising of the sun would be a stupendous miracle to a race of troglodytes, who had lived till then in subterranean caverns, yet not the less would that sun have been the secret source of whatever feeble rays of moonlight or candle-light had previously reached them in their gloomy abode.

The relation of the facts revealed in the Gospels, to the great problem of natural and revealed religion, may be illustrated by the return of Columbus and his companions from their first voyage.   The facts of their landing in Cuba and San Salvador have just the same relation to the great problem of the earth's geography, and the later discovery of the new world and its inhabitants. Those clever persons who refused to credit the report of Columbus and his crew, because ten thousand fishermen and mariners, after skirting the western ocean for

hundreds of years, had never brought any information
worthy of trust concerning its farther shore, have their
exact counterpart in those sceptics who refuse to credit
the testimony of the Apostles and their companions
to the fact, that they saw and conversed with the Lord
Jesus after His resurrection for forty days, because no
such experience, or similar experience, had ever been
recorded before.   For long ages, the shore of the great
ocean had seemed an impassable barrier to human knowledge and exploration, towards the region of the setting
sun ; and so too the grave, "that undiscovered bourn
from which no traveller returns," had seemed to shut
in and enclose all the children of men with a dark and
impassable barrier.   But with the return of Columbus,
the ocean barrier was removed, the great problem was
solved, and the landing of those few voyagers on the
small islet, and their exploration of part of the coast
of Cuba, secured an open pathway of discoveries which
never ceased, till the whole of the American continent
was explored and brought within the range of human
knowledge, and "all the ends of the earth had seen the
salvation of God." So too the facts in the Gospel,
though few and simple, and unlike any previously recorded experience, and in that sense supernatural, were
the key facts to a new and wider range of human knowledge, when man's acquaintance with the works and
the ways of God should no longer be shut in by the
darkness of the grave.   "Life and immortality were
brought to light" by the Gospel.   The resurrection of
Christ was never announced to the world as a solitary
and unconnected fact, out of relation to all that had gone
before, and all that was to follow.   On the contrary, it
was announced from the first as a great germinal fact,
the fulfilment of voices of the prophets from the begin-

ning of the world, and the pledge of the resurrection of all the dead. So St Paul proclaimed it to king Agrippa. "Saying none other things than those that the prophets and Moses did say before should come, that Christ should suffer, and that He should be the first that should rise from the dead, and shew light to the people and to the Gentiles." The resurrection of Jesus was announced as the first-fruits of a glorious harvest that should follow. So when Columbus and his companions announced their landing on the island of San Salvador, that fact was the pledge of the later discovery·of the whole American continent. The resurrection of Jesus was the pledge and earnest of the truth of His words to Martha, "I am the Resurrection and the Life; he that believeth in me, though he were dead, yet shall he live."

A new era of spiritual light began, when man's knowledge of the character and purposes of the Creator ceased to be bounded by the darkness of the grave, and included the blessed certainty of a life beyond, of the resurrection and life everlasting.

The new facts reported in the Gospels were beyond reason in this sense, that no process of abstract reasoning could have discovered them. They needed to be confirmed by clear and full testimony, but when so confirmed, there was nothing whatever to hinder the exercise of the reason and the conscience on their moral features, or to hinder the wayfaring man, though only a fool in natural wisdom, from seeing clearly and with the fullest conviction, that the Son of Man was no agent and accomplice of the father of lies, but a true messenger from the God of love and grace, nay, Himself the great Redeemer promised from the beginning of time. One would think that the sceptic who quotes

admissions of Christian Divines to prove that a message
of supernatural truths is not credible unless supported
by a supernatural guarantee, could scarcely be deceived
by his own sophism, and confound together two things
wholly different, because they are both sometimes expressed by one and the same ambiguous phrase, that
they lie " beyond the range of reason."

CHAPTER V.

Reason and the Christian Revelation.

THE great falsehood that the facts of the Gospel history, because they are unprecedented, and do not come within the range of previous experience, are therefore outside the range of human reason altogether, instead of forming the highest, noblest, and widest sphere for its perfect exercise, is reinforced by a special charge against the contents of that Revelation. The author affirms that a revelation of supernatural truths to promote the salvation of men from the consequences of their own sin is "antecedently incredible and contrary to reason." To prove this, he supplements the difficulties and mysteries of natural religion by various misrepresentations of the doctrines of Christianity. He says first that the existence of Satan, and the Temptation and Fall are not accounted for, and are incredible. Yet the ablest and most candid of modern sceptics, in his latest efforts to solve the great problem of the universe by the light of natural reason alone, is brought back to the very verge of the doctrine thus proclaimed incredible, a mitigated Manicheanism ; or the doctrine of a God, vast and unsearchable both in wisdom and goodness, but, in some way we cannot understand or explain, limited in power, or counteracted and thwarted in His efforts and intentions for the good and happiness of His creatures. The difficulty then is plainly in the facts themselves, not created by the statements of Scripture. But the writer adds this explication of those statements, that

"the evil spirit succeeded in frustrating the designs of the Almighty," that the "sweeping purification of the world by the Flood was as futile as the original design." "We are asked to believe in the frustration of the Divine design in Creation, and the fall of man into a state of wickedness hateful to God, requiring and justifying the Divine design of a revelation, and such a revelation as this, as preliminary to the proposition, that on the supposition of such a design, miracles would not be contrary to reason." "Nothing," it is said, "can be more absolutely incredible or contrary to reason than these statements, or the supposition of such a design." P. 48.

Dr Mozley is quoted as admitting that "as human announcements the doctrines of Christianity would be the wildest delusions, which we should not be justified in believing." He sums up in the words

"incredible assumptions cannot give probability to incredible evidence;" and concludes, "the whole theory of this abortive design of creation with such impotent efforts to amend it, is emphatically contradicted by the glorious perfection and invariability of Nature; it is difficult to say whether the details of the scheme, or the circumstances which are supposed to have led to its adoption, are the more shocking to reason and to moral sense." P. 49.

These additions of the author to the doctrines and teaching of the Bible, are in flagrant opposition to its own express and repeated statements. The whole scheme of redemption, instead of being a mere afterthought, a patchwork addition to a baffled scheme of creation, is expressly declared to have been "foreordained from before the foundation of the world." The fact is repeatedly proclaimed that unto God are "known all His works from the beginning of the creation;" that the mystery of redemption from the beginning of the world had been " hid in God, who created all things by Jesus Christ;" and that what this writer blasphemously calls, " incredible folly," is a declaration of " the manifold wisdom of God, according to the eternal purpose which He purposed in Christ Jesus our Lord." The Scripture does indeed announce a power, inveteracy, and wide diffusion of moral evil among both men and angels, the rational and responsible creatures of God, which constitute a " mystery of iniquity," a kind of dark and malignant shadow and opposite of that great " mystery of godliness," the mystery of God the Father and of Christ, wherein are " hid all the treasures of wisdom and knowledge." When these great and solemn mysteries are approached in the spirit of unbelief and of pride, the result is a most " dangerous downfall," as the Article says. For a time at least the same sentence lights upon such inquirers which fell once in Cyprus on Elymas in his laborious opposition to the Gospel message, "there fell upon him a mist and darkness, and he went about seeking for some one to lead him by the hand." May there be an opposite issue in the present case. May the unhappy man who sets out in his professed search for truth as a Sadducean Atheist, and ends almost exactly where he began—yet receive from God " repentance to the acknowledgment of the truth."

The words of Dr Mozley are quoted to convey a meaning almost the exact reverse of what he himself designed. Dr Mozley (p. 13) puts the case of a person of eminent integrity and loftiness of character, but unattested by any miracle, or similar guarantee beyond the statement itself, affirming that He had existed before His natural birth from all eternity, and that the world itself had been made by Him. He says that no rational being could accept a just, benevolent

life alone as proof of such astonishing announcements.
The words of Dr Mozley, so strangely torn from their
context, are merely the statement of our Lord Himself,
cast into a different form; that a naked assertion of the
possession of Divine attributes, or of being the promised Redeemer of the world, disjoined from acts of
Divine power, and a fulfilment of predictions shewing
the presence of superhuman wisdom, would have been
undeserving of credence. Such would exactly be the
contrast between the true Christ and a false antichrist.
" I am come in my Father's name and ye receive me
not ; if another shall come in his own name, him ye will
receive." Naked self-assertion, unsustained by the testimonies and evidences which should fitly attend it and
confirm its truth, would be the characteristic of antichrist, and not of the true Christ. It is in the harmony
of words of surpassing wisdom, purity and grace, of
works surpassing the power of common men, and even
the gifts of the old Prophets, and these works themselves marked by features of surpassing bounty and
grace ; and the fulfilment of manifold predictions, all
centering in the world's promised Redeemer, from the
days of Paradise to Malachi, John the Baptist and
Caiaphas, and the Evangelists, and express and repeated
claims to be that Messiah of whom Moses and the
Prophets did write ;—It is in the consilience of these
various inductions, these converging streams of evidence,
into one glorious and luminous centre, that the Christian
faith is really founded. This threefold cord of superhuman power, superhuman knowledge and superhuman
goodness, has its strands so wonderfully and mysteriously
interwoven, that no art of man, though they may be
distinguished in thought, can practically sunder them
from each other. The miracles are evidences of Divine
grace and mercy as well as of Divine power ; the fulfilled

prophecies are not only marks of superhuman wisdom but of Divine condescension and grace. The three glorious perfections of the Godhead all co-exist and must co-exist in every work of power, wisdom or goodness, by which the Godhead is revealed, yet each attribute in turn may have a special prominence. The Trinity in Unity of the Divine Persons has its counterpart in the mysterious triunity of the Divine perfections. In a miracle, the Divine power of the Son of God is especially manifested; in the fulfilment of the earlier prophecies, and their completion by His own prophecy on the Mount, and announcement of His own resurrection, and the future resurrection of all men, the attribute of Divine Foreknowledge is specially revealed. In the rest of His discourses, through the Gospels, in the Sermon on the Mount, in the parables of the Prodigal Son and of the lost sheep and the lost piece of money, in the washing of the feet of the disciples, the discourses at the Last Supper, and in all the words full of grace and truth throughout the Gospels, such as the words spoken to the woman who was a sinner, the promises to Martha and her sister Mary, and the precedence given to Mary Magdalene among the witnesses of His resurrection, we have manifold and overflowing tokens of Divine goodness, grace and compassion. Well did He say to His Apostle, " Have I been so long time with you, and hast thou not known me, Philip ? he that hath seen me, hath seen the Father." " I and my Father are one." And very solemn is His comment upon the sin of the Jews, and the equal or greater sin of those, who having received the full message of His love in the Gospels, and seen it confirmed and unfolded by the whole course of the world's history for 1800 years, can still shut their eyes to the light of His Divine glory, and strive to persuade their fellow-men to put out the eyes of their soul, and involve themselves in utter darkness once more. "If I had not done among them the works which none other man did, they had not had sin ... but now have they both seen and hated both me and my Father."

CHAPTER VI.

THE PERFECTION OF NATURE, AND FOUR MOCK DEITIES OF SCEPTICISM.

THE conflict of Faith and Unbelief in the last times is often said in Scripture to be "like the day of Midian." There were two striking features of that day. The first was an extreme illustration of the impotence of mere numbers when opposed to faith and the fear of God. Gideon's little company of three hundred light-bearers went forth by divine command to encounter the Midianite host, four hundred times more numerous, who were slumbering in darkness, and the overthrow was complete and entire. "The host ran and cried and fled ... and every man's sword was set against his fellow throughout all the host." In the hour of panic they perished by mutual self-destruction. So, in the immense confederacy of unbelief in the last times, there is no unity, but endless self-contradiction, and all the materials are already prepared for the overthrow of sceptical speculations through intestine collision and conflict. Thus one leading sceptic prophesies that "the reign of matter must extend till it is co-extensive with knowledge, with feeling, and action." Another, still more eminent, assures us, that " Philosophy refuses to admit the very existence of matter," and that there exist nothing but "permanent possibilities of sensation." M. Comte tells us that the era of forces and causes is past with the childhood of

science, that faith in God and in supernatural powers
is only the stage of its infancy, and that Positivism,
which simply registers phenomena, is its full manhood.
Dr Tyndal assures us the exact reverse : that to pass
from phenomena to the forces by which they are produced, is the first requisite of philosophic thought. The
author of Positivism in the very work where he repro-
bates the introduction of forces, laws and causes, contradicts his own principle two hundred times within
ninety pages. Mr Spencer refers all theology to the
Unknowable, and says that the "power which the
universe manifests is utterly inscrutable." Mr Mill rejoins, and tells him that he admits an immense amount
of knowledge of the Unknowable. What is equally
clear is that he lays down the indestructibility of
motion as an *à priori* truth, and tells us in the same
work that the universe, by evolution and the law of
equilibration, is tending to a state of perfect rest, and
to the reign of omnipresent death.

" If equilibration must end in complete rest, what is the fate towards
which all things tend ? The solar system is slowly dissipating its forces,
the sun is losing its heat at a rate which will tell in millions of years.
If man and society are similarly dependent on this supply of force
which is gradually coming to an end, are we not manifestly progressing
towards Omnipresent Death ? That such must be the outcome of the
processes everywhere going on seems beyond doubt...That the proximate end of all the changes we have traced is a state of quiescence,
this admits of *à priori* proof." Spencer's *First Principles*, p. 514.

These contradictions of different sceptical theories,
and different parts of the same theory, might be multiplied almost without limit. Never perhaps, since the
beginning of time, was there so large a brevet as in
Mr Spencer's philosophical works, by which direct self-
contradictions are promoted to the rank of *à priori*
truths. One German atheistic theory professes to build

up the universe without a God out of atoms which are not atoms at all, but little whirlpools of revolving matter.

With regard to Nature, and its perfection, we have the like antithesis. The writer before us, having corrupted the Christian faith by patchwork additions of his own, directly opposed to the statements of Scripture, then contrasts the compound, with what he calls the "glorious perfection of nature." This anti-supernaturalism encounters its direct opposite, in what may be called the hypo-physicism of Mr Mill.

"Nearly all the things which men are hanged or imprisoned for doing to one another are nature's every-day performances. Killing, the most criminal act recognized by human laws, nature does once to every creature that lives. Nature impales men, breaks them as if on the wheel, casts them to be devoured by wild beasts, burns them to death, crushes them with stones like the first Christian martyr, starves them with hunger, freezes them with cold, poisons them by the quick or slow venom of her exhalations, and has hundreds of other hideous deaths such as the ingenious cruelty of a Nabis or a Domitian never surpassed. All this nature does, with the most supercilious disregard both of mercy and justice, emptying her shafts on the best and the noblest, indifferently with the meanest and worst. She mows down those on whose existence hangs the well-being of a whole people, perhaps the prospects of the human race for generations to come, with as little compunction as those whose death is a relief to themselves, or a blessing to those under their noxious influence. Such are Nature's dealings with life...A single hurricane destroys the hopes of a season; a flight of locusts, or an inundation desolates a district; a trifling chemical change in an edible root starves a million of people; everything, in short, which the worst of men commit either against life or property, is perpetrated on a larger scale by natural agents. Nature has noyades more fatal than those of Carrier; her explosions of fire-damp are as destructive as human artillery; her plague and cholera far surpass the poisoned cups of the Borgias. All which people are accustomed to deprecate as disorder and its consequences, is precisely a counterpart of nature's ways: anarchy and the reign of terror are overmatched in injustice, ruin, and death by the hurricane and the pestilence." Mill's *Posthumous Essays*, p. 31.

Such, according to Mr Mill, is that "glorious perfection of nature," which the author of "Supernatural
Religion" uses as a foil, to demonstrate by contrast,
that the Christian faith is a contradiction to reason
and the moral sense. Mr Mill, on the contrary, insists
strongly that

"the morality of the Gospels is far higher and better than that which
shews itself in the order of nature."

What is nature in the creed of Atheism, and apart
from the vicegerent rule and action of man, ruling over
the earth, and bringing outward things into subjection
to his own will? Mr Mill gives only two meanings to
the word, nature; the first is

"the aggregate of the powers and properties of all things, of all
phenomena and the causes which produce them." "In another sense
nature means, not every thing which happens, but only what takes
place without the voluntary and intentional agency of man." "This
distinction," he adds, "is far from exhausting the ambiguities of the
word."

It does not in fact include the most fundamental
meaning; it leaves Mr Mill quite unable to explain why
"unnatural" in every language should be a term of
strong reprobation; or why the foremost school of
Greek philosophy came to make "living according to
nature," the first and chief maxim of duty and wisdom.
Nature, by its derivation, does not properly apply at
all to mere matter, but to things that are born and live.
It may be extended, by analogy, to God, the self-existent,
who does not come into being; and by a further analogy,
it may be extended, in the opposite direction, to things
that are not born, such as lifeless atoms. The nature
of any particular thing or being is properly that distinctive character wherein its being consists; the fundamental law imposed on it in the hour of its birth, the

specific gift of being it has received from the Creator; when Nature is spoken of as a collective whole, it is plainly a term of extreme ambiguity. It may either include or exclude the perfect being and nature of the self-existent Creator. It may include or exclude the being and dominion of man, the vice-gerent of the Creator in this lower world. It may include all the unknown worlds throughout the universe, or be limited to the world of human experience alone in this terrestrial life; it may include only that which is known, shut in by the grave on the one side, and by two or three thousand years of known history on the other; or it may comprehend both all past ages and a coming eternity. When both the nature of God and of man are excluded, all the unknown future, all the unknown or unseen regions of the universe, and earthly life and experience for the last two or three thousand years alone is considered, it is plain that Nature so defined denotes a very small and infinitesimal part of the vast scheme of universal Being. When Nature within these narrow limits, is extolled as "invariable and perfect," and its "glorious perfection" is made the warrant for the rejection of the Christian faith, the moral teaching of the Gospel, the doctrine of the resurrection and the blessed hope of immortal life beyond the grave, this is indeed an illusion as well as a blasphemy, "shocking both to reason and to moral sense."

How far is Mr Mill's counter indictment of the utter immorality, injustice and cruelty of nature, valid and well-founded? The constancy and perfection of nature to which the appeal is made in the sceptical argument, is really nothing more than our limited human experience of terrestrial changes on the earth's surface from the dispersion of the sons of Noah till the birth of Christ for two thousand years; excluding the beginning, and

the flood of Noah and all previous ages, the resurrection and the life to come, the future judgment, and
all the prospects of a coming eternity; all that is unseen,
or visible only in other worlds beyond our own planet,
and all the actings of the will of men through successive generations, to subdue the earth and bring it into
subservience to the wants, and desires, and spiritual
instincts and aspirations of their own nature. This
terrestrial nature, shut in by these narrow limits, is a
minute and almost infinitesimal fragment of the great
scheme of universal being. The information which it
supplies may be clear and express, and adequate, to the
present guidance of life, with regard to individual men,
animals and plants; and supply also some glimpses and
vistas of thought leading us onward into the abysses
that lie beyond. But to complete it into an adequate
key to the future hopes of man, and prospects of the
human race, and the vast scheme of universal providence,
it needs to be pieced out and completed, if supernatural
revelation be excluded, by infinite guesswork, blind conjecture, and baseless speculation. An inverted pyramid
has to be constructed of prodigious dimensions, resting
on a minute apex, little more than a mathematical point,
of certain truth and well-attested experience. As we
recede from this apex, conjecture is heaped on conjecture,
and Pelion is piled on Ossa, in the vain attempt to scale
the skies, and pull down the Almighty Creator from the
throne of the universe, where He sits enthroned in glory
for evermore. A hundred shadowy and spectral coun-
terfeits are set up by the pride of unbelieving philosophy,
to take the place of the Supreme and Eternal King.

One of these is M. Comte's new Supreme Being, collective Humanity, that is the sum total of all the sinners
of mankind, who have fought with and murdered each
other through the last 6000 years, or fallen under the

stroke of death by wasting disease, and includes almost every variety of moral enormity, with bright exceptional instances of imperfect goodness and nobleness of being. What a hideous folly is this worship of collective humanity, this new god that has lately come up! A second counterfeit is physical force, a mock trinity of indestructible matter, persistent motion, and continuous force, and undiminished and unalterable solar energy. A third counterfeit makes this new divinity of Solar Force dissipate and waste itself continually in the regions of infinite space, till at length, after millions of ages, the new god of physical science is reduced to utter bankruptcy, and the Sun will become a stagnant mass, drained of light, and heat, and all its life-sustaining stores of energy, and nature sink under a reign of utter darkness and omnipresent death.

A fourth counterfeit and rival of the Living God has two different names—"Evolution" and "Natural Selection." The first, as one of its main worshippers allows, ought rather to be called Involution, and denotes the process by which a diffused nebulous mass gradually condenses, while the light and heat that may result from this condensation are dissipated, and lost in infinite space. It is a process of cooling carried on slowly through millions of ages, till instead of sun, stars, and planets, and animated worlds, the universe becomes one vast, inert, black mass of lifeless matter. The other name of this modern Divinity is "Natural Selection," that is, as expounded by its own author, "the course and sequence of events as perceived by us," choosing out through successive ages, what forms of life are fittest to endure; then, like Saturn, devouring all its children in swift succession; a selection in which there is no one who selects, and no real existence to be selected, and the lives selected for endurance disappear like bubbles in

the great ocean of being, as soon as the selection is
made.   A "survival of the fittest," where no one is fit to
survive at all except for a few passing moments, and
then each has to melt away in its turn into the "infinite azure of the future," the gulf of evanescent and
perishable being.   The true and self-existent Jehovah
being denied, there is set up in His place the Buddhist
Maya, or universal illusion, an endless phantasmagoria of
evanescent sensations, without beginning and without
end, an infinite waste of empty shadows.

The author of "Supernatural Religion," after defaming the Gospel of Christ, the glorious message by
which principalities and powers in heavenly places
learn the manifold wisdom of God, and are lost in
adoring wonder, as "shocking to reason and moral
sense," takes up the first substitute that comes to hand.
This happens to be the third of Mr Spencer's three
à priori schemes of the knowledge of the Unknowable,
and the mode of action of the Unknowable through
countless ages to come.   The theory thus adopted is a
climax of unreason.

CHAPTER VII.

Mr Spencer's Three Theories of the Universe.

Mr Spencer defines Philosophy as

"completely unified knowledge. This is the meaning we must give to the word philosophy if we use it at all." (*F. P.* p. 134.) "This," he says, "is tacitly asserted by the simultaneous inclusion of God, Nature, and Man within its scope." (P. 131.)

His next step is wholly to exclude the knowledge of God, and he then attempts to frame a philosophy or scheme of completely unified knowledge, from which the principle and source of unity is wholly excluded. Total ignorance of God, is the first maxim of this philosophy. He claims for it to be more religious than any actual religion.

"Those religions," he says, "are partially irreligious, because they profess to have some knowledge of that which transcends knowledge, and so contradict the teachings of religion." (*Ib.*)

This monstrous folly, that there is no medium between Omniscience and utter Nescience is the foundation and corner-stone of the whole system. The author cannot even state his own first principle without a plain self-contradiction.

"Religion has established the doctrine that all things are manifestations of a power that transcends our knowledge" (p. 100),

but a power of which we can know nothing at all plainly cannot be manifested.

"Religion," he adds, "has ever been more or less irreligious, because it has claimed to know something of a power which transcends knowledge,"

or cannot be exhaustively known.

Having thus rejected Christianity as irreligious, because it does profess to teach us definite truth with regard to the nature and purposes of the great First Cause, how does the author build on this negative foundation? He offers his readers confidently, not one only, but three alternative theories of the universe, that is of the plans and purposes of this Unknowable God through ages to come. The first is the theory of endless Involution or condensation. It is a process by which satellites drop into their suns, and the suns by successive collisions fall into each other, till the whole universe will become one great mass of dull, dead matter, a monstrous extinguished sun, from which heat and light have disappeared and lost themselves in infinite space.

"We are manifestly progressing towards Omnipresent death. That such a state must be the outcome of the processes everywhere going on, seems beyond doubt...That the proximate end of all the transformations we have traced is a state of quiescence, this admits of *à priori* proof." (P. 514.)

This "prodigious amount of knowledge of the unknowable," that all the changes of nature are beyond doubt tending to a reign of Omnipresent death, is Mr Spencer's first offered substitute for the Gospel. It is made up of two *à priori* truths,—that motion is indestructible, and that all things are certainly tending to a state of perfect quiescence. His second theory in the same work, replaces the first by an endless oscillation theory—

"An unmeasurable period, during which attractive forces predominating cause universal concentration ; and then an unmeasurable period, during which the repulsive forces predominating cause universal diffusion, alternate eras of evolution and dissolution." (P. 537.)

Thus the whole scheme of universal Being is supposed, like the stone of Sisyphus, through millions of years or ages to be raised to a higher pitch of dignity, perfection, and multiplied vitality, and then when it has nearly reached some summit of ideal perfection, to bound downward, by a reverse process, and dash itself to pieces at the foot of the mountain, the whole creation resolving itself into diffused nebulous vapour and nothingness once more. This reverse process, it should be observed, is introduced purely by guess, in contradiction to all the laws of mechanics, to provide some escape from the dreary monotony of the first theory.

In " Social Statics," Mr Spencer propounds a third *à priori* theory of the universe distinct from, and inconsistent with, both the others. This is the self-perfecting theory of nature. It is embodied in these maxims :

"Advancement is due to the working of universal law, and, in virtue of that law, must continue till the state we call perfection is reached. These are the steps of the argument. All imperfection is unfitness to the conditions of existence. This unfitness must consist in having a faculty or faculties in excess, or deficient, or in both. A faculty in excess is one which has no opportunity for full exercise ; and a deficient faculty is one from which circumstances demand more than it can perform. The principle of life is, that a faculty which cannot obtain full exercise diminishes, and one on which excessive demands are made, increases ; while this excess and deficiency continue, there must be decrease on one hand and growth on the other. Finally, then, all excess and deficiency, and unfitness and imperfection, must disappear. Thus the ultimate development of the ideal man is logically certain. Humanity must, in the end, become completely adapted to its conditions ; progress therefore is not an accident, but a necessity ;...As surely as a passion grows by indulgence, and diminishes when restrained, so surely must the things we call evil and immorality disappear, and man must become perfect." (S. R. from S. S., p. 50, 51.)

This *demonstration*, Mr Spencer says, removes the doctrine "out of the region of probability into that of

B.

5

certainty." Let us now examine the data and premises of which this grand discovery consists. First, a novel definition of moral evil and immorality; that it consists in a living creature having one or more faculties with no opportunity for their exercise, or not having all the senses or faculties he could exercise if he had them. The ridiculous and entire falsehood of such a definition is so plain that it is needless to develope it further. The one grain of truth in the mock demonstration is, that a faculty is commonly strengthened by repeated exercise, "as the eye tends to become long-sighted in the sailor, and short-sighted in the student, and a clerk acquires rapidity in writing and calculation." But another assumption is required to set the argument on its feet ; that every living creature acquires instinctively, and of course, all the senses and faculties for the exercise of which there is a present opportunity. By this rule all animals should have a faculty of articulate speech. According to all experience man alone has this faculty, while different kinds of beasts and birds have their distinctive notes, cries, and inarticulate sounds. Next, men so far as experience goes, have five senses only, sight, hearing, touch, smell, and taste ; and these within narrowly defined limits. If every one possessed, by natural necessity, every faculty he could exercise if he had it, every one must have a natural telescope for seeing objects more distant, and a microscope for seeing objects more minute, than come within the range of ordinary eyesight. He must have also a natural thermometer, hygrometer, anemometer, and micrometer. All these represent faculties which never would want opportunities for their exercise, but their spontaneous growth is flatly opposed to universal experience. If all living creatures had this prodigal supply of all conceivable senses and faculties, there would be nothing in this to secure their right use and application. Many senses and faculties must be still more liable to abuse than a few only. If circumstances underwent no change, some faculties might be enfeebled by lack of exercise, and others be quickened and made more perfect and acute. If circumstances changed, even this limited amount of variation would be suspended or reversed. The decay of faculties or senses, either by lack of opportunity or of will to exert them, would be likely to have a wider range than the perfecting of others under the concurrence of three conditions; the will to exercise them to the utmost, circumstances favourable to their exercise, and the continuance of those circumstances unaltered for a long course of time. The demonstration starts from a definition of moral evil so prodigiously absurd, and involves an assumption with regard to the senses and faculties of men and living creatures, so utterly opposed to all experience, that the acceptance on such grounds of a self-perfecting tendency in all nature, seems the furthest possible limit of unreasoning credulity. When propounded as an *à priori* demonstration by the same author who assures us, as another *à priori* truth beyond doubt, that all nature is progressing towards the reign of Omnipresent Death, and as another *à priori* truth, that the power working behind all phenomena is wholly "unknowable," and that it is the main defect of all religious creeds to pretend to know something of a Being of whom nothing can be known,—the ridiculous folly of these assertions seems scarcely to admit of increase. We may know, it seems, how "the unknowable" will act, through countless ages to come, and may know as "an *à priori* truth" that He or it will act in three different ways, each contradicting the two others. He will crush up the whole universe, with all its suns and planets, into one vast mass, which will cool down into icy frost and blackness of darkness, so that the self-perfecting tendency of Nature will result in the extinction of all life, leaving behind utter wasteness and desolation. Or He will peradventure assume the task of Sisyphus, and go on through countless ages laboriously raising the universe near to some mountain summit of ideal perfection, only to see it roll down and bury itself in an abyss of ruin and darkness in a later period of utter dissolution. Of such theorists it may well be said in the indignant words of the Prophet, "They have rejected the word of the Lord, and what wisdom is in them."

Mr Spencer's third theory of the universe is further unfolded in the following passage, in which a great truth of Scripture is so misconstrued, as to change it into its own exact reverse.

"The survival only of the fittest is the stern decree of nature. The invariable action of law of itself eliminates the unfit. Progress is necessary to existence, extinction is the doom of retrogression. The highest effect contemplated by the supposed revelation is to bring man into perfect harmony with law, and this is ensured by law itself acting upon intelligence. Only in obedience to law is there life and safety. Knowledge of law is imperatively demanded by nature. Ignorance of it is a capital offence. If we ignore the law of gravitation, we are dashed to pieces at the foot of a precipice, or are crushed by a falling rock; if we neglect sanitary law, we are destroyed by a pestilence; if we disregard chemical laws, we are poisoned by a vapour. There is not, in reality, a gradation of breach of law that is not followed by an equivalent gradation of punishment. Civilization is nothing but the knowledge and observance of natural laws. The savage must learn them or be extinguished: the cultivated must observe them or die. The balance of moral and physical development cannot be deranged with impunity. In the spiritual as well as the physical sense, only the fittest eventually can survive in the struggle for existence. There is, in fact, an absolute upward impulse to the whole human race supplied by the invariable operation of the laws of nature acting upon the common instinct of self-preservation. As on the one hand, the highest human conception of infinite wisdom and power is derived from the universality and invariability of law, so that universality and invariability, on the other hand, exclude the idea of interruption or occasional suspension of law for any purpose whatever, and more especially for the correction of supposed original errors of design, which cannot have existed, or for the attainment of objects already provided for in the order of nature." (S. R. from S. S. 51, 52.)

Now in a scheme which pronounces God to be unknowable, and minds and material objects unknowable also, so that what are called phenomena of matter or of mind, are only "faint" and "vivid" manifestations of "the unknowable," (which is a self-contradiction,) so that human action is the fatal and inevitable result of material circumstances, there are no laws but those of matter and physical change. Now these laws are never broken, and never can be. The man who is dashed to pieces at the foot of a precipice, or crushed by a falling rock, obeys the law of gravitation just as much as the person who lies quietly in his bed. The laws of chemistry are obeyed as much by the choke-damp or fire-damp which causes the death of hundreds, as by the atmosphere which sustains the life of millions. Physical laws, the only laws which exist under the theory, are never broken, and never can be, because their subjects are atoms or masses of matter devoid of choice and reason. The only laws which can be broken are those which the theory excludes as unreal fictions, moral laws imposed by God on rational, conscious, and responsible creatures. Transferred to these real laws which can be broken, and have been broken on the largest scale, the remark is true, "only in obedience to law is there life and safety." Such is the statement of Christ Himself. "I know that His commandment is life everlasting." Ignorance of these real laws of God for man is "a capital offence." Such ignorance, utter and complete, is the starting-point and boast of this wretched mock philosophy. Breaches of the laws which it admits, are impossible, and have never occurred; breaches of the moral law which it

refuses to recognize, and of which it counts the knowledge impossible, have occurred and do occur continually,
and to these transgressions the words do apply, "there
is no gradation of the breach of God's law that is
not followed by an equivalent gradation of punishment."
A great Scriptural truth is borrowed by a godless and
immoral philosophy in which it has no real place, and
then, is so disguised as hardly to be recognizable.
"The wages of sin is death." "In the way of righteousness is life, in the pathway thereof there is no death."
"The righteous shall be recompensed in the earth, much
more the wicked and the sinner." "The commandment
of God is life everlasting."

CHAPTER VIII.

Nature without Man or God.

THE indictment of immorality which Mr Mill has brought against Nature, that idol of modern physicists, suggests a deep inquiry, which may throw light on the whole question of anti-supernaturalism. There are four classes of action of which we can conceive. (1) The direct action of God Himself, the supreme intelligence and perfect goodness, doing as He will among the inhabitants of heaven and the dwellers upon earth. The exclusion of all such direct action of God Himself, as unreasonable if not impossible, is the main dogma of anti-supernaturalism. (2) The second class of activity consists of the conscious voluntary actions of good or bad men, who are subject to a law of moral duty, and the similar action of good or bad spirits, or rational beings in other parts of the universe, supposing us to have access to them, and means of ascertaining their reality, and of discriminating them from all lower activities. (3) Thirdly, the actings of the animal creation, or of vegetable life. None of these can have a strictly moral or anti-moral character. It is not surprising that in brute nature no traces of moral action should be found, though there are near approaches to it, and close resemblances in the nobler animals, when humanized by association with man. (4) Fourthly, there are the

actings of all material creatures, things devoid either
of animal or vegetable life, which yet are most intimately
connected with the welfare or continued existence of
living things. Many indeed hold that lifeless matter
has no active power whatever; that action is the distinctive character of conscious mind; so that what we
popularly call the actings of material objects, are really
the direct actings of the Creator Himself. This view,
I think, is erroneous, and that activity of some kind is
essential to a real existence. That which cannot act in
some way or other cannot be acted upon, and that very
passivity and sluggishness which is imputed to lifeless
matter, still requires us to admit in it activity of some
kind. The wind acts when it blows upon us, fire when
it burns us, a stone when it bruises us, the earth itself
when it pinions us to its surface by its attraction. The
difference is that in the actings of lifeless things, or material
objects of all kinds, there is no spontaneity or element
of choice, but the action is determined by distance and
position alone. The immense disproportion, in amount,
of unorganized matter in the universe as known to us,
compensates in a certain sense for the inferior and more
passive form of its activity. Its actings, because they
are lower in kind than even those of the brutes themselves, cannot possibly reveal moral features of choice
or discrimination, with reference to moral ends or purposes. There seem to be three laws at least to which
all matter is subject. (1) The first is that of universal
appetency, each atom of matter tending to approach
every other, with a force or intensity determined by the
distance alone. (2) The second is a law of special appetency, determined by the union and interaction of matter
and self-repulsive ether. On this second law, probably,
all cohesion, electric affinity, and chemical structure
depend. (3) The third is a law of ethereal repulsion,

on which all the phenomena of light, electricity, magnetism, heat, and the more subtle agencies of nature depend.

If then we deny all direct action of God, the Supreme Intelligence, and shut out the Creator from His own universe, and then speak of nature in contrast to man, of the natural in contrast to the artificial, it is idle to look for moral qualities in the actings of brute creatures, or the limited activities which alone belong to unorganized creatures, or material objects in all their diversities. At the same time, these lowest creatures must have had their limited powers defined by the Creator in the moment of their creation, and out of infinite possibilities, the same Creator must have decided all those conditions of place, number, mass, concentration, or diffusion, on which, by the very law of their being, all their later activities and operations one upon another, and upon the living things with which they co-exist, will really depend. So far then as any semblances of choice, moral purpose, or moral preference seem detected in the changes of mere matter, it can be due to no present purpose or choice in the things themselves, but only be a remote consequence of the wisdom of the Creator, in His wise arrangement of the material universe in the hour of its creation. Thus, brute or unorganized lifeless nature cannot possibly reveal moral preferences in its separate actings. Those actings are linked with each other by a law that extends through distant ages, and which is determined by distance and position alone ; but the actings of brute or inanimate nature are modified continually by the voluntary actions of all mankind, into which the elements of spontaneity, choice, love, and hate, or moral preference and aversion do continually enter. The same is true of the actings of all moral and spiritual intelligences, in whatever part of the universe they may exist, and the laws which link together the whole material universe would make it impossible for such actings of spiritual being, in however remote a region, not to extend their influence to the earth and terrestrial changes.

That changes on the earth should be determined solely by physical laws would require two great conditions; that the Living God should, by a self-denying ordinance, bind Himself never to stretch forth His Almighty hand, whether for judgment or for mercy, to interfere with the mechanical working of the laws of brute and inanimate nature, and that He should equally shut up in eternal inaction all rational and spiritual creatures, in every part of the created universe. It is not surprising then that Mr Mill should find Nature, as defined by himself, nature, that is, exclusive both of Man and God, guilty of strange enormities and moral crimes, when he tries each separate event in which material agents are concerned, by the same test as if they were the separate and independent actions of a moral agent. He exacts, in short, from nature the unnatural; from things not endowed with the power of choice, the proper results of choice and spontaneity; from creatures that cannot choose, the virtue of choosing well. It is not surprising, when God Himself and all moral and spiritual creatures, have been excluded from the definition of nature, that the residuum should be found devoid of moral excellences and perfections. Two questions alone remain. First, whether the general laws appointed for the lower creatures, and for the whole material universe devoid of life and moral preference, disclose any proofs of wisdom and goodness, in Him by whom they were first appointed. Now it is the wisdom and excellency of these laws which tempt atheistic speculators to embrace the strange hypothesis,

that it is useless for the Creator Himself ever to interfere with their undisturbed operation. The other question is, whether the special arrangement of the material
constituents of the universe might have been so ordained in their original creation, as to secure the benefits, and escape all the inconveniences and mischiefs,
which result from time to time from their invariable
operation. Those who affect to solve this great and
mysterious problem more perfectly than the Allwise
Creator has done, shew the extreme of folly and presumption into which it is possible for sinful creatures
to fall. They are well rebuked by that voice of God
to the patriarch: "Hast thou an arm like God? or
canst thou thunder with a voice like Him? Shall
he that contendeth with the Almighty instruct Him?
He that reproveth God, let him answer it." "Look on
every one that is proud and bring him low, and tread
down the wicked in their place, then will I also confess
unto thee, that thine own right hand can save thee."
Surely one glance on the grandeur, immensity, and marvellous variety of the wonderful works of God, ought
to silence those rash and audacious speculators, who
would affect to improve on the counsels and works of
God the Only Wise!

The author of "Supernatural Religion" says that
miracles, or the direct action of God Himself, are "emphatically contradicted by the glorious perfection and
the invariability of the order of nature; the imperfection thus ascribed to the Divine work is derogatory to
the power and wisdom of the Creator." The hypo-
physicism, as it may be called, of Mr Mill, is a curious
contrast to this anti-supernaturalism. Having excluded
from nature all direct agency of God Himself, and of
all moral agents, men or spirits, and left only a residuum
of unmoral agencies, we see what is his conclusion as

to the moral perfections of this residual nature. All the worst crimes recorded in history are surpassed, he says, by this idol of modern atheism. These two tribes of the great Midianite camp effectually destroy each other.

CHAPTER IX.

The Unnatural in contrast to the Supernatural.

The term Nature when used comprehensively, includes a vast variety of beings and of natures widely different from each other. We may distinguish six main classes of natures. First, the nature of material things; secondly, of plants; thirdly, of animals; fourthly, of men; fifthly, of rational beings not human; sixthly, the Nature of God, the Self-existent First Cause. Now in each of these there may be first, natural or normal actings; secondly, unnatural, and thirdly, supernatural actings, above or beyond the ordinary standard and mode of action. This last term may be extended, so as to include unusual and extraordinary actings of the Creator Himself. It will be enough to notice two forms of the Unnatural and two of the Supernatural. First, the brutish unnatural. "What they know naturally, as brute beasts, in those things they corrupt themselves." Man may thus be self-degraded below his own nature to the level of brute beasts. Secondly, the animal preternatural, when some lower creature, plant, or animal, is raised to a mode of acting above the usual range of animal faculty. (1) "The dumb ass speaking with man's voice forbade the madness of the prophet." (2) "The Lord spake unto the fish, and it vomited out Jonah on the dry land." (3) "Cast an hook and take up the fish that first cometh up, and when thou hast opened his mouth, thou shalt

find a piece of money."   (4) "Cast the net on the right
side of the ship and ye shall find. They cast therefore,
and now they were not able to draw it for the multitude
of fishes."

One form of the unnatural in contrast to the Supernatural is included as a main article of the Creed of Anti-
Supernaturalism. The Nature, of which the " glorious
perfection and invariability" are extolled, as excluding the
miracles and truths of the Christian Faith, is a Nature,
in which death reigns supreme and undisturbed from
age to age. It is that nature of which Mr Mill says
pithily, " Killing, the most criminal act recognized by
human laws, Nature does once to every being that lives."
It is that nature of which, according to Mr Spencer's
first theory, the undoubted tendency is " to a reign of
omnipresent death." This apotheosis of death is so complete that according to Strauss, "the statement that a dead
man has returned to life is composed of two contradictory
elements." Thus the living God is dethroned, and His
existence is either denied, or thrust wholly beyond the
reach of human knowledge, and DEATH, the last enemy,
is enthroned in his place. This most monstrous and
unnatural of all creeds, is gravely propounded as a pre-
ferable substitute, more agreeable to reason and the
moral sense, than the glorious and everlasting Gospel
of redeeming love. Sinful man flings back the unspeakable gift of God, in the face of Him who offers it, and
chooses rather to sit down in blind and slavish subjection to the worst and foulest of all false gods. The
most degrading of all conceivable superstitions, is that
which shuts out God from the right to interfere, by a
message of redeeming grace, with a world over which
death reigns supreme, the "lazar house" of Milton's
description. (Bk. XI. 480.)

2. Another form of the Unnatural is the refusal to

see any signs or proofs of a superhuman Intelligence, or of the working and dominion of a conscious First Cause in the whole system of created things. The message of God to sinful men, by the Prophet whose lips were touched with a coal of fire from the heavenly altar, begins by denouncing the more than brutish blindness of this practical atheism, into which his own people had so widely fallen. "Hear O heavens, and give ear, O earth, for the Lord hath spoken; I have nourished and brought up children, and they have rebelled against me. The ox knoweth his owner and the ass his master's crib, but Israel doth not know, my people doth not consider." (Is. i. 2, 3.) The speculative atheism which openly professes to know nothing at all with regard to the Being, works and character of God, is thus defined by His own lips, to be a degradation of man below the level of the brute creatures. The great Apostle of the Gentiles applies the same truth specially to the case of those with whom modern Agnostics would prefer to be classed, the old philosophers of the heathen world. "They are without excuse, because when they knew God, they glorified Him not as God, neither were thankful, but became vain in their imaginations, and their foolish heart was darkened; professing themselves to be wise, they became fools." Moral degradation, and the influx of a tide of degrading lusts and passions, is declared to be the Divine Nemesis on this ungrateful and foolish blindness. "Even as they did not like to retain God in their knowledge, God gave them over to a reprobate mind... filled with all unrighteousness, full of envy, murder, debate, deceit, and malignity."

Atheistic speculations, spreading like a canker in any one generation of mankind, are almost sure to breed gigantic and unnatural wickedness in the generation that

follows.   The mock philanthropy which sets out with
atheistic contempt for the living God, will be sure to
set in a sea of blood.   And "when the kindness of
God the Saviour towards man," has been despised and
rejected, the "New Supreme Being" of M. Comte's
blasphemous philosophy, will be sure ere long to develope his historical attributes, "foolish, disobedient,
deceived, serving divers lusts and pleasures, living in
malice and envy, hateful and hating one another."
(Tit. iii. 3.)

The first form of the Supernatural is the Prophetic.
This supposes that God, the Supreme Intelligence,
singles out amongst men some individuals, through
whom He would give messages of heavenly truth, and
announcements of His will to their fellow-men: that
He then bestows upon them gifts of power, or foresight,
to attest and prove the commission which they have received.   These supernatural gifts, exceeding the power
or wisdom of ordinary men, are tests and signs of
their divine commission.   So it was said to Moses,
"take this rod in thine hand wherewith thou shalt do
signs."   So St Paul writes to the Corinthians, "the
signs of an Apostle were wrought among you, in all
patience, in signs and wonders and mighty deeds."
The idea that though MAN at his will can make known
his thoughts and wishes to his fellow-man in writing,
yet the Lord of Heaven and of earth, the Architect
and Builder of all things, is unable so to do, is the
strange paradox of some modern sceptics.   If God is
pleased to make known His will by speech or writing
to men, reason requires that the messengers He em-
ploys should have clear credentials to confirm their
commission.   So the same Apostle says at the close of
his letter to Thessalonica, "The salutation of Paul with
mine own hand, which is the token in every epistle, so

I write." Thus a distinct proof that the writing was his, and that he had a divine commission, attested by supernatural works, was given with each epistle. So "no prophecy," we are told, "came at any time by the will of man, but holy men of God spake as moved (or borne along) by the Holy Ghost;" and of these messengers we are further told that "God also bare them witness, both with signs and wonders, and divers miracles, and gifts of the Holy Ghost, according to His own will." Such a witness then, either in works of superhuman power, directly wrought by them, or linked with their message, has been the constant law of revelation by prophets, from Adam in Paradise to the beloved disciple in Patmos. To make the contrast more conspicuous between Christ and His forerunner, "John did no miracle." But his birth was announced by the message of an angel, and his work and character by a second prophecy uttered by his own father, and his message was essentially only a preface to that of Christ Himself. Works and sayings, preternatural in common men, are natural, and essential to their work and character, in men singled out to be prophets, messengers, apostles, and ambassadors of the God of heaven.

But beyond this prophetic form of the supernatural, there is one still higher. Should the living God Himself appear in human form, the words and acts of such a Divine Person, conversing with men upon earth, must be supernatural in the highest sense. They must transcend not only the words and works of average men, and of righteous men, but even of prophets; a wisdom, a power and a goodness surpassing those of human prophets would be needful to justify the claim to be such a Divine person. Such a claim, if advanced with an entire absence of any such proofs, would be incredible. So our Lord says, "If I bear witness of myself

B. 6

my witness is not true; the works which the Father
hath given me to finish, the same works that I do, bear
witness of me, that the Father hath sent me." "Had
ye believed Moses ye would have believed me, for he
wrote of me." "If I had not done among them the
works which none other man did, they had not had sin,
but now have they both seen and hated both me and my
Father." And again when the messengers of the Jews
were asked "why have ye not brought him?" they answered, "Never man spake like this man." Thus
works of divine power, and words of divine wisdom,
were joined with signal manifestations of divine goodness. "Ye call me Master and Lord, and ye say
well, for so I am. If I then, your Lord and Master,
have washed your feet, ye also ought to wash one
another's feet." "Peace I leave with you, my peace I
give unto you, not as the world giveth, give I unto
you. Let not your heart be troubled, neither let it be
afraid." "When He was come near, He beheld the city
and wept over it." "Then said Jesus, Father, forgive
them, for they know not what they do." "He said, It
is finished, and He bowed His head, and gave up the
ghost." This threefold cord, of which the strands are,
works of superhuman power, words of divine wisdom,
and acts and tears of divine compassion, condescension,
and grace, is intertwined to guarantee this glorious
truth, that Jesus is the Christ, the Son of God; and
that "the Father sent the Son to be the Saviour of
the world;" and that "all men should honour the Son
even as they honour the Father;" and again, that
"He that honoureth not the Son, honoureth not the
Father which hath sent Him." This great truth of the
divine glory and perfection of the "Sun of Righteousness," the Incarnate Redeemer, shines out above all
other truths, with a brightness like that of the vision

seen by Saul on the way to Damascus, "a light from heaven at midday, above the brightness of the sun." And whenever the eyes of men are closed to this divine and supernatural light, and they prefer to sit down content with the thick darkness of that course of nature, in which death reigns supreme for evermore, the same Apostle has taught us the secret cause of a preference so unnatural. "If our Gospel be hid, it is hid to them which are perishing, in whom the god of this world hath blinded the minds of them which believe not, lest the light of the glorious Gospel of Christ, who is the image of God, should shine unto them."

CHAPTER X.

The Constant Element in Nature.

The Bampton Lectures of Dr Mozley on Miracles (1865) are, in the main, one of the most valuable contributions which Oxford has given within the last forty years to the defence of the Christian faith. I have shewn elsewhere, that Professor Tyndall, in his reply to them in "The Fortnightly," where he warns off the clergy as "noble savages" from the field of physical science, has himself committed two great errors, one with regard to the views of Newton, and the other with regard to the fundamental basis of all inductive science, as illustrated and confirmed by the "Principia." But while he is thus wholly wrong in the issue he has raised, a serious defect mingles with that part of the Lectures which has occasioned his strictures. Dr Tyndall makes it the first principle of real science, that the forces of nature and the laws which men of science investigate, "are necessary,"

"that if the force be permanent, the phenomena are necessary, whether they do or do not resemble anything that has gone before."

Dr Mozley says on the other hand, that our faith in the order of nature

"is an impulse which rests on no rational grounds, and can be traced to no rational principle ; which possesses no intellectual character," and that "the proper function of the inductive principle, or belief in the order of nature, is to act as a practical basis for the affairs of life, and the carrying on of human society."

Professor Tyndall rejoins effectively by enumerating a series of scientific discoveries.

"What," he asks, "has the planet Neptune, or the belt of Jupiter, or the whiteness about the poles of Mars, to do with the affairs of society, or how is society affected by the fact that the sun's atmosphere contains sodium, or that the nebula of Orion contains hydrogen gas? What practical interest has society in the fact that the spots on the sun have a decennial period, and that when a magnet is closely watched for half a century, it is· found to perform small motions which synchronize with the appearance and disappearance of the solar spots?" He continues, "We hold it to be an exercise of reason to explore the meaning of the universe to which we stand in relation, and the work accomplished is the proper commentary on the methods pursued."

The truth lies almost midway between Dr Mozley and his critic; though the error of Prof. Tyndall is the more complete, and is one which would extinguish that very process of induction on the value of which he so strongly insists. Prof. Tyndall's writ of eject-ment against all theologians, and nine-tenths of the clergy, as ignorant savages, from the field of physical science, as involving questions with which they are in-competent to deal, and where they are ill-informed, self-deluded, and likely to delude others, rests on two data. The first is a direct inversion of the facts with regard to Newton's own doctrine; the other is an assertion of the necessary character of the laws of nature, which is opposed to every page of the reasoning in the Principia, and would turn that immortal work into a tissue of laborious folly. It affirms the laws of force to be ne-cessary truths, and thereby stultifies the whole course of experimental science, and reverses the plainest facts in the history of discovery. The other ground of the charge is the maxim, that

"a truly scientific intellect can never be satisfied till it reaches the *forces* by which the succession is produced...In judging of the order of nature, our enquiries relate to the permanence of force."

This principle is true, but Prof. Tyndall has misdirected the writ of ejectment which he founds upon it; its proper address is not to the Christian clergy, but to M. Comte and all the Positive Philosophers. His statement is a point blank contradiction of the fundamental maxim of that philosophy. For its first principle is the exclusion, not only of supernatural powers, but of such abstractions as cause, force, substance, and vital power, from the researches of science, which in its positive stage must be confined to the bare classification of phenomena. The whole course of reasoning by which Dr Mozley has brought on himself and the clergy the reproach of being ignorant savages, is not drawn from theology, but wholly borrowed from the speculations of sceptical philosophers. By a rash acceptance of their premises, he has greatly impaired the value of lectures which contain much striking and valuable thought. Dr Mozley's conclusion is, that the inductive principle belongs to the irrational part of our nature, that it is an unreasoning impulse or mechanical instinct, by which we expect that future changes will be like the past; that it is simply a

"mechanical expectation of the likeness of the unknown to the known," that it is "unreasoning, and no part of the distinctive reason of man." He says that "step by step, philosophy has loosened the connection of the order of nature with the ground of reason, befriending in the same proportion the principle of miracles. Science has itself proclaimed the truth, that we see no causes in nature; that the whole chain of physical succession is to the eye of reason a rope of sand, consisting of antecedents and consequents, but without a rational link or trace of necessary connection between them; we know of law only in the sense of recurrences in nature."

Here Dr Mozley starts with assuming the truth of the first principle of the positive philosophy, that science has to deal with phenomena and their recurrence alone, the relations of likeness and unlikeness.

The only connection of this view with theology is of a secondary and accidental kind. Bishop Berkeley deceived himself with the notion that, by adopting the current philosophy of ideas, and reasoning it out to the sceptical conclusion of the non-existence of matter and the material universe, he could gain a fresh argument for the existence of God. This strange paradox, by which he contradicted both Scripture and common sense, was taken up by successors of a very different spirit, and worked out to its natural issue. First, Hume adopted his reasoning, and applied it to all *mental* phenomena. Instead of material objects, Berkeley left us floating in an ocean of momentary and evanescent phenomena. Hume completed the process, and instead of minds, left nothing but an interminable series of states of consciousness, or sensations, or perceptions, or internal phenomena, with no minds, any more than things, to which they belonged. The denial of the reality of matter being thus followed by a like denial of the existence of mind, there could be no room left in this abyss of darkness, for faith in the existence and attributes of God, that is, of a creative and supreme Intelligence. Bishop Berkeley, unhappily, took the first step towards burying science and religion in this thick jungle of sceptical philosophy, a double contradiction of common sense and of Scripture. But its patrons have not been the Christian clergy or theologians, who have almost unanimously rejected it by a healthy instinct, but sceptical philosophers. From Hume onward, this phenomenalism has been the favourite creed of modern sceptics.

Mr Mill, in his " Logic," makes this the main basis of his Metaphysics, and adopts it fully with regard to the non-existence of matter, which he would replace by the new term " permanent possibilities of sensation." With regard to mind, the phenomena of memory make him hesitate. He owns that philosophical consistency would make us deny the existence of minds, as well as of material objects. But the phenomena of memory forbid him fully to acquiesce in this view; so he counsels a compromise, by which we may use the popular language which implies their existence, with the reserve of a secret doubt and philosophical uncertainty whether they exist or not. Mr Spencer adopts the very same theory with a new phraseology. All the material phenomena which Berkeley left in their endless succession, when matter itself was abolished, are with Mr Spencer an indefinite series of " *vivid* manifestations of the Unknowable." Again, all the series of states of consciousness which Hume left to us after minds were abolished, are with Mr Spencer an interminable series of " *faint* manifestations of the Unknowable." Thus, in this grand funeral procession, Bishop Berkeley led the way, under the guidance of a false philosophy, by abolishing the whole world of matter, Hume followed, and completed the funeral rites, by abolishing the whole world of created minds, leaving us floating in an abyss of material and mental changes, without any things or persons, material objects, or conscious minds, to which they belong. Well may Mr Spencer say that

"Metaphysics of this type usually produce a sceptical state of mind, and are ordinarily followed by a sense of universal illusion."

His proposed remedy however for this great evil only aggravates the disease. It is to introduce a new definition of reality, that reality means only "persistence in consciousness," a definition truly "unthinkable," and never known or heard of till his "First Principles" appeared. Hume has frankly acknowledged this inevitable result of his own extension of Berkeley's reasoning on the non-existence of matter to include mind also.

"These principles," he says, "may flourish and triumph in the schools, where it is difficult to refute them, but as soon as they leave the shade, and by the presence of the REAL OBJECTS (!) are put in opposition to the more powerful principles of our nature, they vanish like smoke, and leave the most determined sceptic in the same condition as other mortals."

The constancy of Nature has a different meaning with Prof. Tyndall, Mr Spencer, and the author of "Supernatural Religion." In the author of the Belfast address it means the *necessary* character of the laws of physical science : the doctrine that

"Nature has never been crossed by spontaneous action, or a state of things ever existed which could not be rigorously deduced from the preceding state."

Prof. Tyndall boldly ascribes this doctrine to Newton himself, and makes it the test of the scientific mind. A startling contradiction of notorious facts, since this is the very doctrine which Newton expressly denounces at the close of the Principia, as unscientific and unreasonable. The doctrine is indeed the most palpable of scientific errors : it destroys the deep contrast between abstract sciences, and concrete sciences which rest upon the evidence of facts, and deal with concrete realities; it stultifies the whole course of experimental science as laborious trifling, and reverses the plainest facts in the history of discovery. It annuls that process which is the essence of scientific advance, a comparison of the results of different hypotheses with observed facts, so as to detect which out of several hypotheses is actually true. The binding of nature by modern science "in the bonds of fate," spoken of in the Belfast address, is nothing else than the contradiction of the fundamental principle of M. Comte and the positive philosophy, which bids us

set aside the research of *forces* and real entities, and
classify phenomena alone. On this view, we have an
infinite multitude of phenomena through successive
moments of time, but the phenomena of each moment
are quite independent of those of the previous or se-
quent moments.

The only indeterminateness which is set aside by
the progress of physical science, is the false inde-
pendence of the phenomena of each separate instant
of time, which would result from the positivist or
phenomenal philosophy. The indeterminateness which
still remains, and which separates the actual universe
and its physical laws, from that system of necessity with
which Prof. Tyndall confounds it, consists of the places
of all the atoms in the universe, containing three times
as many indeterminates, as there are atoms of matter
or of ether in the whole universe. These data cannot be
supplied by the laws themselves. They must be supplied
by the choice of a will, prior to and above the laws;
till they have been thus supplied, the law of gravitation,
and any similar laws depending on the distances of the
atoms, cannot operate. The atoms must exist, and be at
definite distances from each other, and in definite directions, before any one of these laws can take effect. The
result of excluding all spontaneous action, of man or of
God, is not to supersede will by physical laws, but to
restrict the action of will to the first moment of creation, and to confine the choice of the number, properties,
and positions of all the atoms of the universe to that
moment of creation. The whole infinite spontaneity or
element of choice would be concentrated in one moment
of time; thenceforward will and choice in the Creator
would be dormant and idle for evermore. And no will
or choice in any creature would be permitted to interfere
with the perfect and eternal development of the ever-

changing positions of the innumerable atoms. Such is
the senseless view of the history of the universe which
this mechanical theory sets before us. Its laws cannot
work, or come into existence at all, without the previous exercise of choice and will on the part of the
Supreme Lawgiver, and this choice once made, the
faculty of spontaneity is supposed to sink into an everlasting sleep; and the blinded Samson of the material
universe has to grind on in a prison-house of fated and
inevitable change for evermore. Had Prof. Tyndall
read with due care the Lectures he praises so justly,
and followed this by a study of the Principia and the
Scholium at its close, he would have escaped falling into
these blunders. But Dr Mozley's statement, that the
inductive principle, and our faith in the order of Nature,
is an unreasoning impulse, a blind and "unreasoning
instinct," and his further explanation in these words, that

"our nature, though endowed with reason, contains constitutionally
large irrational departments, and includes in it many processes which
are entirely spontaneous, irresistible and of the automaton kind"
(p. 46),

seem to have provoked the rejoinder that "as regards
the knowledge of Nature, which is here the one thing
needful, nine-tenths of the clergy are noble savages
and nothing more," with the further advice, "keep away
from physical nature." The fault of Dr Mozley is, that
he has adopted blindly the main principle of the
phenomenal or idealistic school of sceptical philosophy,
and has thereby greatly impaired and perplexed a course
of argument, marked in other respects by much ingenuity
and force of reasoning. Prof. Tyndall's writ of eject-
ment from the studies and researches of physical science
ought to have its superscription altered, and instead
of being served on theologians and the Christian clergy,
so as really to include with them Bacon, Newton, Milton, ⹀

Barrow, Faraday, Whewell, Sedgwick, and most physical discoverers of real eminence, should be addressed to his own allies, the positive philosophers and Nihilists of modern times. The inductive principle according to Dr Mozley is the expectation that the future will be like the past; this he regards as a blind instinct, having nothing to do with the reason, and implanted to assist us in the practical conduct of life. Now, instead of settling whether this expectation belongs to the rational or irrational part of our nature, there is a prior question whether it exists at all. No one, either peasant, philosopher or divine, really expects that to-morrow will be exactly like to-day in all its events, and the third day exactly like both. As the Bishop of Exeter has well said, in the first Essay (p. 2),

"A series of recurring cycles, however conceivable to the logical understanding, is inconceivable to the spirit, for every later cycle must be different from every earlier by the mere fact of coming after it and embodying its results."

No one ever did believe the course of Nature, or any portions of it, to be mere facsimiles, and perfect repetitions of previous events without any change. On the other hand, to suppose that the events of to-morrow or any later day will be wholly different from the events that are past, with no elements common to both, is incredible and inconceivable. It would imply the annihilation of the actual universe around us, and of ourselves, and the creation of another wholly new. Since no one, then, expects the future to be like the past in all respects, and every one expects it to be like the past in some respects, there is plainly a wide range for the exercise of reason, to decide how far it is probable the likeness will extend, and what will be the degree of unlikeness, variation, and change. The first step in the exercise of reason on this subject, is to renounce as wholly false the first principle of the positive philosophy; that we have to deal with a vast phantasmagoria of phenomena alone, and not with real entities, things, persons and places. The element of permanence, on which we confidently and reasonably rely, has this ground, that the persons, the animals, the trees and plants, and the places and material objects of which we have had experience to-day, will form the main part of our experiences to-morrow, unless we travel away from our present to a wholly different locality. There are various changes on which we reasonably calculate amidst this general identity; death and dissolution in the case of some; growth and insensible vital progress in all; and births, introducing fresh persons, animals, and plants, besides those which were known before. There are other changes of a periodic kind. The regular succession of day and night, of spring, summer, autumn, and winter, of seed-time and harvest; and besides these, changes which we cannot precisely predict or anticipate, of a more exceptional kind; partial or complete catastrophes, such as sudden deaths, earthquakes, explosions, thunderstorms, destruction of life by lightning, river-floods and oceanic inundations, and other violent and extreme changes, to which Nature is liable in every part of her wide dominion. The cultivation of our reason, and the practical habits of human life, depend on the permanent elements in Nature, and on those quiet and regular changes which come within the range of reasonable expectation and practical forecast. All exceptional changes, which we cannot foresee or anticipate by our knowledge of second causes, come practically under the head of the miraculous; there is no blinding influence of custom to hinder our minds from passing at once, in these, to the recognition of that Divine Agent, on whom all second causes really depend.

"Miracles viewed as evidences for a revelation, are unusual events not within the ordinary power of man, nor capable of being foreseen by man's actual knowledge of second causes, and wrought or announced by some professed messenger of God, to confirm the reality of the message; the definition has a negative and a positive side. There must be no second causes, at least within human knowledge, that will account for the event, and there must be an apparent connection with a plain moral object or more professed message from God. Wherever these two conditions meet, we have a case of miraculous evidence; some of these, possibly, by an increase of man's insight into natural changes, or of his power over nature, in some later age might cease to be miraculous. Others may surpass not only human, but super-human power. ..Whenever, through the power of sin, creation has grown opaque to the eyes of men, and the physical course of nature conceals from them the presence of the great Lawgiver, miracles are needed to form an antidote to blind nature-worship, and to reverse the blinding spell of unbelief. This end may be secured either by acts of Divine power suspending or reversing some particular law of nature, or by combining these in such an unusual way, and with such marks of a moral purpose, as to force on reluctant minds the conviction that Nature is only the servant and handmaid of the Living God, the Creator and moral Governor of the universe." (*Bible and Modern Thought*, p. 76.)

The Most High, when He answers the patriarch out of the whirlwind, speaks of these extraordinary changes in Nature, as His own treasures,—"which I have reserved against the time of trouble, against the day of battle and war" (Job xxxviii. 23). And again, with regard to the bounds of the ocean, the circuits of the earth, the ordinances of heaven, and the lightnings, "Who brake up for it a decreed place, and set bars and doors, and said, Hitherto shalt thou come, but no further, here shall thy proud waves be stayed? Hast thou commanded the morning, and caused the dayspring to know its place, that it might take hold of the ends of the earth, and that the wicked might be shaken out of it? Canst thou lift up thy voice to the clouds, that abundance of waters may cover thee? Canst thou send lightnings that they may go and say unto thee, Here we are ?" All that is vast, unforeseen, unusual, and magnificent in Nature, constitutes the secret treasure-chamber of the Most High, that He may " withdraw man from his purpose, and hide pride from man."

The constancy of Nature, or as he styles it, "the perfection and invariability of Nature," with the author of "Supernatural Religion" is a third thing, distinct from both the extremes of Mozley and Tyndall. It is a passive adoption of the third of Mr Spencer's three inconsistent theories of the future manifestation of the unknowable. It is neither the necessary character of natural laws, nor the likeness in all respects of the future to the past.

The author of "Supernatural Religion" in accepting as a first principle the predicted Creed of the scoffers of the last days, that "all things continue as they were since the fathers fell asleep," under the title of the "glorious perfection and invariability of the order of Nature," seems never to have taken the least pains to analyze or define to himself that constancy of the laws of Nature to which he appeals. It is plain that the endless variation of natural phenomena, and of the changes of the visible universe, is quite as conspicuous as that constancy of natural law to which the appeal is made. Let us consider the matter a little more closely. There may be said perhaps to be nine great laws or principles which reveal themselves in the constitution and changes of the universe. (1) First, the law of Permanence; the continuous existence of all the creatures which God has made, and which come within the range of our observations; man, animals, and plants, and the innumerable atoms of lifeless matter. Our knowledge refers to things and persons that do really exist, and not to perishable evanescent sensations or phenomena which

expire in the moment of their birth.   The first step then
of genuine science, is to renounce the Idealism of Berkeley, and the Sensationalism of Mr Mill in his "Logic."
This first law of permanence in all natural objects, results
directly from the fact of creation.   THINGS abide and
endure, but sensations and phenomena expire from moment to moment.   There is an element of permanence
in Nature, because "in the beginning God created the
Heavens and the Earth," and "they continue this day
according to His ordinance."   (2) The second law is
that of Progression, or the successive stages of life and
growth in all living things.   Thus, all men, animals and
plants, beginning with the embryo or the seed, pass
on through successive stages to maturity and old age.
This law of progress, and continual passage from infant
weakness to mature strength and fully-developed life,
extends through the whole range of animated being.
It has its defined periods, which extend from the ephemeral life of the insect tribes to the millennial duration
of the trees of the forest.   (3) A third law, which accompanies the second, as a kind of negative counterpart
or dark shadow, is the law of Death or dissolution, what
the apostle calls "the law of sin and death."   Life in all
plants and animals and even in man himself, after a
period of growth or maturity of varying length, is followed by disease, death, and dissolution of being.   This
law we accept as a fact, universal within the limits of
terrestrial existence, but reason protests against the
acceptance of it as a fundamental and absolute law of
universal being.   (4) Fourthly, there is a law of Periodicity including three main elements, on which the
course of human history and the measurement of time
depend ; 1. The period and ceaseless alternation of day
and night, resulting from the daily revolution of the
earth, and revealing itself in every sunrise and sunset,

fulfilling the decree, "While the earth remaineth, day and night shall not cease." 2. The second period is that of the natural year, depending on the motion of the earth in its annual orbit, and revealing itself in the succession of the seasons; this is ratified by the same divine decree, "While the earth remaineth, seed-time and harvest, cold and heat, winter and summer, shall not cease." 3. A third period, less conspicuous than these, but still playing an important part in natural science and all human history, is the month, or lunation of the moon. With these are connected many secondary periods, of a more complex and dependent kind; the tides and ocean currents, the trade winds and other changes of the ocean and the air. The heavens supply other periods in the revolutions of the planets and their satellites, and binary and variable stars. But all these are very subordinate, in practical importance, to the three fundamental periods of the day, the year and the month. Nearly all the cases of man's limited power of predicting future events depend on this law of periodicity.

There are four other natural laws of mutation, dependent on the inter-action of the two elements of water and fire. First, the law of evaporation, by which water under the influence of heat evaporates and disappears, and the whole aqueous system of the earth is maintained. Secondly, the law of freezing, by which water solidifies with cold, and the snows of winter and the mountain glaciers are formed. Thirdly, the law of induration, by which bodies imperfectly solid are hardened, and changed to a rocky texture. Fourthly, the law of combustion, by which, under the application of intense heat, the texture of material masses, either great or small, is completely changed, and they are either entirely dissipated or assume wholly altered forms, while life is extinguished in all living things. To these eight main principles or laws of material change, we may add a ninth, the law of occasional catastrophes, or non-periodic changes of an exceptional and peculiar kind. Phenomena of this kind are, explosions, sudden conflagrations, floods and inundations, shipwrecks, earthquakes, volcanic eruptions, pestilences, tornadoes, and hurricanes. Though not infractions of natural laws, they are exceptional results of a combination of those laws beyond the range of human foresight, but foreseen and pre-arranged by the great Governor of the universe. The constancy, then, of natural laws is an ambiguous term. The sameness of a law itself is one thing, and the sameness of the conditions under which it operates is something wholly different. While fundamental laws are the same, the conditions under which they operate, and by which their effects are determined, vary ever from hour to hour, from year to year, and still more from age to age.

The geological reasonings of Sir C. Lyell are wholly based on a confusion of these two different things; the sameness of laws, and of the conditions under which they operate. He professes to aim at explaining all geological changes through many past myriads of years, by causes that are now in operation, as inferred from the experience of the past hundred years. The causes themselves, now in operation, are the attractive, cohesive and ethereal forces of the actual atoms or masses of matter in the solar system. The action of the law of gravitation, and doubtless of cohesion and electric repulsion also, depends for its amount on the position of the different atoms or masses; but those positions have changed and are changing from hour to hour, by the action of those laws themselves; these changes in the course of long ages may have been, and indeed in the course of long ages must have been, so great and various as practically to annul the sameness of the law, by utter diversity and entire contrast in the conditions under which it is exercised. To strive to account for all past changes, whether on the earth's surface, or throughout its entire mass, by "causes now in operation," if by these are meant present laws, operating under present conditions, is an attempt which is sure to fail. It assumes sameness of conditions and circumstances through myriads of past years, where all experience and reason conspire to demonstrate the fact of a wide, indefinite and almost immeasurable diversity. It is true of the life of each individual man, that he "is cut down as a flower, and fleeth as it were a shadow," while it may be said of the universal frame of Nature, and of the earth itself in past ages of geological change, and in the promised ages of the world to come, that it "never continueth in one stay." " In the midst of life we are in death,"' and terrestrial experience since exact records began, is confined within far too narrow bounds, to allow us to determine thereby the working and the limits of the two contrasted laws of life and death. We need for this all the further light which Divine revelation can supply, and in part has supplied. When we go a little further back than three thousand years, we are confronted at once by the two great facts of which unbelievers are "willingly ignorant" —the creation of "all things in the beginning by the word of God," and the Flood which came "upon the world of the ungodly." And for the last eighteen hundred years, the whole history of our world has been determined and moulded by those two facts which the Gospel history alone sets before us, the actual resurrection of Christ, and the promise which He has given of a future hour when "all that are in the graves shall hear His voice,

7—2

and shall come forth." The moral and even the physical history of all Christian nations, that is, of the dominant and ruling part of the earth's population, has been determined and moulded by these two great facts, which the sceptic in his blind worship of the constancy of natural causes, would set aside as dreams of superstition.

The course of Nature may be said to be compounded of three elements : the fixed or permanent, the periodic, and the ever varying. Man's power of forecast depends on the second. The elements of change and variation outnumber and exceed those of fixity and permanence. The further we recede from present time, the more complete is the change, and the fewer are the unchanged and abiding elements. In less than a hundred years, the whole generation of living men will have passed away, and in a thousand years, only a few forest trees and the everlasting hills will remain, of all the objects that now meet the eyes of man on the surface of the earth. What is permanent and enduring is a very small fraction indeed of that which existed once, and will soon have passed away. For permanence and constancy we need to mount higher, and look to Him who is the Self-existent and the Unchangeable, and to those elements of created being which partake most largely of these Divine attributes ; to the spiritual being of man, in those who, by partaking of a Divine nature, are raised above the sphere of death and corruption, and the darkness of the grave, into a higher region of blissful hope and expectation of an immortal life to come. " He that doeth the will of God abideth for ever."

CHAPTER XI.

THE MIRACULOUS ELEMENT INVOLVED IN THE WHOLE COURSE OF NATURE.

A DOUBLE confusion of thought with regard to the meaning of Nature, and of miraculous evidence, forms the basis of that monstrous tissue of sophistry, by which the author of "Supernatural Religion" seeks to blot out the light of the Gospel, and of the blessed Dayspring from on high, and to bury the whole world in midnight darkness once more. Let us examine the meaning of three cognate terms in connection with the whole course of Nature: the mysterious, the unusual, and the miraculous. Man's knowledge of the course of Nature, and of the universe around him, is a very small fragment of a vast and mighty whole. The little island of human knowledge is shut in and surrounded by a vast ocean of the unknown, and that unknown ocean is the home of infinite and unsearchable mysteries. The range of common and ordinary experience includes mainly two things: certain known objects or permanent existences; human beings, animals, plants, portions of the earth's surface, the atmosphere, the lights of the sky, the sun, moon and stars; and certain usual changes, of birth, growth and death, and of the circuits of the heavens, and that succession of the seasons, and of day and night, of which he has constant experience. Within these narrow limits, custom, indolence, and moral torpor weaken the sense of mystery.

and make it possible for men to forget the Author of
their being, the great Cause on whom both they and all
things around them depend.   Our own existence, and
that of the persons and things immediately around us,
is itself a great mystery.   Whenever we reflect upon it
seriously, reason cannot pause, till it reaches the footstool
of the throne of God.   Since we and things around us
exist, there must be self-existence somewhere, a First
Cause of all things.   Again, not only the existence of the
things around us, but the ordinary circuit of changes
which they undergo, is highly mysterious.   To thoughtful
minds "the Heavens declare the glory of God, and the
firmament sheweth His handiwork."   When the Psalmist
considered the sun, moon, and stars, he was lost in ad-
miration of the greatness and glory of the Creator, and
of His condescending goodness towards the children
of men.   "What is man, that Thou art mindful of him?
and the son of man, that Thou regardest him?"   The
sense of mystery, though it may lie dormant for a time
while we abide within the narrow sphere of man's daily
experience, wakens up afresh when his understanding
returns to him, and he begins to reflect seriously on the
wonders of the universe which surround him on every
side.   Even the known and familiar objects of Nature,
and their customary changes, are full of mystery, and
ought to lead the thoughts of men upward to the
presence of God.   Still more is this true of that immense
abyss of unknown, undiscovered truth, by which the
islet of our actual knowledge of Nature and outward
things is shut in and enclosed on every side.   The
unusual and unfamiliar in Nature has a far wider range
than the familiar and the usual.   As soon as men travel
from place to place they become acquainted with fresh
groups of terrestrial objects; and the men, animals, and
plants, of which any one has had a personal experience,

and gained a familiar knowledge, are a very small part
of the whole range of earthly existence.   Growing study
of the skies opens a still wider range of celestial mysteries,
of worlds and systems, wholly inaccessible to the footsteps of man in his present state.   The unusual, the unfamiliar in Nature, is thus the appointed pathway, by
which man is conducted out of the littleness of his own
actual ignorance, into the contemplation of the infinite
vastness of that universe which is on every side, and is
raised to a growing apprehension of the wisdom, power,
and goodness of the great Author and Parent of the
whole.   "All we behold is miracle, but seen so duly, all
is miracle in vain."   The unusual and unfamiliar, then,
is that by which the deadening effect of custom and habit
is overcome.   It is God's surgical instrument for re-
moving the scales and couching the cataract, by which
the eyes of the soul are darkened; till men are content
to live on in thoughtless unconcern, in a constant round
of day and night, seed-time and harvest, summer and
winter, forgetful of all the mysteries of human life, and
of the wonderful world around them, never asking,
Whence am I, and whither am I going?   What means
this gift of life, this "vapour, which appears for a little
time and then vanishes away?"   It is the unusual and
unfamiliar which wakens man from the dull sleep of
custom, to draw once more the conclusion of the wisest
of men, "Fear God and keep His commandments, for
this is the whole business of man."   The awakened
conscience will then soon pass on to accept the further
truth, "God will bring every work into judgment, with
every secret thing, whether it be good or whether it
be evil."

But this wide range of the unusual and unfamiliar in
Nature, this Divine pathway, which leads man out of his
own littleness into fellowship with the full grandeur and

magnificence of the universe, admits of a twofold distinction. It includes changes foreseen and anticipated, and changes wholly unforeseen, unexplained, and unexpected. These two classes of the unfamiliar and unusual are very dissimilar in their operation on the human mind. Changes however unusual, which man can foresee and anticipate, because he can trace them to some special concurrence of second causes in usual and daily operation, do not awaken in him the impression of witnessing an immediate operation of Divine power, a direct effect of supernatural agency; the tendency is rather to enlarge and enrich his impressions of the order and method that reigns in the universe, and of the wide range and complexity of those laws by which the Creator governs and regulates all the works of His hands. The phenomena of a total eclipse of the sun are impressive and startling in the highest degree; they must arrest and absorb the attention of all who witness them, and they even disturb the accustomed instincts of the lower creatures. But, when observed as a consequence of calculations made beforehand, which determine with the greatest accuracy the moment of its occurrence, and its short continuance, it can produce no such impression as it does amongst savages, on whom it bursts without any warning; an impression of the direct action of some malignant demon, blotting out the whole light of heaven in pure malice, and awakening a fear that this may never be restored. On the other hand, the strange occurrence, being foreseen, and referred to a specific combination of second causes, serves to crown and complete the evidence of the wide range of natural laws, and of the constancy of their operation, not only in the regular succession of day and night, and summer and winter, but in an immense variety of celestial changes that, on a superficial view, seem irregular and arbitrary.

But unusual and unfamiliar changes, not foreseen or anticipated, have an opposite effect. They waken men equally from the trance of custom, but their further lesson is not of the greatness of human knowledge, and the wide extent of natural laws, but on the contrary of the narrow limit of man's knowledge, and the vast range of Divine power, optional and not confined and fettered by any law that man can trace or discover, but still at the free disposal of the Almighty Creator, to hide pride from man, and bring him to worship in humble reverence at the footstool of the Almighty.

Now what is the relation of the miraculous, in the scriptural sense of the phrase, to this wide range of un-familiar and unforeseen elements in the course of Nature ? It is a selection from amongst all the changes that might arrest attention, of a limited number, to connect them by some plain and specific marks with a moral pur-pose, and the manifest presence of the Supreme Creator. This connection may be secured in three different ways. First, by an alteration and modification of the instincts of the lower creatures, such as can only be reasonably assigned to a superhuman cause. Secondly, by special powers or gifts imparted to individual persons, the bearers of a Divine message ; or, thirdly, the Most High God may reveal Himself, as a Person, by personal acts of Divine power, or by words of Divine wisdom and goodness, speaking to men face to face, as a man speaketh to his friend, with a presence of condescending love in the midst of the creatures He has made.   All these different forms of the miraculous are set before us in the messages of the Bible.   First, we have cases of the miraculous control and elevation of instinct in the lower creatures.

A wider range of Scripture miracles is that of signs and wonders, wrought by a long series of prophets,

commissioned to bear God's messages to the people of
Israel, from Moses to Malachi, and the prophets and
apostles of the New Testament. Three signs were given
to Moses at his first commission, as the pledges and
proofs of its reality—Then "he put forth his hand and
caught it, and it became a rod in his hand...that they
may believe that Jehovah, the God of their fathers, the
God of Abraham, of Isaac, and of Jacob, hath appeared
unto thee."..."Thou shalt take this rod in thine hand,
wherewith thou shalt do signs." So St Paul says to the
Corinthians, "Truly the signs of an apostle were wrought
among you in all patience, in signs and wonders and
mighty deeds." But the crowning glory of the Gospel,
and the fullest form of miraculous self-manifestation of
God, is in the person, ministry and presence on earth
of the incarnate Son of God, and the like manifestation of the Holy Ghost, the Comforter, in the manifold gifts of the Spirit on the day of Pentecost, and in
the later history of the Church. Hence reasons the
Apostle, "How shall we escape if we neglect so great
a salvation, which at the first began to be spoken by the
Lord, and was confirmed unto us by them that heard
Him; God also bearing them witness with signs and
wonders, and with divers miracles and gifts of the Holy
Ghost, according to His own will." Thus, from the
insect plagues of Egypt, through the barren fig-tree, and
the fishes of the ocean depths, upward to the throne of
God, all departments of the creation, and the Supreme
Creator Himself, give consenting testimony, by signs,
wonders and mighty deeds, to the truth, reality and
excellency of the everlasting Gospel of the grace of
God to sinful men. Those who venture to defame and
denounce this glorious message of redeeming love and
grace, as "shocking to their reason and moral sense,"
and contradicted by "the glorious perfection" of that

order of Nature, in which death reigns supreme without a Redeemer; show merely the depth of moral darkness into which it is possible for men to sink, even in the midst of the noonday brightness of "the Day-spring from on high," the "Sun of Righteousness," the only true and eternal Light of the souls of sinful men.

CHAPTER XII.

The Threefold Inconstancy of Terrestrial Nature.

THE free thinkers of the last days, who make the constancy of Nature, within the limits of earthly experience, "since the fathers fell asleep," a warrant for their disbelief of the Creation and the Deluge in time past, and of the solemn warning of a Judgment to come, overlook three great limitations of that constancy to which they appeal as a first principle; three scientific refutations of their uniformitarian philosophy. In our own days, a whole school of geological speculation, with many disciples, has been founded on the misconstruction of a single ambiguous phrase, "causes now in operation." First, the constancy of terrestrial nature for indefinite ages past, and countless ages to come, is disproved and forbidden by the nature of man, and the known course of human parentage and descent. The habitable surface of our earth is of known and definite extent, about fifty millions of square miles. The present population of our globe is either a thousand or twelve hundred millions of human beings; or from twenty to twenty-four for every square mile, whether barren or fertile, locked in eternal frost or scorched with torrid heat, from the North to the South Pole. This surface is a fixed, invariable quantity, but the law of human life is one of geometrical progression.

It is not unlikely that the present population of our globe is ten times greater than at the beginning of the Christian era. With the same rate of increase forward, or decrease backward, the population might be from eight to ten millions, eighteen hundred years before Christ; now it is quite easy to conceive of an increase a million-fold of the sons of Noah, in five centuries, when the unpeopled earth lay all before them, open for their occupation. But such a relation between the earth's surface and its population is incapable of being produced indefinitely, either backward or forward, except under conditions quite contrary to this assumed constancy of terrestrial nature. One possible alternative is, that the whole race might be placed under a law of comparative barrenness and sterility, so that with few exceptions no parents should have more than one son and one daughter. But this, according to the past experience of human nature, could only be by a constant miracle, operating through successive millennia of the world's history, and therefore flatly opposed to the constancy of laws purely physical. The second alternative is, such an increased prevalence of pestilence, bloodshed, violent war, and other causes of human mortality, as might reverse and nullify from age to age, the tendency, in more peaceable and prosperous times, to a constant increase and overflow of the world's population. The third alternative is one, in which the moral and spiritual elevation of the whole race would bring the higher elements of our nature into such activity, as to overcome all its lower instincts and passions, and prevent all marriages but those guided by a Christian ideal, social forethought, and a full sense of paternal and maternal responsibility. In the absence of these three alternatives, none of which agrees with past experience, the constancy of Nature, instead of continuing unbroken through many millennia of coming time,

must terminate in a few centuries, or else require a
communication to be opened miraculously with other
worlds, to provide space for overflowing multitudes of
the earth's population.   The laws of human increase
wholly exclude a doctrine of the constancy of terrestrial
nature, even for a single millennium.   They supply
also a scientific presumption of great force, against that
hypothesis of the extreme antiquity of the human race,
for many myriads of years before the time of Moses
and Noah, which many have lately espoused, in entire
contradiction to the plain teaching of the word of God.
A miraculous process by which men and women had
been developed out of apes or monkeys, must have been
succeeded by a law of unnatural sterility and barrenness,
and by a further law of preternatural indolence and
inaction, so that through successive ages many generations were born and died like ephemera, without
leaving behind them any visible and palpable signs of
their existence.   All the strongest instincts and characteristics of man, as unfolded in the last two or three
thousand years, must have been reversed, or wholly
wanting, in these thousand or ten thousand generations
of pre-Adamite men, bred and reared in the fertile brains
of a few inventive speculators of the present or the
last century.

A second limit to the constancy of terrestrial nature,
is that which depends on the earth itself.   The earth, as
explored by modern science, seems to be throughout
its crust, or the parts nearest the surface to the depth
of a few miles, an immense cemetery, with strata
superimposed one upon another, of systems of plants
and animals which have existed in succession and
then passed away, whether through a great number of
partial catastrophes and violent changes, or a smaller
number almost total.   Now, our earth being thus con-

stituted, a constancy of terrestrial nature for many past myriads of years, and still more, through myriads of past centuries, is a manifest contradiction of the known facts. The disciples of the uniformitarian scheme of geology, in striving to account for all changes of the earth through the eras of geology· by causes now in operation, merely deceive themselves with an ambiguous phrase. The causes now in operation are certain atoms of matter which constitute the mass of the earth, and certain laws of terrestrial change, and relations of place, distance, density, rest or atomic motion, and heat, under which the forces operate at the present time. Now the known law of gravitation, and most probably the unknown laws of cohesion and repulsiòn, are functions of the distances. The force exercised by every atom or body, on every other, varies with every change of distance. The causes in operation ten thousand, or a hundred thousand years ago, if the mass of the earth and its component atoms were the same, and the laws of force the same, must have been different, and could not have been the same as the forces which are in operation now. The theoretical sámeness would be that of the atoms composing the mass of the earth, and of the abstract laws, but the forces would probably differ in all the following respects. First, the mean density of the earth must probably have varied from age to age, if it was condensed from a primitive nebula ; and if the moon, which is of less density, was parted from it many millennia ago. Also the mean temperature of the whole has plainly varied from age to age ; the pressure on every stratum from the surface to the centre ; the density of each stratum, resulting from that pressure ; the more or less intense resistance to further condensation, or the modulus of elasticity ; the coast lines, or separations between land and sea, the bed or depression of

the ocean; the heights and position of all the different
mountain ranges; the total amount of light and heat
received from the sun; the electric and magnetic conditions of every part of the surface, and of the whole
mass.   These are only a few of the elements which
almost certainly have varied from age to age, throughout all past time, since the crust of our earth became
solid.

To found a scheme of geology, then, on the assumption that the causes in operation in all past time, were
the same which operate at present in the nineteenth
century of the Christian era, is to build a pyramid of
guess-work on the foundation of a demonstrable falsehood.   At the same time, within a limit of two centuries, it may be highly probable that the structure of
the earth, and the main elements of its constitution, on
which local changes, their nature and direction, would
chiefly depend, would not differ much from those which
operate at present.   But with every century that we
remove from the present time, the differences must increase; probably at least in the ratio of the square, and
more probably in the ratio of the cube, or some higher
power of that interval.   For the difference in each of a
dozen different elements of the great problem reacts on
all the rest, and multiplies their compound effect.   Thus
it will be probable that the differences a millennium ago,
compared with those of a single century, are not tenfold
but at least a thousand-fold, and more probably a million
times greater.   Never surely was a scientific theory built
in the dark, on a more demonstrable falsehood, than the
uniformitarian doctrine of some modern geologists, at least
in its most extreme form.   At present, the known and
really scientific elements of the vast problem, to determine
what was the state, configuration and chemical structure,
of every part of the earth's crust, and its fauna and flora

to the depth of one mile from the sea level, a thousand or ten thousand years ago are only as one in a million, compared with the data which are purely conjectural and still unknown.   The constancy then of terrestrial nature in past ages, is excluded and disproved by the whole structure of the crust of the earth, as far down as science has been able to penetrate.   The lesson taught is the very opposite ; inconstancy, change and perpetual variation, only with some fixed and permanent elements in the midst of a vast series of indefinite changes.   But the elements of permanence bring out into fuller relief the predominence and manifold complexity of the causes of change which were in ceaseless operation.   The whole structure then of the earth's crust, from the Laurentian strata of Canada upwards, is one continuous protest against that doctrine of the constancy of terrestrial nature, which the scoffers of the last days make the excuse for their rejection of the statements of Scripture with regard to the Creation and the Flood, and of its solemn warning of a future Day of Judgment, when the earth and the works therein shall be burned up and dissolved, and be followed by new heavens and a new earth according to the Divine promise.

A third proof of the inconstancy of terrestrial nature may be drawn from the relation of our earth and its whole system to the sun, the great source of light, heat, and central attraction.   On no reasonable view can we assume the thorough constancy of terrestrial nature, wholly dependent as it is on the sun, for immense and limited ages, either in the past or the future.   In fact, several different theories and conjectures are prevalent among scientific men on this subject, and all of them alike are incompatible with an unlimited constancy of terrestrial nature.   One very prevalent view, at the present time, is that the sun is a great spendthrift, send-

ing out his light and heat throughout space never to
return to him, a prodigal wasting his substance in riotous
living,—the stock of primitive energy on which the
light, warmth, and life of the whole system depend.
They predict that in ten, twenty, or four hundred millions of years, this stock will probably be exhausted, in
which case the whole system must issue in a glacial
period, very different from that which geologists think
they have deciphered in the boulder drift age; and the
whole planet remain covered for ever with a frozen
ocean, or mountain glaciers, with all life extinct, for
evermore.   This is the basis of the first of Mr Spencer's
three incompatible theories, or *à priori* conclusions, with
regard to the future mode and scheme of action of the
UNKNOWABLE through millions of ages to come.   Half a
dozen kindred theories might be named.   The sun is
speeding fast through the realms of space.   He is rapidly
losing energy, light and heat, by sending out his rays
through all surrounding space.   He is gaining fresh
light and heat by the constant dropping in of streams of
meteors.   Or again, by a ceaseless condensation of his
mass from age to age.   Many think that his present
light, heat, and mass have been attained in millions of
years by condensation from a vast nebular cloud.   Others
conjecture that as the sun and Sirius are now approaching each other at the rate of some hundreds of millions
of miles each year, they will probably, in less than a
million of years, end their course by a violent collision,
which certainly would involve the destruction of both
systems; of the Sirian planets, if any, and of the earth
and all its sister planets as far as Neptune.   Thus modern
men of science offer us almost as many alternative
theories of change, inconstancy, and probable destruction
in store for the sun, as they have detected dark lines
in the solar spectrum itself.

When therefore we consider the nature of man as a living being, the constitution of the earth's crust, and the probable past and future history of the sun, we have a threefold refutation of the maxim of the scoffers of the last days.   " Since the fathers fell asleep, all things continue as they were from the beginning of the Creation," and will so continue for ever.   They further affirm that "the universe is unlimited and immeasurable, it is eternal and it is infinite," so that in fact there was no creation, and there has been no beginning, and will be no end[1]. Thus the physical theory of the bankruptcy of the sun some millions of years hence, has been anticipated in the higher sphere of morals.   In the souls of some modern atheists a state of moral darkness has been reached already, in which the " Sun of Righteousness," the true Light of the world, is quenched in utter darkness.

[1] Haeckel's " History of Creation," p. 324.

CHAPTER XIII.

The Witness of all Nature to the Being and Perfections of God.

THE author of "Supernatural Religion" in his Introduction, professes to deplore the general eclipse of faith, and the inconsistencies of those Christian Divines, who pick out scraps and fragments from the Christian Revelation, and reject the rest, or dilute it into seeming agreement with modern currents of unbelieving thought. Yet the one great object of his work is to render that eclipse total, permanent and irreversible, and his chief implement in this melancholy task, is a gathering up and collecting into one focus of those concessions and partial surrenders of divine truth of which he complains. The apparent success is almost complete. The impression left after reading his first chapter, is, that if Nature or revelation yield any evidence for the existence and perfections of a personal God, it has been so effectually disguised, frittered away, mixed up with confused thought, and surrendered or contradicted in detail, as to be robbed of all moral power, and practically to be equivalent to the entire absence of all real evidence whatever. The first step of his argument is a statement that faith in miracles and the supernatural is almost entirely rejected by continental divines and philosophers, so that its defence is made to rest on English writers alone, and certainly the admissions or contradictions which he quotes from these, are of a very startling kind. The concessions he affects to condemn, constitute the whole sinews and strength of his own argument. I will first state separately the negative elements, by the union of which the testimony of Nature to a God is wholly abolished, and then reverse the process, and expound briefly what is the cumulative force of that testimony.

A first negative element is borrowed from Sir W. Hamilton and Dean Mansel. They both in their peculiar phraseology, do not hesitate to affirm

"that the kind of cause we denominate a Deity is exclusively given in the phenomena of mind, and that the phenomena of matter do not warrant any inference to the existence of a God." (S. R., p. 55.)

Here at one blow the whole universe, except the living generation of men, is pronounced to be destitute of any voice to bear witness to the existence of its Author, His power, wisdom, or goodness. In the second part, the author adopts the creed of the ancient Sadducee, and counts it a sufficient proof of the blind credulity of the apostles, that they believed in a resurrection, in angels and spirits. This increases the effect of the first admission, and confines the testimony for a God exclusively to the living generation of men upon earth, since it is held that no other minds, either spirits of men or angels, have any existence. The testimony, even of these, is limited to their minds alone, and excludes wholly their bodily organization.

Meanwhile, another school of sceptical philosophers are busily engaged in striving to prove that mind is nothing whatever but a product of material organization, and that the phenomena of mind are only a sub-province of the phenomena of matter, and that the mind of man in fact is only a condensed bundle of transformed solar force. Dr Mozley next makes the strange admission that

"the argument from miracles for the truth of a revelation begins and ends with an assumption ; we assume the existence of a personal Deity prior to the proof of miracles in a religious sense...the question of miracles is thus shut up within the enclosure of one assumption, that of the existence of a God...When we state this, it is replied that this very conception of God as a Personal, Omnipotent Being, is one for which there is no evidence in material nature."

Thus revelation, real or supposed, merely assumes His existence, and proves nothing; the idea it is said further, has never been practically derived from the study of Nature, but has resulted from a supposed revelation, and that the philosophers who held a universal first cause never thought of that cause being a proper object for worship. He holds however that though the idea was never actually derived from reason and the works of Nature, and revelation never proves it, but begins by assuming it, still the idea, once possessed, is seen to rest on some ground of reason. This ground is thus explained, that when we see marks of design in Nature issuing in the production or existence of personal beings,

"this implies a personal being at the other end of the chain of causes ; from personality at one end, we may infer personality at the other. We cannot suppose that the existence of that which is contrived can be personal, and the contriver a blind, irrational force." (B. L., pp. 24, 99.)

This is certainly true, but the truth is so hemmed in by needless limitations, that the whole argument seems in danger of vanishing away. All Nature, except some individual human minds, is owned to yield no evidence for the being of a God. All revelation, true or false, is owned to yield no evidence or proof, but to begin and end with assuming it to be true. If physiologists were to succeed in reducing mind itself to be merely brain or cerebral organization, then the sole evidence for the Divine existence, according to these writers, would wholly disappear. But this is not the last step of surrender. We are carried still further by Dr Westcott's admission, apparently borrowed from Mansel and Hamilton, but expressly rejected by Dr Mozley,

"the only approximately adequate conception we can form of a Divine Being is in the form of a contradiction." ("Gospel of Resurrection," p. 21, S. R. 69.)

Now a contradiction is to say a thing, and straightway to unsay it. If then human minds alone, with or without revelation, yield us any evidence for the existence of a God, and the only idea of a God of which they yield any evidence, is made up of contradictions, a series of assertions completed by as many more assertions which contradict them, such evidence must be a mere zero. These human minds, which alone furnish any evidence for the existence of God, furnish no evidence of any real being whatever, but only of a blank of total darkness within them, as well as in the universe around them. Such is the logical issue of these various concessions and surrenders of truth when combined together.

Let us now turn to the clear light and plain testimonies of the word of God. "The invisible things of God from the creation of the world, are clearly seen, being understood by the things that are made, even His eternal power and Godhead" (Rom. i. 20). The first step of the proof, is our knowledge of our own existence, and of that of our fellow men, and of the various objects and real existences of the world around us. From this real à posteriori knowledge, however limited and partial, of an actual universe, reason at once infers concerning each of these, that it must either be self-existent, or

formed by a self-existent Being.   But all the things
we know by experience, including ourselves and our
fellow men, have many features of change, weakness,
littleness, passiveness or recent birth, which exclude the
notion that any one of them is a self-existent being,
the cause of all other beings.   Since then there must
be a self-existent Cause, distinct from each and all
the particular beings, things, or persons we know by experience, what light do these supply with regard to the
nature of that First Cause ?   Our knowledge of all actual
things is joined with a clear conviction, that there are
many possible beings besides those which are actual, and
that even of real existences, those known to us are only
a very small part.   Our knowledge of the First Cause,
to be complete and exhaustive, would require a double
extension of our thoughts, from the beings actually known
to us to all the unknown, and from all actual existences
known or unknown, so as to include also all unknown
possibilities of being.   Only then do we attain to a full
conception of the universe of non self-existent being on
the one side, or of the self-existent uncreated First
Cause, the Author of all actual and possible creatures,
on the other.   What then are the steps by which we
may rise from our limited and partial knowledge of
ourselves and things around us, to a right and true conception, of the great First Cause ?   There is no creature
great or small, living or lifeless, which is not able to
contribute some spark of light towards this, the final
cause of its own creation, a fuller manifestation of the
great Creator.   Such is the consenting voice both of
reason and of the word of God.   "All Thy works shall
praise Thee, O Lord."   Some of those works may be
mute for a time, or men may be deaf and fail to catch their
heavenly melody.   "Every creature which is in heaven
and on the earth, and under the earth, and such as are

in the sea, heard I saying, " Blessing, and honour, and glory, and power, be unto Him that sitteth on the throne, and unto the Lamb for ever and ever." A first principle of reason is that the Creator may be greater and nobler, but cannot be weaker and more imperfect than any of His creatures. The nature of each creature then, is a kind of inferior limit to our conception of the great Creator. We must sum up the separate elements of power, intelligence, or goodness of any kind, which each creature supplies, excluding in this summation whatever attaches to each of limitation, feebleness, littleness, and natural or moral evil, through this summation to gain the nearest approach to an adequate conception of the nature and character of the First Cause.

First, what materials or elements for such a summation, does matter and the whole lifeless universe supply ? We can resolve that universe imperfectly in our thoughts, into an immense multitude of atoms; and these, so far as our present knowledge extends, are of two opposite kinds, self-attractive matter, and self-repulsive ether. All distinct and definite material objects are composed chiefly of the first; and light, heat, electricity, magnetism, and all the more subtle influences of nature, usually classed as the imponderables, depend on the other. Now what is the testimony of this material world, by its bare existence, apart from all the special features of its cosmical arrangement, with regard to the existence, works, and perfections, of the self-existent Being ? First, they bear a distinct and clear testimony that they are not themselves, or any one of them, the self-existent Cause and Author of the universe. Not one of these atoms could possibly create itself, still less the trillions of its fellow atoms; nor could any one of them choose for itself whether it should be an atom of matter or of ether. Two elements, it seems, must co-exist in each: a force,

or law of force, by which it acts on many or all the rest,
and a place, or position, where it is at each particular
moment of time.   One of these is an active and the
other a passive element of its being.   The law of
force and its variation can never determine itself, but
must have been determined by the will and choice of
the great Creator.   The position, the passive element
of its being, that it is in one particular spot or point
of infinite space, in contrast to a threefold infinity, of
other spots or points of infinite space, must equally be
referred to the will, choice, and appointment, of the
First Cause alone.   We cannot conceive either a point
or a mass of matter placed nowhere : but the place
where it is, is a contrast to an infinite number of places
where it might have been and is not.   This contrast
between the one actual place of each material object,
and millions of possible places, where it might have
been and is not, when multiplied by the whole number
of those objects, and of their component parts, forms
a vast and infinite abyss which separates our conception
of the actual world, from that of a fatal necessity.   For as
Newton says, " blind necessity, which is certainly the
same always and everywhere, could produce no variety
of things."

From this first truth, that matter is created, and not
self-existent, we may infer a second truth, the Divine
Omnipresence.   The Being who created all these countless atoms, must be present wherever those atoms exist,
and the words of the Psalmist must be absolutely true,
" Thou knowest my downsitting, and mine uprising ;
Thou understandest my thought afar off...whither shall
I go from Thy Spirit, or whither shall I flee from Thy
presence ?   If I ascend up into heaven, Thou art there.
And if I make my bed in hell, behold Thou art there ;
if I take the wings of the morning, and dwell in the

uttermost parts of the sea, even there shall Thy hand lead me, and Thy right hand shall hold me." But a farther truth taught by the material universe and the atoms of lifeless matter, is the unity of a vast scheme of Providence which reaches to the farthest range of the stellar universe. This is why Mr Mill says, that

"Monotheism is the only Theism which can claim for itself any footing on scientific ground; every other supernatural theory is inconsistent either with the carrying on of the government of the universe according to fixed laws, or with the inter-dependence of each series of natural antecedents on all the rest, which are the two most general results of science." (P. E., p. 133.)

The law of gravitation, reaching as far as the remotest binary stars, proves a unity of plan, extending throughout a sphere with a radius of several billions of miles, and thus confirms strongly our conception of all material things, as creatures of one great super-mundane Intelligence. But the same facts teach a further lesson with regard to the range and vastness of that supreme Intelligence. The course from moment to moment, of each atom of matter, as determined by that law alone, depends on the position and distance, at the same moment, of every other atom in the universe. Now to know all these with infinitesimal accuracy at any one moment, would almost require Omniscience. But, supposing the fact known for that moment, what is the knowledge that would be required to calculate, according to that law, the motion of a single atom for a single hour? It would infinitely surpass the combined powers of all the ablest mathematicians who have ever lived, from Pythagoras down to Adams and Leverrier. The number of the atoms of matter included within the range of that law, must be many trillions, and probably many trillions of trillions. But it is notorious that the problem of tracing out the motions and courses of three spheres or bodies only, when their initial places and motions are given, and they are acted on by the law of gravitation alone, baffles the efforts of all modern analysis to solve it, except by imperfect approximations. How clearly then, from the world of matter alone, which according to the foolish dictum of Sir W. Hamilton and Dean Mansel, can "teach us nothing whatever with regard to the cause we denominate a Deity," are we forced irresistibly to the conclusion that the Supreme Intelligence, who has ordained the law of gravitation, and thereby bound in unity countless worlds, and who is able to enforce that law in an ever changing universe through successive ages, must correspond to the description of patriarchs, apostles, and prophets, " I know that no thought can be withholden from Thee." Job xlii. 2. " Thou knowest all things." Joh. xxi. 17. "Such knowledge is too wonderful for me; it is high, I cannot attain unto it." Ps. cxxxix.

Let us pass on from the evidence of the Being and perfections of God, taught us even by the world of matter, to the higher and fuller message conveyed to us by all the varieties of living creatures, and most of all by man, created at first by God in His own image. It must be remembered that the world of matter itself cannot be known or studied without one mind at least, by whom that process of inquiry shall be carried on. The question, therefore, can never really arise, what lessons could be learned from the material universe wholly apart from the experience and consciousness of any mind whatever. But if the question be asked,—What lessons may be learned from the material universe by any one rational intelligence, studying it without assistance from other minds ? Then the rational inferences from the contemplation of the material universe cannot be confined to the intellectual perfections of God only, but must include some knowledge of His moral perfections also. In the study of Nature we must have a Person at the lower end of the scale, before that study can begin, and therefore the requirement of Dr Mozley is already satisfied. If there were only one person, one conscious intelligence capable of discerning moral truth, and recognizing a law of duty, this would be as sure a warrant for ascribing moral perfections to the author of that universe, as if there were a thousand such beings; but of course the larger the number of known beings, endowed with these higher attributes and faculties, and the more important the influence which these have exercised on the whole course of known physical change, and the actual state of the world in which we live, the stronger is the presumption for the prominence which moral truths, motives and aims may be expected to have from age to age in the whole scheme of universal being. That prominence, however, in the eye of reason must depend mainly on the essential dignity of moral truth, duty, and moral goodness in themselves, and only in a secondary degree on the number of individuals, within the range of our knowledge, who have this nobler and higher gift of moral being.

Let us next consider the further inferences which may be drawn from a contemplation of the wide range of living creatures, plants, and animals, exclusive of man or creatures endowed with reason, and voluntary choice as well as life. Here we must seek to abide in the clear daylight of conspicuous facts, and avoid losing ourselves in the mists and jungle of modern physiology and metaphysics. What foothold for reason or inference of any kind can we find in this vast range of the living universe, by starting from Mr Spencer's proposed definition of life?

"Life," he instructs us, "is a definite combination of heterogeneous changes, simultaneous and successive, in correspondence with external co-existences and sequences."

Every word here is either an ambiguity, an unexplained assumption, or a self-contradiction. First, life is a combination of changes; it is not the source or cause of changes, but those changes themselves; how many of these changes then are needed to satisfy the definition? Through how many changes must a living plant or animal have passed in order to be really alive? Again, of what are they to be the changes? Of some millions of atoms, which had pre-existed for countless ages before the birth of this living creature, and have been changing ever since through every moment of their existence? Next, life is said to be a "combination" of these changes. How is this possible? How can these changes combine at all, since any one state of this set of atoms must have ceased before the next comes into being? Life then it seems, is a combination of past, present, and future changes of countless atoms, all co-existing at the same moment. But if life is a combination of past, present, and future changes, who or what is to combine them? The theory and definition are framed to exclude the need of any reference to a Creator. The phrase itself, "persistence of force," instead of its preservation, is framed to avoid the risk of suggesting an idea foreign to this atheistic creed, of a Divine Preserver and Sustainer of all things. The definition further excludes the unity of a living plant or animal, distinct from the atoms that compose it. Do the changes combine themselves? The successive changes then must either all exist before they combine, or combine themselves before they exist. Or is the combination nothing more than the bare fact of the successive occurrence of these different states? What claim can such a series have to the title of combination? Life again is a "definite" combination of changes. By whom or what is this to be defined? What severs these special changes from an innumerable multitude of other changes adjacent to them in place, and contemporaneous with them in time, which it is meant to exclude? The changes which are to constitute life, when they have been combined, without any combiner, and defined, in the entire absence of any power able to define them, are further said to be "simultaneous and successive." This can be no special character of *vital* changes, but must be true alike of the changes of all things, living and lifeless. The millions of atoms cannot fail to have simultaneous changes, since they all co-exist throughout their successive changes. Those changes cannot be "heterogeneous," or unlike in kind, unless we . introduce surreptitiously that idea of definite *kinds* or species, which forms one of the plainest elements in the Bible account of creation, but which it is one main object of the modern theory of evolution wholly to exclude. Let us return from this morass of obscure verbiage, where our feet sink deeper and deeper in contradiction at every step, when we attempt to tread upon it, and contemplate the facts themselves.

A living plant or animal implies and requires a unit of some kind, associated with an organized system, composed of a vast multitude of material or ethereal atoms, in some special relation to that unit and to each other. The first question is, what is the characteristic feature of these various units, living plants and animals, as distinct from the multitude and manifoldness of the structures of material atoms with which they are associated? Vegetable and animal life, except in their lowest forms, have many features of contrast with each other, and in each class the varieties are almost innumerable; but in both, some kind or degree of spontaneity, or the power to originate certain changes at its own choice or pleasure, seems inseparable from the conception of life. The power of each living thing to originate changes directly, is limited to its associate organism; indirectly through the changes of its own organism, it may produce changes in other living creatures and in the lifeless world around.   The amount or range of power to effect change may vary immensely, from the animalcule, of which there are millions in a drop of water, to the elephant, the hippopotamus, the whale, or the mammoth.   But a power of spontaneous motion seems as clearly revealed in the most minute, as in the most ponderous, and massive. Spontaneity then, or a power to vary the motions or positions of its own frame within certain limits, by an internal choice or preference, not determined from without, but depending on its own secret nature, seems to be the essential and defining feature of life in all living things.   In plants, this character is more obscure and less developed than in animals, yet we speak instinctively of a tree struggling towards the light, and of the sun-flower as turning to seek and meet the rays of the sun, and of the sensitive plant, as shrinking, by a kind of instinct, from any contact of foreign bodies. Spontaneity, or action not determined by mechanical laws, seems to be a main feature in the whole universe of life, from the animalcule, detected only by the microscope, up to man himself, the lord and head of the visible universe.   It is thus a startling assertion of Prof. Tyndall, in the advocacy of his statement in the Belfast address, that "modern science has bound nature fast in the bonds of fate to an extent before unsuspected," that from Galileo and Newton to our own time, while eager eyes have been pondering the phenomena of the universe,

"Nothing has ever intimated that nature has been crossed by spontaneous action, or that a state of things at any time existed which could not be rigorously deduced from the preceding state."

One would have thought that to watch the sportive flutterings of a single butterfly on a summer day amidst the flowers and trees, or the gambols of a kitten, when it coils itself up for rest on some favoured spot, or starts up suddenly into fresh and free activity of manifest enjoyment, would be enough to shew the utter baseless-ness of this statement. Life, in all its forms, is one vast range of activity, chequered and intersected by countless conditions and laws of a mechanical and purely material kind, but intertwined in every part, and through the whole range of being, with the elements of choice, freedom, spontaneity; and this vital action is determined in all its details by reasons and motives which are not mechanical, which indicate the internal preferences of conscious or semi-conscious existences, that is of things that live and feel and choose. The range of choice in many of these creatures is almost infinitesimally small, but internal choice and preference, and activity depend-ing upon it, seems almost inseparable from the very conception of a living creature. What then are the main inferences with regard to the Divine nature, which in the view of sound reason, result inevitably from the contemplation of the whole universe of living things? The general conclusion must be that the great First Cause possesses in the fullest measure, and to the great-est extent, every excellence which may be seen in any of His creatures, but free from the endless imperfections and limitations and negative characters by which those different creatures are distinguished from, and contrasted with, each other. We are bound then to ascribe to the First Cause, in our thoughts, the highest conceivable degree of spontaneity, or freedom from bondage to cir-cumstances and physical determination from without, and a mode of activity as far removed as is possible or conceivable from dull, blind, unalterable, and fatal

necessity, without lapsing into the other extreme of
mere caprice, or changes and mutations devoid of any
kind of reason from within or from without ; the highest
degree of liberty consistent with our ascribing to Him
reason in its fullest perfection, and all-perfect goodness.
Again, since we see throughout the whole universe of
living things, instincts of various kinds, often of extreme complexity, which tend to the preservation of the
individual life, and in many cases to the preservation
of an association or fraternity of living things, as in the
case of the hive-bee, and the ant, and colonies of the
beaver, so we may reasonably attribute to the Author
and Source of all these countless instincts, a will or
purpose tending to the preservation or bettering of the
whole community of living things, subject only to those
conditions which may be involved in the nature of the
gifts bestowed on each part, or such as may be involved
in the nature of the whole, as a universe of derived
and dependent existence.   Each part of this universe,
and all parts combined, must form a contrast in many
unknown respects, to the perfect, indefectible goodness
of the self-existent God from whom their existence is
derived.   Subject to this condition, the range and extent
of which we can never determine by *à priori* reasoning,
we may with the highest reason infer from the countless instincts in the living universe of lower creatures,
and their common tendency to the preservation of individual life, or of partial communities of living things,
the largest measure of the like instinct in the First
Cause and Author of the great world of life, tending
towards the preservation, comfort, and well being of the
whole.   Thus every sentient and intelligent creature has
the highest warrant of reason for faith in the overflowing
bounty and benevolence of God ; and for following the
instruction of the Apostle, to those who suffer, " to com-

mit the keeping of their souls to God in well-doing, as unto a faithful Creator."

What conclusions with regard to the existence and perfections of God may be drawn from a contemplation of the moral universe; that is, of all mankind, creatures endued with reason and choice, and with a power of discernment between good and evil, created at first in the image and after the likeness of God? The first and simplest conclusion is of this kind. We are bound to ascribe to the Supreme God, a wisdom greater and more vast than the combined intelligence of the wisest and most gifted of His creatures; a knowledge of mathematical truth far greater than that attained by man, from the earliest Greek geometers down to the latest French, German and British analysts, combined and summed up in one prodigious and superhuman intelligence; and instinctive possession of a wide range of mathematical truths, theorems, and certainties, compared with which their combined discoveries are only like a drop out of the abysses of an inexhaustible and infinite ocean. We are bound also to ascribe to Him as the supreme, uncreated Wisdom, a like pre-eminence over the combined knowledge of the various forms of animal life attained by modern naturalists, and over the knowledge of past changes in the depths of earth and ocean reached by all modern geologists. This is the true description of the uncreated Wisdom by the wisest of men: "The Lord possessed me in the beginning of His way, before His works of old. When there were no depths, I was brought forth; when there were no fountains abounding with water. Before the mountains were settled, before the hills was I brought forth: while as yet He had not made the earth, nor the fields, nor the highest part of the dust of the world. When He prepared the heavens, I was there: when He set a compass upon the face of the depth : when He gave to the sea His decree, that the waters should not pass His command : when He appointed the foundations of the earth : then I was with Him ; I was daily His delight, rejoicing always before Him ; rejoicing in the habitable part of His earth ; and my delights were with the sons of men." (Prov. VIII. 22—31.) And we are bound to complete this sublime description of the uncreated Wisdom, who was with the Father before all worlds, by the further statement of the Apostle, concerning this beloved Son of God, " in whom we have redemption through His blood," that " HE IS BEFORE ALL THINGS, AND BY HIM ALL THINGS CONSIST," and " He is the Beginning, the First-born from the dead ...in whom are hid all the treasures of wisdom and knowledge." (Col. I. 14—18 ; II. I—3.)

Reason, from a contemplation of the moral universe, compels us further to ascribe to the Creator, a moral goodness greater than that of the best man whom we have personally known, and greater even than the collective goodness, purified from all adherent faults and imperfections, of all the best men of whom we have learned by the testimony of others, and whose names meet us, as recorded in the ample scroll of human history from the beginning of time. The various sparks of goodness, benevolence, and virtuous activity, that have appeared separately in a Howard, a Livingstone, a Washington, an Aurelius ; in Cato, Socrates, Plato, Noah, Daniel, Job, Lycurgus, Justinian or Moses, must all, when combined and freed from their several imperfections, faults and errors, be far exceeded by the goodness of that Divine Being who is the secret fountain from which flows forth every rivulet of human virtue ;— the Sun of Righteousness, to whose uncreated and inexhaustible brightness all the stars of human and created excellence " repairing, in their golden urns draw light."

Full and various indeed is the testimony to His own greatness and Divine perfections, to His eternal power and Godhead, which the living God has provided for Himself in the things which are made. Truly says the Apostle, " He left not Himself without witness in that He did good, and gave us rain from heaven, and fruitful seasons, filling our hearts with food and gladness." There is indeed a strange blinding power, which may conceal the bright evidences of wisdom and goodness in the whole range of creation, from the hearts of sinful men, an effect which in its worst and most extreme forms can only be fitly described by three different figures of the Word of God. First, the second woe, when "there arose a smoke out of the pit, as the smoke out of a great furnace, and the sun and the air were darkened by reason of the smoke of the pit." The second, the "mist and darkness" which fell in Cyprus upon the unhappy Elymas, when he sought to turn away the deputy from the faith ; and the third, the same Apostle's description of the secret cause of the rejection and contempt of the Gospel by its open opposers, "In whom the god of this world hath blinded the minds of them which believe not, lest the light of the glorious gospel of Christ, who is the image of God, should shine unto them."

The author of "Supernatural Religion," while extolling the "glorious perfection" of the order of nature, which Mr Mill has so oppositely described, ventures to affirm of this glorious Gospel,

"It is difficult to say whether the details of the scheme, or the circumstances which are supposed to have led to its adoption, are more shocking to reason or to moral sense." That "it is derogatory to the power and wisdom of the Creator, and degrading to the idea of His moral perfection." (P. 49.)

So thick is the darkness and mist which has fallen upon him with regard to that very message, of which the apostle, who had been caught up into Paradise, assures us, that therein "unto principalities and powers in heavenly places are made known by the church the manifold (many-varied) wisdom of God, according to the eternal purpose which He purposed in Jesus Christ our Lord," and of which he solemnly proclaims that "therein are hid all the treasures of wisdom and of knowledge."

CHAPTER XIV.

THE CENTRIFUGAL AND CENTRIPETAL TENDENCIES OF FALSE AND GENUINE SCIENCE.

A KIND of rival to the Christian doctrine of Creation, with its corollary in the unity of the whole universe, has been devised of late in the doctrine of Evolution. This, however loudly extolled, is very vague and indefinite, so that many of its disciples seem to attach no definite meaning to the phrase. Mr Spencer, one of its great admirers and patrons, confesses that it ought rather to be called a doctrine of involution, that is of the winding up and involving, rather than evolving, the great complex cotton-ball of the universe. By his definition, Evolution is really nothing more or less than a process of cooling, by which a primitive nebula, excessively rare at first, is condensed, and all the heat and motion generated by that condensation are dissipated and lost in infinite space; so that the result would be a great sluggish central mass, a kind of monstrous extinguished sun. If we strive to define the doctrine, as a substitute or rival for the doctrine of creation, we must view it as shewing the necessary consequences of physical change in the whole universe of life and lifeless matter, when once the conceptions of a Creator, of a creation, of a Supreme and Guiding Intelligence, and all specific laws ordained by such a conscious intelligence have been set aside and excluded. Evolution will thus express the results of motion and perpetual

change in all actual existences, when special acts of creation, and all special laws instituted by the wisdom of the
Creator, have been excluded.   Then the universe will
exhibit to us nothing but a Proteus without reason or
intelligence, going through a series of endless changes,
without conscious design, or any intelligible end and
purpose in those changes.

Now what must be the demonstrable result of an
evolution consisting in endless motion, without any
guiding law or superior intelligence ?   Let us conceive a
universe consisting of an almost infinite number of material atoms; some associated in the forms of living things;
the greater part not so aggregated, guided by no intelligence, and subject to no optional law appointed by such
an intelligence, but simply moving on continually without
rest, under the first law of motion alone.   That law is
that every atom or body, unless deflected by some force,
will persevere in its actual motion uniformly in a
straight line.   To trace the result of Evolution, we must
take every point or spot in which there is any atom of
matter in the universe, and draw from it a straight line
in the direction of the actual motion of that atom, reaching out infinitely into empty space.   The effect then of
evolution must be to transfer all the atoms of the universe from their actual places, to some spot in the further
extension of these lines, and to transform the whole into
some semblance of an immense hedgehog piercing infinite space with mathematical lines diverging from each
other in all conceivable directions.   The atoms in no
finite time would reach any end of their expanding and
diverging progress, but this must lead them farther and
farther apart from each other, since the directions of
their actual motion are infinitely various.   If any two
were moving in parallel lines, and there were the least
difference in their velocities, they might approach for a

short time, but must ultimately diverge, and be wider and wider apart. What then must be the result of an evolution in which there is simply continuous and interminable change, with no guiding and controlling law? The whole universe would expand and separate into a rarity greater than that of the most rarified gas, and every part of it, severed from the rest, would be lost for ever in outer darkness.

To escape from this inevitable result of a doctrine of pure evolution, we must re-introduce by stealth, some of the elements which the atheist professes himself able to dispense with; either special acts of creation, or special laws ordained by a superior intelligence, or other theistic elements, introduced by mere caprice or blind guesswork, or from the inventive imagination of the speculator, to disguise the utter nakedness of a theory of evolution pure and simple. We must re-introduce the notion of a guiding intelligence, capable of choosing some one out of many alternative laws or positions, and of guiding changes towards definite and rational results. As for instance, a law of "natural selection," when there is no intelligence capable of an act of choice, and when selection of any kind must be a self-contradiction and a chimera. Or again, a law of the "survival of the fittest," when life has been pronounced to be a combination of successive changes without any one to combine them, and any survival would be a continuance of one series of changes of ever-changing atoms, longer than another series, while neither series has any limit but a past or future eternity. *Survival* is impossible in a scheme of the universe where there is nothing but sets of atoms that have existed from eternity, and will co-exist for ever. A survival of the *fittest* is equally a contradiction in the scheme of the atheist. There can be no degrees in the fitness of a set of atoms to fulfil any definite purpose, when a creator, and special acts of creation, have been set aside as dreams of superstition; and a new term, "persistence of Force," is expressly invented, lest the phrase, preservation of Force, should let in the unwelcome idea of a Supreme Intelligence, who is at once the Creator of all things, and the Preserver of men. These phrases then are only fig-leaves stolen from the trees in the Paradise of God, that field where fitness, choice, life, intelligence, and beauty, are prodigally revealed on every side, so as to disguise the utter nakedness of a creed which admits no choice, or fitness, or moral beauty, no creative power, or providential wisdom. This is the latest birth of the spirit of unbelief, in which a universe that had its beginning some way or other, without any First Cause or Beginner of its existence, is left by its unknown author, to evolve or involve itself through interminable ages of change; and the wisdom of the Creator, if there be a Creator, is supposed to be best maintained, by denying His interference with the great machine which has proceeded from Him, when He has once set it going. He is thus likened to the bird which He singles out as lowest in the scale of animal intelligence. " The ostrich which leaveth her eggs in the earth, and warmeth them in the dust, and forgetteth that the foot may crush them, or that the wild beast may break them," and whose conduct He thus describes : "She is hardened against her young ones, as though they were not hers ; her labour is in vain without fear; because God hath deprived her of wisdom, neither hath He imparted to her understanding." (Job xxxix. 13— 17.) What is that glorious perfection and invariability of the order of nature, which the author before us says, is emphatically contradicted by the Christian doctrine of redemption, and by the Resurrection of Christ, and the promise of the life to come after death ? It consists in

imputing to the only wise God that very course of conduct towards the noblest works of His hands, which He
Himself pronounces to be the proof of a folly and lack of
understanding which falls below the average standard of
the birds of the air.

There is a tendency towards unity in all true Science.
No part of it can be wholly isolated from the rest; any
branch broken off from the common stem of truth withers
and ceases to grow. The first and highest source of this
unity is found in the doctrine of creation. The MANY
are all made by ONE. The multitude of derived existences, with all their laws, circumstances and conditions
of being, are derived from the will of the one Perfect and
Self-existent Being. We find a reflection of this truth,
this unity of all creation, as created, in the law of universal gravitation. The usual mode of expressing this
law seems to me doubly defective. It seems to place the
action of every atom of matter in every place where it is
not, and to represent the nature of that action as a
selfish tendency to attract and absorb every other being
or atom into itself. Newton did not give this name
to the law he discovered. He expressly states it as
capable of three different modes of expression, Impulse,
Attraction, or Appetency. When A tends towards B,
it is surely more natural to regard A than B as the seat
and centre of that tendency, and that the tendency is not
that of B to pull A into itself, but of A to transport
itself out of its actual place, and unite itself with B.
The law then of attraction is really a law of universal
appetency, a tendency of each material atom to link
itself in turn with every other atom of the material universe, to travel out of itself into nearer fellowship with
each of its neighbours in turn, and that in proportion to
their nearness. It is thus analogous in the lowest field
of nature to appetite in higher creatures, and to the moral

law of universal love in those still higher. This great
law, always observed in the material world, and existing
in a higher form, whether obeyed or disobeyed, in the
moral world also, is plainly a uniting principle that
secures evermore the unity of the material and the
moral universe. The same unity may be seen further in
the great law of subordination. There are not only
many creatures of one common Creator, but the multitude of each class of creatures seems to increase with
our descent in the scale of being. The mass of dull
lifeless matter in the universe immensely exceeds, so far
as our knowledge extends, the mass of organized matter,
or living objects; or to speak more exactly, the multitude or number of the atoms of lifeless matter or ether
is immensely greater than the multitude of all living
things. The multitude again of the lowest microscopic
forms of vegetable and animal life, is far greater than that
of the blades of grass, or of insects perceptible to our
senses. The tribes of insects again, and of low parasitic
forms of life, are far more numerous than the tribes of
birds, and fishes, and living creatures upon the earth.
The number of each class of creatures seems to diminish
as we rise nearer to the great source and fountain of
all Being. When we mount to man, the highest of
God's creatures here on earth, though the actual number of human beings is very great, we are compelled
by the known laws of life, and human experience and
parentage, to travel back in thought to a time when there
were only a few pairs, or even a single pair of human
beings. Thus even where the actual unity of the universe is at present disguised and hidden by its vastness and multiplicity, it shines out more brightly, when
we travel out of the present into past time. The unity
of a common origin is linked with the unity of gradation,
order, and subordination. The solar system has its one

central sun, its revolving planets, its satellites and aste-
roids, its comets, meteoric streams, and diffused nebulous
patches of unformed matter, in regular series, descend-
ing from the one great central orb, to the innumerable
multitude of loose, unformed, and floating atoms. This
unity of gradation seems crowned and completed, by the
further unity of a common aim and purpose extending
throughout the whole creation.

Unformed and lifeless matter, massed together
throughout the universe, fulfils the evident purpose of
supplying a dwelling-place for the various ranks and
orders of the sentient and living creation. So we are
taught by the Prophet, "Thus saith the Lord that
created the heavens, God Himself that formed the earth
and made it: He hath established it, He created it not
in vain: He formed it to be inhabited." (Isa. xlv. 18.)
The whole animal creation is sustained by nourishment,
derived from the products and results of vegetable life.
The higher orders of the animal world in their turn,
depend for their nutriment on creatures below themselves
in the great scheme of creation.

The various fields of science are rather distinguished
than severed from each other, and whenever a logical
distinction is mistaken for a real severance, fresh truths
come to light to correct the error, and establish the unity
of the whole, once more. Thus theories of light, heat,
electricity, galvanism and magnetism, of crystallization and
chemical attraction, have been more and more traced to
a common source by the successive advances of science.
The wide contrast laid down by M. Comte, between
Chemistry and Astronomy, began to disappear under
the influence of new discoveries of the spectroscope,
almost as soon as he had laid it down as a fundamental
truth of science. All creatures, from the highest to the
lowest, through all their gradations of being, as they

proceed from a common source, minister to one common purpose, and are sustained by the power, wisdom, and goodness, of one Supreme Intelligence. It is truly said of Christ our Lord, " He is before all things, and by Him all things consist; He upholdeth all things by the word of His power." And the tribute of praise ascends ever to the Lord of heaven in this double ascription, " Thou hast created all things, and for Thy pleasure they are, and were created." " Blessing, and honour, and glory, and power, be unto Him that sitteth upon the throne, and unto the Lamb for ever and ever."

CHAPTER XV.

THREE HEADLESS PHILOSOPHIES.

THE first of three Philosophies, which are alike head-less, by reason of their common Atheism, is Positivism, or the scheme of M. Comte and his disciples. Its first princi-ple is, that the manhood and perfection of science consists in rejecting all supernatural ideas, or faith in God, as the mark of a childish or puerile stage of thought. It pro-fesses further to exclude all metaphysical ideas, such as law, force, and causation, and pretends to restrict it-self to the registration and classification of phenomena alone. It thus not only excludes wholly Theology from the scheme of knowledge, but makes its admission the sign of intellectual childishness: excluding meta-physical ideas also, it brings on itself the curse of utter emptiness and vanity, even in those fields of thought with which it professes to deal. Professor Tyndal has truly said, that to pass from bare " sequences and phe-nomena, to forces or causes by which the succession is produced, is the first law and necessity of the scientific intellect." In fact, M. Comte, in a hundred pages of the appendix, in which he lays down this absurd law of scientific progress, contradicts himself two hundred times, and by introducing one of the very ideas which he makes it a mark of manly science to exclude.

The second headless system, misnamed philosophy, is the Agnosticism of Mr H. Spencer. This system, pre-tending to unify all human knowledge, and develope a consistent theory of the universe, takes for its first principle a bold assertion that Theism, or faith in a First Cause and intelligent Governor of the world, is an untenable and unthinkable hypothesis, and that the nature of God is wholly and for ever inscrutable. Theology is thus made a synonym for nescience, and midnight dark-ness in which nothing can be seen or known.

Besides Comtism or Positivism, the French variety of Atheistic philosophy, and Spencerism or Evolutionism, which may be called the English variety, there is a third, which Scotland has furnished, the Nihilism, or philosophy of the unconditioned, of Sir W. Hamilton. This philosophy, like the two others, pronounces Theology an impossible science, fruitful only in chimeras and direct contradictions. This theory, whatever the good intentions of its author, fixes a gulf of eternal separation between the Infinite God and every creature, across which no ray of genuine knowledge and real light can ever come.

Let us inquire what are the social or physical merits of Positivism, the first form of godless philosophy. I know of no physical discovery that it can claim as its own. It plainly involves two great physical mistakes. First, in M. Comte's classification of the sciences, he placed a line of utter separation between Astronomy and Chemistry, and affirmed that we could never gain any light as to the chemical constitution of the heavenly bodies. Within a few years, this prediction was falsified by the researches of the spectroscope. Another great mistake was the denial and rejection of the existence of an ether, dis-tinct from ponderable matter. The admission of this, M. Comte placed in the same category with the vortices of Descartes. The whole course of later science has tended to prove the utter baselessness of this dictum of the Positive Philosophy.

Secondly, what is the result of Mr Spencer's ambitious attempt to build up a complete scheme of philosophy and history of the universe, setting out, as a first principle, from the extinction and denial of all theology, and an utter rejection, as unthinkable and unreasonable, of that fear of God which is the beginning of wisdom, and that knowledge of the Holy, which alone is understanding? His success in the field of zoology may be inferred from his definition of life already examined. His like success in the field of physics, or of lifeless matter, may be inferred from the utter inversion of notorious facts, and of logic, which stood sentinel fifteen years at the entrance to his physical speculations; that Newton and men of science had adopted the law of the inverse square for that of gravitation, as an *à priori* truth, because any other was unthinkable. This was a plain warning to any thoughtful reader, that in this system the reign of darkness would not be confined to theology alone, but extend impartially to the whole range of material and physical science.

The third variety of headless philosophy, that of Sir W. Hamilton, is equally barren of any trace or sign of success in the discovery of any new truth, in physics or sociology. This is the less surprising when we remember the profound contempt expressed by Sir W. Hamilton for mathematics, that one sphere of thought, below the region of morals, where clear and certain truth has been attained, and is still attained by all patient inquirers, and which alone supplies master keys for its progressive attainment in all the rest. All these three philosophies have supplied a large and indefinite amount of flat self-contradictions, thinly disguised and veiled from superficial readers by learned phrases and metaphysical abstractions; but I doubt whether any one of the three has contributed a single grain to our know-

ledge of the laws of Nature and of the material universe.
Certainly in every age the King of Heaven has reserved
his chief gifts, of new insight into the laws of Nature
and the system of the material universe, for men of a
serious and reverent tone of mind.   Copernicus, Kepler,
and Newton, the two Herschels, Lord Bacon, Boyle,
Cavendish, Dalton, Davy, Faraday, Cuvier, are examples
of this general law of the Divine government.

The three Anti-theologies of Comte, Spencer, and
Hamilton, have one common feature, a darkening and
benumbing effect on the study of physical science.   M.
Comte's first principle with regard to the stages of science
is the exact antithesis of the real truth.   The only manly
and mature stage of scientific thought is that which he
defames as its puerile and infant stage; when men cease to
grovel on the ground like the brutes, or Nebuchadnezzar
in his madness, and in their study of God's works lift up
their eyes unto heaven, their understanding returns to
them, and they bless, praise, and honour the Most High.
Having mistaken the highest and only truly human stage
of science for the lowest and worst, he inverts the relation
of the two others, and honours with the name of youth
that mere infancy in which men renounce the study of
second causes, along with the knowledge of the great
First Cause, and reason itself goes to sleep, and the mind
of man is degraded to a mere *camera obscura*, to register
passing phenomena as they occur.   The stage M. Comte
extols as the maturity of science, answers either to its
mere babyhood, or its extreme old age and decrepi-
tude, in which it has been smitten with utter palsy.   The
effect of the atheistic starting-point, in Spencer's system,
is a like confusion, perplexity, and darkness.   Even
when he borrows facts from the discoveries of others
to weave them into his system, they are so disguised
by some cloak of metaphysical mist, that their definite

meaning is obscured. The same is true of the Hamiltonian system. Some degree of light is needed even for the healthy growth of a plant, and some clearness in the apprehension of fundamental ideas is essential to real progress in all natural science. What results can be expected to follow, when in the highest and noblest field of thought, the proper home of light, to multiply direct contradictions, to say things and straight unsay them, the fit character in Milton of the father of lies, is proclaimed to be the highest possible achievement of human reason. Now this is the common feature of the Scotch, French, and English varieties of atheistic speculation, and the same principle applies, doubtless, to other German theories. Thus the atheistic theory of Haeckel and Helmholz starts from a self-contradiction at the lowest point of its scheme of being, besides ending in a blank of darkness at the summit. It professes to build up the whole universe out of atoms, which are vortices of revolving matter, made unalterable by some artifice of mathematical calculation, when from their very definition it is plain that they are not atoms at all, but an immense multitude of smaller atoms, ever changing, and to which permanence can be ascribed by a blunder of reasoning alone. The clearness of vision, on which progress in natural knowledge depends, can never be gained by putting out the eyes of the soul, till it becomes blind to the simplest and highest of all truths, that there must be Self-existence somewhere. So that it starts, like Mr Spencer, with affirming two opposites at the same moment, that to think of Self-existence *anywhere* is impossible, and yet that we cannot help thinking of Self-existence *somewhere*. A philosophy which starts in such mental dizziness, can hardly reach a greater depth of confusion at its close, than that with which it begins.

CHAPTER XVI.

The Four Maxims of Modern Nature-Worship.

Anti-Supernaturalism, in striving to sweep away Christian faith and all revealed religion, as a fraud and gigantic delusion, and to prove the four Gospels forgeries of a late date, which gained general acceptance by some unaccountable delusion of the early Christians, has a rival creed of its own, based on four main principles.

> " Just are the ways of God...unless there be
> Who think not God at all,
> If any be, they walk obscure ;
> For of such doctrine never was there school
> But the heart of the fool,
> And no man therein doctor but himself."—*Sam. Agon.*

The first is the old doctrine of the "fool," who says in his heart, " There is no God." It is unfolded by the help of "Science falsely so called," into two great maxims. First, that Theism, Belief in a personal God, is one of three untenable attempts to explain the mystery of the universe ; and that the great First Cause which sits concealed behind all phenomena is, and must ever remain, wholly inscrutable. Next, that all pretended revelation merely assumes without proof the existence of a God, and that all Nature is mute, and supplies no real evidence whatever. Its starting-point is thus the same which the Psalmist long ago described, " Understand, ye brutish among the people, and ye fools when will ye be wise ?"

A second main principle of Nature-Worship, borrowed from the creed of the Sadducees, is the eternal and irreversible reign of death; for it proclaims "the glorious perfection and invariability of the order of nature;" this order includes as a matter of fact the universality of death; and its sure tendency, according to one of its exponents, is to a reign of omnipresent death. Dr Strauss, in his "Life of Christ," tells us that the proposition,

"'A dead man has returned to life,' is composed of two contradictory elements; that in the attempt to maintain the one, the other threatens to disappear; if he has really returned to life, it is natural to conclude that he was not wholly dead; if he was really dead, it is difficult to believe that he has really become living." "Thus that unbelief alike in God's power and God's goodness, which it must be one main aim of revelation to remove, is found to centre in one gloomy doctrine, the omnipotence of death. The Christian revelation, in its central truth, the Resurrection of Jesus, directly meets this great evil, and thereby satisfies the moral conditions of a message of God. A revelation would be a mockery, which left men at liberty still to continue Sadducees, worshippers of the powers of Nature, believers in no supremacy but that of death and the grave." ("Horae Evangelicae," p. 467.)

How deep-rooted is the evil to be overcome, a slavish prostration of the mind before the despotism of Death, is clear from this statement of Strauss. The Gospel, according to the author of "Supernatural Religion," "is emphatically contradicted by the glorious perfection and invariability of the order of Nature." "That perfect and invariable order" by which death has reigned supreme from Adam to Moses, and from Moses to Christ; of which he seems as enamoured, as Satan is described by Milton to have been, of SIN, before he saw her hideous offspring and his own. What an outrage on all reason! to speak of the glorious perfection of an order of Nature, in which death reigns for ever supreme. What a blessed contrast are those gracious promises, "I will ransom

them from the power of the grave; I will redeem them
from death. O death, I will be thy plagues; O grave, I
will be thy destruction." " The last enemy that shall be
destroyed is death." The first principle then, of the
Creed of Nature-Worship, is an expansion of the voice
of the "fool" in Ps. xiv. into a developed theory of the
non-existence of God, our Heavenly Father. The second
is the glad tidings of the invariable and gloriously perfect
supremacy of death and the grave.

The third main principle is the other half of the Sadducean creed, or the doctrine that there is no angel or
spirit. The Apostles are adjudged wholly incompetent
witnesses of the fact, that they ate and drank with the
Lord Jesus forty days after His crucifixion, because they
shared with the other Jews in the belief that there are
angels, and spirits, good angels, and demons. The sceptic,
who after crawling on the surface of our earth like an
insect for a few years, never able to leave it, assures
us that there are no moral agents or rational intelligences
in any part of the wide universe except himself, and his
fellow insects on this one little globe, thereby evinces
an audacious folly, hardly less than that of the "fool"
who rejects the testimony of all Nature, when she
bears witness to a supremely good and wise Creator.
Surely, even apart from the express testimony of Him
who is the Lord both of angels and of men, and who
will assuredly return with His holy angels, to execute
judgment "in flaming fire on those who know not God,
and obey not the Gospel," there is every presumption
from natural reason alone, that all the abysses of infinite
space are not wholly bare and devoid of intelligent and
rational existence, except this one little planet, which is
a million times less than the central orb around which it
revolves. There is no conceivable presumption of abstract reason, in favour of the doctrine that no spiritual

intelligence exists in the universe, which is not weighted and tied down, by a few stones weight of material substance, to one planetary prison.

The fourth principle or pillar of the system of Nature-Worship, is the constancy or perfect uniformity of the course of Nature, as determined by the earthly experience of men for a few past generations, bounded and shut in by the grave; and thence extended conjecturally to all ages of past time, and to a coming eternity; and from the surface of our own planet to the whole range of the material universe, but so as to exclude all faith in things beyond the range of our senses, "unseen, and eternal." This attempt to elevate the insect-like experiences of some myriads of men of the last two or three thousand years, ended in each case by the gloom and darkness of the grave, into the adequate foundation for a theory of universal being, and of the whole course of cosmical change through myriads of ages, and throughout myriads of starry systems, is surely almost the widest conceivable aberration of unreasoning folly. Especially when we remember that, even within these narrow limits, a constancy of variation, by which the past never repeats itself in the future, is still clearer than the partial resemblance which links past with future changes. The partial constancy of Nature, even within the narrow limit of two or three generations, is chequered by many striking catastrophes of various kinds. When we go further back, the whole globe of the earth from its surface to its centre seems, in the eye of science, like a stereotyped record of many catastrophes and changes, wholly different from the present quiet and orderly state of things, within the experience of the present or recent generations.

The three first principles of the anti-christian creed, which denies the Father and the Son, are gigantic falsehoods of a negative kind. The first blots out and annuls the Living God, the good, wise, and intelligent Author and. Disposer of the universe, and leaves the whole a sightless Samson, with no light either as to its own origin or issue. The second provides a gloomy substitute for the Living God, whom the first has dethroned, the eternal prevalence and unlimited supremacy of Death, thus turning the universe into one gigantic valley of the shadow of death, one bottomless gulph of dissolution and decay. The third is almost equally prodigious in its negative character. It affirms, without a grain of evidence, after abolishing the Creator, and enthroning Death in His stead, that nowhere in the wide universe, except on the surface of our planet, are spiritual and rational creatures to be found. The fourth principle degrades still further that little fragment of a godless, death-dominated universe, of which it admits the existence, by making it repeat itself in cycles of unending recurrence to all eternity. The dethronement of God, the enthronement of death, and the extinction of all rational creatures but men now living upon the earth, needed only this further element, to complete its emptiness and degradation, as a creed of utter vanity and hopeless despair.

CHAPTER XVII.

THE ATTEMPT TO REVIVE HUME'S ARGUMENT.

THE famous dictum of Hume, that it is not contrary to experience that testimony should be false, but is contrary to experience that a miracle should be true, has been answered and refuted a dozen times by as many authors; Campbell, Somerville, Penrose, Dr Chalmers, Bp. McIlvaine, Dr Mozley, Archbp. Trench, Paley, myself, and many others. The author strives to revive it out of the grave, in which it had lain for forty years, after being pierced through and through many times. Dr Farrar says,

"Its logical consistency has been shattered to pieces by a host of writers, as well sceptical as Christian."

This is quite true. Our author retorts that

"Apologists find it much more convenient to evade the arguments of Hume than to answer them, and where it is possible, they dismiss them with a sneer."

This monstrous inversion of the facts is worthy of one who spends a thousand pages in the effort to prove the Gospels forgeries, and the Gospel itself a series of incredible falsehoods. Instead of apologists evading the argument they have repeatedly laid bare its emptiness.

"The argument consists of two premises, that the falsehood of testimony is not improbable, since it is of frequent occurrence; and that the truth of a miracle is impossible, because it opposes a fixed and unalterable experience. Each of these is a sophism of the grossest kind.

"And first, that some testimony is false, can never warrant the inference that all testimony alike is deceitful and uncertain. This is a return to worse than childish ignorance. It is the very test of growing wisdom to be able to discriminate between different kinds of testimony, according to the moral character of the witnesses and their means of information. But the force of the objection depends on a rejection of all these distinctions, the fruits of a ripe and manly reason. 'The error,' Dr Chalmers observes, 'lies in this, that all testimony is made responsible for all instances of falsehood, whereas each kind should be made responsible for its own. Divide the testimony into its kinds, and the sophistry is dispelled. It were thought a strange procedure in ordinary life to lay on a man of strict honesty any portion of the discredit which is attached to an habitual impostor, or even to one who has been detected in one instance of fraud or falsehood. It were equally strange to lay upon testimony, marked by all the characters, and accompanied by all the pledges of sincerity, the burden of that discredit which belongs to testimony of a different kind.'

"The first sophism then of the sceptical argument has been answered long ago in that one brief sentence of the wisest of men, 'A faithful witness will not lie : but a false witness will utter lies.' To confound together these moral contrasts, in order to shake our faith in the Gospel, is not only a wicked perverseness, but a childish folly. The other premiss is, if possible, still more strange. Miracles are said to be impossible, because they contradict a firm and unalterable experience. In other words, God cannot suspend any law of Nature, or reveal his will by supernatural tokens to mankind, because unalterable experience proves that this has never been done. This is the boasted argument against Divine revelation ; to assume it false, to derive from that assumed falsehood a most absurd inference, and then by that absurdity to prove the falsehood again ! The moral blindness implied in such reasoning seems almost incredible. To say that miracles contradict universal experience, is merely to beg the question that they never have occurred, or can occur. To say that they contradict our experience is simply untrue. They may lie beyond it, as the battles of Thermopylæ and Salamis, or the death of Cæsar ; but they contradict it only if they are asserted to have happened before our eyes, and we did not see them. Miracles are unlikely, prior to actual experience, only so far as it is unlikely that God should reveal His will to mankind. They are likely to be frequent, only if it be likely that God will often suspend the laws of Nature to attest new revelations of His will, or to confirm others already given. And hence the fact, that none may have occurred within our own experience, yields not the slightest presumption against their reality in other cases. The sceptic can draw no just inference against them from his own limited experience, unless there be good reason to suppose that God would select him, or some one in his circle of friends, for his agent or witness, in conveying a supernatural revelation to mankind. When it is said, however, that a fixed and unalterable experience disproves all miracles, it is plain that an inference from a partial and limited experience, is confounded with the proper teaching of experience itself, whether particular or universal."—(Appendix to Paley's Evidences, BIRKS, p. 376, 377.)

Paley's two or three pages on this subject are marked by that lucid simplicity and clearness, and plain common sense, which are the characteristics of his style. In force of reasoning they immensely outweigh the twenty pages of confused thought which our author spends in a vain attempt to refute them. His self-satisfied comment on them is,

"It seems almost incredible that arguments like these should for so many years have been tolerated in the text-book of a University."

The ground of this censure is a gross misinterpretation of one expression in Paley's statement of the case. Paley's words are these :

"If twelve men whose probity and good sense I had long known, should seriously and circumstantially relate to me an account of a miracle wrought before their eyes, in which it was impossible they should be deceived, and if the governor of the country, hearing a rumour of this account, should call these men to his presence and offer them either to confess the imposture, or submit to be tied up to a gibbet, and if they should refuse with one voice to acknowledge that there existed any falsehood or imposture in the case; if this threat was communicated to them separately, yet with no different effect, and it was at last executed, and if I myself saw them one after another consenting to be racked, burned, or strangled rather than give up the truth of their account, still if Hume's rule be my guide, I am not to believe them. I undertake to say that there exists not a sceptic in the world who would not believe them, or who would defend such incredulity."

The words of Paley " in which it was impossible they should be deceived," are interpreted by this writer to mean an ascription to the twelve witnesses of indefinite and unlimited infallibility on all subjects whatsoever. It is self-evident that Paley means nothing of the kind. What he means is plainly something very different : that their testimony in this particular case was based on such ample testimony of their own senses, so full and various that no suspicion of their being deceived would have arisen, if the fact to which they bore witness had not been of an exceptional and peculiar kind, and such as would commonly be called miraculous. The gloss of the writer, and his scoff at Cambridge University, proves nothing but the readiness with which a cloudy and pre-judiced writer may import his own mistiness of thought into a clear and simple statement.

I have endeavoured to complete Paley's argument, and make the precise force of it plain in the following words :

"What is the strength of the evidence which results from the con-currence of many distinct eye-witnesses, as in the fact of our Lord's Resurrection ? Two alternatives have here to be considered, illusion or imposture. Now the first of these may be reckoned absolutely impossible. Let us suppose, what is far too great an admission, that our senses may commonly deceive us, in a single look, once in a thousand times. If now we combine all the appearances of our Lord that are men-tioned, the numbers present, and the time occupied in each appearance, the whole number of distinct observations by sight, hearing, and touch, will amount to some thousands. And hence the possibility of decep-tion will be expressed by the inverse of a number, formed of at least six thousand figures, a quantity inconceivably small, and practically nothing. Illusion, then, is absolutely impossible. The supposed con-flict of probabilities is thus reduced simply to these two questions. Is it more likely that the Almighty Creator would, or would not, reveal His will to mankind? Is it more likely that the Apostles, who laid down their lives in spreading the Gospel, were honestly persuaded of our Lord's Resurrection, or all leagued in a wicked conspiracy of fraud and imposture. The answer to both inquiries is plain. There is here no contest of improbabilities, because they are both of them on the same side. It is most unlikely, *à priori*, that God would leave all mankind in sin and ignorance, without some message of warning or of mercy from on high. It is most unlikely, nay, morally impossible, that the witnesses who endured scorn and mockery for their faith, and laid down their lives for the sake of Jesus, were merely confederates in a vile imposture, and that they who denounced judgment speedily to come on all iniquity, were themselves monsters of fraud and deceit. The infidel, who rejects and denies the resurrection of our Lord, is thus guilty of a double folly. He prefers to believe that God is careless about the highest good of His creatures, rather than to own that He regards them with the compassion of a father and the vigilance of a sovereign. He imputes the foulest crime to good and upright men, rather than own himself so ignorant as to need a Divine Teacher, or so guilty as to require the atoning sacrifice of the Son of God. The charge he brings against the Christian believer applies fully to his own case. His unbelief in the midst of Gospel light is a miracle and a marvel which subverts all the principles of his understanding, and gives him a sullen determination to believe what is at once most dishonourable and blasphemous towards God, and most false and calumnious towards the best and holiest of his fellow men." (Appendix to Paley's Evidences, p. 381.)

The sound part of Mr Mill's comment on Hume's argument (" Logic," Vol. II. pp. 170—180), consists in marking the contrast between the improbability of a mere guess being right, and of an alleged fact being true.

"This," he says, "has been overlooked by Bishop Butler and several of the writers against Hume, in their anxiety to destroy what appeared to them a formidable weapon of assault against the Christian religion."

Now in my appendix to Paley I have devoted three pages to an exposition of this very distinction between mathematical and historical probability, which Bishop Butler and Dr Price both felt, without clearly explaining it. Mr Mill says that

" Hume's argument is merely this very plain and harmless proposition that whatever is contradictory to a complete induction is incredible. That such a maxim as this should either be accounted a dangerous heresy, or mistaken for a great and recondite truth, speaks ill for the state of philosophic speculation on such subjects." (II. 262.)

Hume's argument, if we accept Mr Mill's gloss is, as he owns,

"in fact, a flagrant *petitio principii*, used to support a wholly unphilosophical assertion."

What is astonishing is, that our author should charge Dr Farrar with misinterpreting and misstating Mr Mill's remarks, and say that

"far from shattering to pieces the logical consistency of Hume's reasoning, Mr Mill substantially confirms it"!

Mr Mill has no right to despise Christian apologists for dealing with Hume's real argument and not with the fictitious substitute of his own invention, yet with the help of this friendly gloss, it still remains exactly what he says, "a flagrant *petitio principii*." Our author thinks it astonishing that Dr Farrar should take Mr Mill's own words, quoted *verbatim*, as expressing Mr Mill's verdict on the logical value of Hume's argument. What is really astonishing is the blindness with which he himself labours to prove the very opposite. Mr Mill's comment is a friendly attempt to attach some meaning not wholly ridiculous to Hume's maxim. After he has mended and tinkered it, he calls it a

"flagrant *petitio principii*, used to support a wholly unphilosophical assertion."

After this our author audaciously affirms that Mr Mill confirms Hume's reasoning. He rejects the true and sound part of that reasoning as quoted by Dr Farrar, and strives to neutralize it by quoting Mr Mill's ridiculous censure of Christian apologists for not aiming their weapons against his own gloss instead of against the statement of Hume himself.

Mr Mill's gloss on Hume is that anything is incredible which is contrary to a complete induction.   Now a complete induction must plainly include the disputed case itself.   Mr Mill's phrase merely brings into full relief a sophism essentially involved in Hume's statement. Our author spends eight pages, (79—87,) in a vain effort to neutralize and undo the effect of Mr Mill's candid admission.   But if he had not been blinded by his unbelief, he might have found in Mr Mill's later remarks a real key to the main question.   Mr Mill specifies one or two cases in which a fact is loosely said to contradict experience.

"One is the case in which the alleged fact appears to conflict with a real law of causation.   But a more common case, perhaps, is that of its conflicting...with the properties of Kinds.   It is with these principally that marvellous stories related by travellers are apt to be at variance: as of men with tails, or with wings, and (until confirmed by experience) of flying fish; or of ice, in the celebrated anecdote of the Dutch travellers and the king of Siam.   Facts of this description, previously unheard of, but which could not, from any law of causation be pronounced impossible, are what Hume characterizes (elsewhere) as not contrary to experience, but merely unconformable to it.... In a case of this description, the fact asserted is the existence of a new Kind; which in itself is not in the slightest degree incredible, and only to be rejected if the improbability that any variety of object existing at that particular place and time should not have been discovered sooner, be greater than that of error or mendacity in the witnesses. Accordingly, such assertions when made by credible persons, and of unexplored places, are not disbelieved, but at most regarded as requiring confirmation from subsequent observers....Of reputed impossibilities which rest on no other grounds than our ignorance of any cause capable of producing the supposed effects; very few are certainly impossible, or permanently incredible.   The facts of travelling seventy miles an hour, painless surgical operations, and conversing by instantaneous signals between London and New York held a high place not

many years ago among such impossibilities." ("System of Logic,"
Vol. II. pp. 167, 169.)

Now the miracles of the Gospel clearly fall under
Mr Mill's description.　They are facts concerning a
person wholly unique, who cannot be classed with ordinary men, nor even adequately with human prophets;
who is essentially the God-man, "Emmanuel," "the man
Christ Jesus," "God manifested in the flesh."　Mr Mill
admits that the prophet of Nazareth, "even in the estimation of those who have no belief in his inspiration," is
a unique man.

"there is in his life and sayings a stamp of personal originality combined with profundity of insight, ... which must place him in the
very first rank of men of sublime genius. ... When this pre-eminent
genius is combined with the qualities of probably the greatest moral
reformer, and martyr to his mission, who ever existed on earth,
religion cannot be said to have made a bad choice in pitching on this
man as the ideal representative and guide of humanity."　("Three
Essays," p. 254.)

Thus this person is a KIND or species to himself.
The miracles of Christ, His sayings, the fulfilments of
prophecy in His life, the angelic messages which heralded
His birth, His birth itself, His rejection by His own
people, His death as the true Paschal Lamb, His lift-
ing up from the earth, like the brazen serpent, to be
a centre of moral attraction to all mankind through
successive ages, His resurrection the third day from the
dead, His appearance to chosen witnesses for forty days
after His resurrection, His ascension into heaven in the
view of those same witnesses, and the promise of His
return in the clouds of heaven to be the Judge of all
mankind; these are not separate and independent facts
out of relation to each other, contradicting that experience by which individuals gain their knowledge of the
characters and properties of the individual objects which

come within the range of the separate experience of each one. They are supernatural facts only in this sense, that they are manifestations of a PERSON never manifested before, whose birth is the great central fact in the whole scheme of universal providence. It is in reality the fulfilment of a prophecy which completes and fills up the long series of the messages of God to man in the Old Testament Scriptures, flowing onward through four thousand years from the opening sentence, " In the beginning God created the heavens and the earth," in an ever-widening stream of Divine truth, till it issues in the long-predicted rising of "the Sun of Righteousness with healing in his wings," to give light to those who were "sitting in darkness and in the shadow of death," and by His own resurrection to "bring life and immortality to light."

CHAPTER XVIII.

The Law of God, and the Created Universe.

The laws of nature are a favourite topic with modern sceptical philosophers. But the phrase in their lips is extremely vague, obscure, and indefinite. The laws are without a Lawgiver, or at least he is removed to an infinite distance. They are not really laws at all, but vain attempts to classify ever changing phenomena, when the great Creator, all created minds, and all things, or material bodies, have alike been consigned to the common gulf of the UNKNOWABLE.

The laws of God include: (1) first, a great law of the sub-moral universe. This is the Newtonian law, commonly styled the law of universal attraction, but more correctly named a law of universal appetency. It applies to all matter, living or lifeless, except so far as it is modified by other laws yet undetermined, of special affinity, or of repulsive self-preservation. It co-exists with, and its effects are modified by, higher laws of life in plants and animals, and by a still higher law of right, wrong, duty, and spontaneous choice of good or evil, in all moral and responsible creatures. (2) A second Law, higher than the self-attraction or mutual appetency of all material masses, is the law of self-preservation. The instinct of life in every plant or animal is to shrink from everything that pains, and to seek everything that pleases, or tends to perfect and expand its own conscious life, so far as the momentary consciousness extends. This instinct is the first germ of rational self-love. It passes into it only when momentary sensation is exchanged for a rational apprehension, on the part of each creature, of the true law and attainable limits of its own being. Then the instinctive shrinking from momentary pain, and pursuit of momentary pleasure, is succeeded by that rational self-love by which each recognizes the true law of its own being, and aims to realize and fulfil that ideal law.

(3) Higher than this law or instinct of self-preservation, is the great moral law, "Thou shalt love thy neighbour as thyself." This is a Divine law of duty expressly revealed, of eternal and irreversible obligation. The duty depends on two conditions only, the possession of a power of choice and faculty of reason by the individual, and the co-existence of a moral universe of creatures similarly endowed, susceptible of having their welfare increased or diminished by the actings of their fellow-creatures. This Divine law constitutes the one sound element in Benthamite Utilitarianism, or the greatest happiness principle, but its truth and Divine authority are there neutralized by transferring it from the heart, as a law prescribing a right state of inward feeling and desire, and turning it into a law of calculation alone. What is the calculation thus enjoined? Supposing three alternatives open in any case, then three positive totals or sums of pleasure would have to be calculated for the whole universe of being through a coming eternity, and as many negative totals of pain. Of the three differences $A - D$, $B - E$, $C - F$, the moral rule prescribed is, to adopt that alternative which makes the excess of pleasure above pain the largest. Each of the six sums is composed of terms not only doubly infinite, but incommensurable, and

incapable of being accurately measured by any common standard. Each sum also involves an infinite number of undetermined quantities, depending on the volitions of an almost countless number of free agents. Such a calculation could never be performed without Omniscience. Even when performed, it could have no binding authority, either from spontaneous instinct or reason, to enforce its fulfilment. The only effect of such a rule must be to throw back the individual on the instinct of self-preservation, or the avoidance of the pain, and the pursuit of the pleasure, of the moment. Still the mere attempt to perform this impossible calculation might remind of the double truth that life is not the present moment, and that we are surrounded by fellow-creatures towards whom we ought to cherish feelings of good-will and not of ill-will. The Divine law applies itself directly to the spring of action, the desires of the heart, "Thou shalt LOVE thy neighbour as thyself." It does not, like its human parody, recommend a choice to be made on arithmetical grounds, after a wholly impossible calculation. The altruism alone is true, being borrowed from the Divine law, and exempts the Benthamite maxim from a charge of total error.

The Divine law includes two elements; the first is altruism in contrast to egoism; that self is to be loved not as self, but "counting as one," on the same ground that every other also is to be loved, for his capacity of happiness. The second element is the law of neighbourhood, that is moral or physical nearness; the law does not command us to love every one alike, but each according to the degree of nearness, that is, our opportunity to do good and impart a blessing. It is so expounded by two apostles: "as we have opportunity let us do good unto all men, especially to them who are of the household of faith." "To him that knoweth to do good and doeth it not, to him it is sin." "Knoweth" seems here the same as "hath opportunity." The law thus explained is the exact moral counterpart of the natural law. Each atom seeks to approach, and so far to unite itself with every other atom, with a force varying inversely as the square of the distance. Not equality, but immense and eternal disparity is a fundamental law of both the natural and the moral universe. The triad of the French Revolution, "Liberty, Equality and Fraternity," exalts a great falsehood between two fundamental truths of the Law of God. For, "where the Spirit of the Lord is, there is liberty;" and the Christian code is, "Love the brotherhood," "all ye are brethren." The real triad of Divine truth is, Liberty, Inequality, and Fraternity.

(4) The supreme Law of duty is that which defines the relation between the Creator and all His moral and responsible creatures. It is "the first and great commandment," "Thou shalt love the Lord thy God with all thy heart and with all thy soul, and with all thy mind." This law of religious duty, like the great law of social duty which resembles it, rests on two data; the presence in the individual to whom it applies, of the power of choice, will, and intelligent action, and the fact that in God the Creator, beyond any of His creatures, or all those creatures combined, there is a vast and immeasurable fulness of Being. Thus, to seek the glory of the Creator is a higher object than to seek the welfare of any one creature, or of all creatures combined. Therefore, love to being in general, Jonathan Edwards's definition of virtue, finds its true explication in both these great commandments of the perfect Law of God. There is first, Self-love, not excluded, but really included by the words, "as thyself." The unreal mysticism which would abolish self-love, must abolish along with it

philanthropy, or the love of our neighbour. Again, the
second commandment, the love of our neighbour, or
universal philanthropy, cannot be severed from the higher
law and obligation of the love of God. Both are
enforced by the same authority, and rest on a common
principle, by which the soul travels out of itself, first
into communion with all its fellow-creatures, and next
into fellowship with the Creator, from whom all things
proceed, and to whom they must return as to the proper
end and purpose of their being. "For of Him, and
to Him and through Him are all things; to whom
be glory for ever and ever."

The love of God, the supreme law of moral duty, has
two opposite aspects, of which one is downward towards
the whole world of possible or actual evil. This is that
fear of the Lord, and keeping of His commandments,
which is the whole duty of man. Of this the patriarch
says, "The fear of the Lord, that is wisdom, and to
depart from evil is understanding." This is that faith
in the Divine warnings by which the soul is deterred
from every evil way. The upward aspect of the same
duty is the grace of hope, not for ourselves alone,
but for the whole world of being, and has respect to
the whole range of possible good to be expected or
looked for from the hand of God. It is that grace of
which the apostle says, "Ye are saved by hope," and,
"rejoice in hope of the glory of God." This love of
God, both in its Old Testament form, the holy fear
of God by which men depart from evil, and dread
all disobedience; and its New Testament form, in which
it has respect to the whole universe of possible good,
the faith which accepts the Divine promises, and the
hope which looks forward to the good things to come;
must rest on a common foundation, the knowledge of
God as a God both of mercy and of judgment. This

great truth that God may be known, and that in such knowledge alone is life, peace, and blessedness, pervades the whole of Scripture from its beginning to its close. "This is life eternal that they may KNOW Thee, the only true God, and Jesus Christ whom Thou hast sent." Again, "Ye worship ye know not what, we KNOW what we worship, for salvation is of the Jews." "God will have all men to be saved, and to come unto the KNOWLEDGE of the truth." "The people that do KNOW their God shall be strong and do exploits." "There is no truth nor mercy, nor KNOWLEDGE OF GOD in the land." "Then shall we know if we follow on to KNOW the Lord." "I desired mercy not sacrifice, and the KNOWLEDGE OF GOD more than burnt-offering." Then "when ye KNEW NOT GOD, ye did service unto them which by nature are no gods, but now ye have KNOWN GOD, or rather are known of God." "He hath given unto us all things that pertain unto life and godliness, through the KNOWLEDGE of Him who hath called us to glory and virtue." And all these testimonies of Scripture are crowned by the words of the beloved disciple, "We know that the Son of God is come, and hath given us an understanding that we may KNOW Him that is true." The truth that the Infinite God cannot be exhaustively or comprehensively known, or understood by creatures who are finite, or the inquiry of the Patriarch, "Canst thou by searching find out God, or know the Almighty unto perfection?" is wide as the poles apart from that monstrous falsehood which an unbelieving philosophy substitutes for it. If nothing at all can be known of anything of which our knowledge is only partial, we must be shut up in utter nescience. The doctrine of the UNKNOWABLE in all its forms dethrones the Most High, annuls all religion natural or revealed, destroys the very foundations of morality, and is high treason against the dominion of the Living God, and the welfare of the whole Universe. No terms are strong enough to express the moral aversion and repugnance with which every disciple of Christ should turn away from it.

Love towards God, the All-perfect Being, who is "blessed for ever," cannot have all the same characters as love towards creatures actually sinful and miserable, or at least exposed to the risk of natural or moral evil, or of both at once. The forms of goodwill and inward love of which the blessed God can be the object, are first, Adoration of His infinite goodness and majesty; next, the desire that His glory may be manifested, and His excellent goodness be owned and understood by every creature capable of such knowledge; that His name may be hallowed, that His will may be done in earth as in heaven, that is, in every sphere of His wide dominion, as perfectly as it is done by those who stand before the presence of His glory. It must include intense gratitude for benefits received, "we love Him because He first loved us." It must include unreserved obedience, or entire conformity of heart and mind to His revealed law. It must include fellowship with God, according to His charge to Abraham, "Walk before me and be thou perfect;" and the experience of Enoch, who walked with God, and "was translated that he should not see death," and before his translation "had this testimony that he pleased God." It should include adoration after the pattern of the Psalmist. "I will praise Thee, for I am fearfully and wonderfully made; marvellous are Thy works, and that my soul knoweth right well. How precious are Thy thoughts unto me, O God! How great is the sum of them; if I should count them, they are more than the sand; they cannot be reckoned up in order unto Thee, they are more than can be numbered."

Its perfect types may be found in those words of the apostle, "Unto the King Eternal, immortal, invisible, the Only Wise God, be honour and glory for ever and ever." And in the fourfold ascription of praise from every creature. "Blessing and honour and glory and power, be unto Him that sitteth upon the throne, and unto the Lamb for ever and ever." And still further, in the sevenfold anthem from the heavenly host, "Worthy is the Lamb that was slain to receive power and riches and wisdom and strength and honour and glory and blessing."

CHAPTER XIX.

FUNDAMENTAL FACTS IN THE HISTORY OF THE MORAL UNIVERSE.

THERE are five fundamental facts in the history of the moral universe which must be recognized by every one who would gain, whether from natural reason alone, or the Christian revelation, a consistent view of the whole scheme of Divine Providence, and attempt the great argument which Milton proposed to himself,

"that...
I may assert Eternal Providence
And justify the ways of God to men."

1. THE FALL OF MAN.

The Fall is no obscure and esoteric doctrine of doubtful speculation, but results directly from a comparison of the actual state of mankind, at present and as far back as the records of history extend, with the standard of uprightness and sinless perfection in the perfect law of God. That law enjoins the love of God our Creator with all our strength, and the love of our neighbour as ourselves. When tried by this perfect standard, the testimony of experience in every age corresponds with and echoes the testimony of the word of God, "All have sinned, and do come short of the glory of God."

The great law of love cannot be reversed or abrogated to suit the practice and low moral state of sinful creatures, but is a direct effluence from Him who is the Father of lights. The standard of perfect love in the stream, that is, in the revealed will and law of God, is a necessary corollary from the perfection of the Divine nature, the fountain from whence it flows. Thus the facts of human experience, if we receive the revealed truth of a judgment to come, point plainly to the further truth that "every mouth will be stopped, and all the world become guilty before God;" and ought to suggest to each one the prayer of the Psalmist, " Enter not into judgment with Thy servant, for in Thy sight shall no man living be justified."

2. GOOD AND EVIL ANGELS.

The existence of other moral and spiritual beings besides men, some good and others evil, is a second main fact in the revealed history of the moral universe. Apart from express revelation, there is the strongest presumption of reason, that men are not the only spiritual beings in the whole range of the created universe. There is also a like presumption of reason that the same conflict of moral good and evil which experience proves to exist amongst men, is not confined to them, but exists also in the other races which together with them constitute the universe of moral and rational being. The express teaching of Scripture that there are angels as well as men, and their number very great, "ten thousand times ten thousand," and that among these angels, some are morally evil, and others pure and sinless, is thus most agreeable to the presumptions of reason. Yet the author before us says it is "shocking both to reason and the moral sense." That among evil and malevolent beings there should be great disparity, both of natural gifts, and of degrees of guilt or wickedness, is in complete harmony with the analogies of universal nature. Now since the nature of man is a little, though but a little, lower than the nature of angels, and the creation of angels was earlier than that of Adam, and the fall of the angels that first sinned was earlier than the fall of man, the foremost and chief of sinning angels must have a natural pre-eminence among all evil beings, whether angels or men, and deserve the titles which he receives in Scripture, "Satan," the great Adversary, the "Wicked One," the "Tempter," the "King over all the children of pride." This solemn truth, taught under a veil in the second page of the Old Testament, and expressly and openly throughout the New Testament, from the opening of the Gospels to the close of the Apocalypse, however repulsive to superficial and thoughtless minds, is in full harmony with the voice of sound reason. The most candid of modern Sceptics, in his latest thoughts, offers this as the nearest approach to an explanation of the actual course of the universe to which by his own reason alone he can attain, that

"The author of the world, wise and knowing, but not all-wise and all-knowing, may always have done the best that was possible under the conditions of the problem; and the Creator, though not Omnipotent in the usual sense of the word, for some inscrutable reason tolerates the perpetual counteraction of his purposes by another being of opposite character, and of great though inferior power." Mill's "Posthumous Essays," p. 183.

The dim guesses of natural reason thus lead men to the very verge of the doctrine expressly revealed in Scripture, and which even there is presented to us as a deep and unsearchable mystery. "The Son of God was manifested that He might destroy the works of the Devil." "He went about doing good, and healing all that were oppressed of the Devil;" and his crowning triumph is expressed in the words, "The prince of this world is judged."

3. TEMPTATION AND THE TEMPTER.

A third great fact, underlying the whole economy of providence, is that all moral and rational creatures, from the highest to the lowest, are liable to be tempted, and turned aside from the path of goodness and uprightness into a downward pathway of sin, corruption, and disobedience. God alone, the All-perfect Being, is in Himself free from this great liability of all created intelligence. "God cannot be tempted of evil, neither tempteth He any man." This is one part of the mysterious condescension involved in the Incarnation, that fundamental mystery of the Christian faith, that God in the Person of His Son, Emmanuel, the God-man, did come within the sphere and range of possible temptation; that the Son of God, our High priest, "can be touched with the feeling of our infirmities, and was in all points tempted like as we are, yet without sin."

Temptation to all men through successive ages is set before us as having three distinct but confederate sources. First, the flesh, or the internal infirmity or wilful perversion of the individual himself, as expressed by the Apostle, "Every man is tempted when he is drawn away of his own lust and enticed. Lust when it has conceived bringeth forth sin, and sin when it is finished, bringeth forth death." The second great source of temptation is the world, by which is expressed the collective amount of moral evil, bad example, and corrupting or degrading influence from mankind at large, "the lust of the flesh, the lust of the eyes, and the pride of life." So that, "the friendship of the world is enmity with God." The third great source of temptation is the Devil, who has this very name, the Tempter. By this is expressed all temptation from unseen powers of evil, beyond the range of our senses and our actual contact with evil in our fellow-men. Now since evil in individual men, through its

own self-contradiction and diversity, tends to conflict and
endless antagonism; hence all confederacies and long-
lasting systems of error and delusion; enduring forms
and modes of idolatry, unbelief, and systematic opposition
to the revealed word and will of God, are everywhere
in Scripture referred to this secret and mighty ultra-mun-
dane source of evil. When the servants of the heavenly
householder inquire, " Didst not Thou sow good seed in
Thy field, whence then hath it tares ? he said unto them,
An enemy hath done this .... The tares are the children
of the wicked one, the enemy that sowed them is the
Devil."

4.   THE CONFLICT OF GOOD AND EVIL.

The whole course of God's providence through the
ages of the world's history, in the word of God as in the
book of human experience, is revealed as a ceaseless conflict and warfare of moral good and moral evil, " Supernal
grace contending with sinfulness of men." So in the first
promise two classes are contrasted, and proclaimed to be
in lasting opposition, " I will put enmity between thee
and the woman, and between thy seed and her seed."
This enmity is then described as a striving of God's
Spirit with sinful man.   " The Lord said, My Spirit shall
not alway strive with man, for that he also is flesh; yet
his days shall be 120 years." So again in later times.
" Curse ye Meroz, said the angel of the Lord, curse bit-
terly the inhabitants thereof; because they came not to
the help of the Lord, to the help of the Lord against the
mighty." And the voice of the first Christian martyr
proclaimed the same truth to his Jewish persecutors. "Ye
do always resist the Holy Ghost, as your fathers did, so
do ye." So the great Apostle found in every step of
his labours for the spread of the truth; "a great and
effectual door is opened unto me and there are many ad-

versaries." He gives this charge to all the disciples of Christ, "Ye wrestle not against flesh and blood, but against principalities, against powers, against the rulers of the darkness of this world, against spiritual wickedness in heavenly places. Therefore take unto you the whole armour of God, that ye may be able to withstand in the evil day, and having done all, to stand." So we are told by the Lord that "the kingdom of heaven suffereth violence, and the violent take it by force."

The first great moral contrast is between the Holy and All-perfect God, who is love, and light, and "in whom there is no darkness at all," so perfectly and essentially good that He cannot even be tempted with evil; and the whole universe of created Being, men and angels and any other unknown races of rational and responsible beings, who either have actually fallen under the power of moral evil, or at least are liable so to fall, but for whom also redemption and recovery are not impossible.

But here again there is a second great moral contrast between the sinless and the fallen, or those who have actually wandered from God into the paths of sin; and again, between the penitent and the impenitent, those who persevere in evil and sin presumptuously, and those who turn their face to God, and seek to return to the path from which they have wandered. This great contrast, among angels, between the elect angels and those who "sinned and left their first habitation;" and amongst men, between the "poor in spirit," the lowly and penitent, who are willing to learn of Him who is "meek and lowly in heart," and the proud, the unbelieving and profane, who turn their back to the light, and walk on wilfully in darkness; between the church of true believers and the world, is set before us through all Scripture as the summary of the moral history of our fallen race. The conflict, though it lasts for long ages, is to be followed by a sure and full triumph of redeeming mercy. The exalted Redeemer at God's right hand is now "expecting until His enemies be made His footstool," and we are taught that "the earnest expectation of the creature, (or, the whole creation with outstretched neck), waiteth for the manifestation of the sons of God."

5. THE SUPREMACY OF DEATH.

A last main feature and law of the economy of providence from the days of Paradise, through 6000 years, is the reign and supremacy of death, summed up in the words, "By one man's offence death reigned by one," and "by one man sin entered into the world and death by sin, and so death passed through unto all men, for that all have sinned." This dark and gloomy reign of death and the grave from age to age, our author perversely and blindly extols as the "glorious perfection and invariability of the order of nature." He is so enamoured of this "law of sin and death," that he counts any interference with its unbroken sway, by the resurrection of the Son of God Himself from the grave, "shocking to reason and to moral sense." He seems so satisfied with the world in which death reigns supreme, that he reckons any communication with the higher world, where moral laws reign supreme, to be superfluous and incredible.

How far more consistent with reason, and moral sense, and true philosophy, is the double description of death which Milton, in his striking allegory, has put into the mouth of Sin and Satan.

> "I fled, and cried out, Death.
> Hell trembled at the hideous name, and sigh'd
> From all her caves, and back resounded, Death.
> ....What thing art thou thus double form'd?
> I know thee not, nor ever saw till now
> Sight more detestable than him and thee."
>   "Paradise Lost," B. ii. 788, 741.

CHAPTER XX.

THE WISDOM OF GOD IN REDEMPTION.

CHRISTIANITY, as expounded and distorted by this author, is a theory of an abortive design of creation, and of impotent efforts to amend it.

"Both the details of the scheme and the circumstances which are supposed to have led to its adoption, are shocking to reason and to moral sense, derogatory to the power and wisdom of the Creator, and degrading to the idea of His moral perfection."..."Not only is the assumption that any such revelation was necessary, excluded on philosophical grounds, but it is contradicted by the whole operation of natural laws." S. R. I. p. 49.

Long ago the Apostle said, "We preach Christ crucified, to the Jews a stumbling-block and to the Greeks foolishness," but he adds, "The foolishness of God is wiser than men." 1 Cor. i. 23, 25. He who had been caught up into Paradise, and "heard unspeakable words, which it is not lawful for man to utter," 2 Cor. xii. 4, thus describes the real character of that message which the 'bats and moles' of earth account so foolish and unreasonable. "To me is this grace given that I should preach among the Gentiles the unsearchable riches of Christ, the mystery which from the beginning of the world hath been hid in God, to the intent that now unto the principalities and powers in heavenly places, might be known by the Church, the manifold wisdom of God, according to the eternal purpose which He pur-

posed in Christ Jesus our Lord." Eph. iii. 8—11. He
expounds the secret cause of the contemptuous rejection
of this mystery by earthly minded Sadducees, "The god
of this world hath blinded the minds of them which believe not, lest the light of the glorious Gospel of Christ,
who is the image of God, should shine unto them."
2 Cor. iv. 4. Not only the message itself, but the
wisdom to discern its excellence, is a gift of Divine grace.
"God who commanded the light to shine out of darkness,
hath shined in our hearts, to give the light of the knowledge of the glory of God in the face of Jesus Christ."
v. 6. The duty of the servants of God is, with patience
and "meekness to instruct those who oppose themselves,
if God peradventure will give them repentance to the
acknowledging of the truth, that they may recover themselves out of the snare of the devil." 2 Tim. ii. 25, 26.

Creation is no abortive work, in which the expecta-
tions of the Creator have been wholly frustrate and
disappointed. The exact reverse is the express and repeated statement of Scripture. (Acts xv. 18) "Known
unto God are all His works from the beginning of the
world." The redemption of the Gospel is the "eternal
purpose of God;" and Christ is the "Lamb of God, who
verily was fore-ordained before the foundation of the
world." 1 Pet. i. 20. It proclaims that "hope of eternal
life which God, that cannot lie, promised before the
world began." Tit. i. 2. It is the "revelation of the
mystery which was kept secret since the world began,"
but then by "the commandment of the everlasting God,"
the "Only wise," to whom be "glory for ever, was made
known to all nations for the obedience of faith," Rom.
xvi. 25—27, and "this is the condemnation, that light is
come into the world, and men loved darkness rather than
light, because their deeds were evil." Joh. iii. 19. Let
us turn from the follies and blasphemies of modern Sad-

ducees, enamoured of the reign of death; and observe the revealed laws and principles of that Gospel, which is the highest and noblest exhibition of the perfect wisdom and love of God, and the subject of adoring praise and devout wonder to ten thousand times ten thousand pure and perfect spirits, dwelling in light and bliss before the throne of the "blessed and only Potentate; whom no man hath seen or can see, to whom be glory and power everlasting." 1 Tim. vi. 15.

(1) The first principle is the great truth proclaimed by Christ Himself, that God is the only Good Being; "there is none good but one, that is God." Matt. xix. 17. This glorious and primary truth, uttered by Christ in reply to a solemn inquiry, and transmitted by the consenting evidence of more than 500 copies of each of three Evangelists, has been replaced in five copies only, of one of the three, by a human substitute which blots out this great truth and substitutes the pointless inquiry, "Why dost thou ask of me concerning the good?" This seems to imply a censure on what is most lawful and praiseworthy, for to inquire after God is one of the first of revealed duties. The great truth proclaimed by our Lord is afterwards expounded by St James, into the double maxim, that all evil is from the creature, and all good from God alone: "God cannot be tempted with evil, neither tempteth He any man. Every good and perfect gift is from above, and cometh down from the Father of Lights." Jas. i. 13, 17. The negative truth, of evil in the creature is expounded both by the apostle and the patriarch: Rom. iii. 23, "All have sinned;" v. 12, "Death passed through unto all men, for that all have sinned;" "Behold, He put no trust in His servants, and His angels He charged with folly." Job iv. 18. "The heavens are not clean in His sight." xv. 15. "It was necessary" that "the heavenly things themselves" should be

"purified with better sacrifices than these." Heb. ix. 23.
As the spots of the sun, though luminous, shew like blots
of darkness in contrast with his still more luminous disc ;
so every creature, compared with the Divine perfection,
reveals either an actual presence of moral evil, or at least
a mournful liability to rebel, and go astray.   Redemption
is a sequel of the truth, that God is the only Good Being,
perfectly and indefectibly good, and of the solemn fact
that both men and angels have sinned.   A fallen creature
is without strength to restore itself, and can be restored
only by Divine power and grace.   "O Israel, thou hast
destroyed thyself, but in Me is thine help." Hos. xiii. 9.
"Without Me ye can do nothing." John xv. 5.   "When
we were without strength, Christ died for the ungodly."
Rom. v. 6.   Such is a first great principle and law of
the Gospel, growing out of the truth that "God is the
only Good," and embodied by St Paul in the words, "By
grace are ye saved, through faith, and that not of yourselves, it is the gift of God."   Eph. ii. 8.

(2)   The second great maxim and law of Providence, is the truth that God is the Only Wise.   Nothing,
even the most minute, can escape from the vision of His
Omniscience and from the control of His providence.
"Even the hairs of your head are all numbered."
Matt. x. 30.   "Gather up the fragments that remain,
that nothing be lost." Joh. vi. 12.   Evil men and angels
may and do rebel against His will, and strive against
Him, but the "counsel of His will," Eph. i. 11, they
cannot disappoint or annul : "there is no wisdom, nor
understanding, nor counsel, against the Lord." Prov.
xxi. 30.   So was it announced to Pharaoh in the height
of his rebellion.   "For this cause have I raised thee up,
to shew in thee my power, and that my name may be
declared throughout all the earth." Ex. ix. 16.   And
Solomon and David both proclaim the same truth : "The

Lord hath made all things for Himself, yea, even the wicked for the day of evil." Prov. xvi. 4. "Surely the wrath of man shall praise Thee, and the remainder (or, excess) of wrath wilt Thou restrain." Ps. lxxvi. 10.

(3)   The third principle or law of the whole economy of Redemption is that God is most Just, expressed by Abraham, in his intercession for Sodom. "Shall not the Judge of all the earth do right?" Gen. xviii. 25. This truth is guarded by the solemn oath, "As I live, saith the Lord God, I have no pleasure in the death of the wicked, but that the wicked should turn from his way and live...why will ye die, O house of Israel?" Ezek. xxxiii. 11. So sternly does God repel the double falsehood that He takes pleasure in the destruction and moral ruin of His own creatures: or that His judgments, however severe, shall exceed the measure of the most perfect equity, and the highest wisdom. "He will not lay upon man more than right, that he should enter into judgment with God," Job xxxiv. 23; and again, "Thou wilt be justified when Thou speakest, and be clear when Thou standest in judgment." Ps. li. 4. "Hear, ye strong foundations of the earth, for the Lord hath a controversy with His people, and He will plead with Israel." Mic. vi. 2. In His own time, God will make "all the hard speeches, which ungodly sinners have spoken against Him," Jude 15, to turn back upon themselves by the testimony of their own re-awakened conscience and reason, according to those words, "Why, even of yourselves, judge ye not what is right?" Lu. xii. 57. "The glory of the Lord shall be revealed, and all flesh shall see it together." Isa. xl. 5. And what that glory is, is thus explained by another prophet: "Let him that glorieth, glory in this, that he understandeth and knoweth me, that I am the Lord, which execute lovingkindness, judgment, and righteousness in the earth; for in these things

I delight, saith the Lord." Jer. ix. 24. The long delay
of judgment is ascribed to the "riches of God's forbear-
ance." "The Lord is not slack concerning His promise,
but is long-suffering to usward, not willing that any
should perish, but that all should come to repentance."
2 Pet. iii. 9. The certainty of judgment in its own
appointed time is assured alike by the perfect truth, the
holiness, and the wisdom of God. It is said of this
message of solemn warning, "At the end it will speak
and not lie; though it tarry, wait for it; because it will
surely come, it will not tarry." Hab. ii. 3. "Yet a little
while, and He that shall come will come, and will not
tarry." Heb. x. 37.

(4) The fourth revealed principle and law of all providence is the Omnipotence of God. The most candid,
and one of the ablest of modern leaders of sceptical
thought, in his latest work, comes much nearer to the
Christian faith than most other sceptics. He holds
that there is evidence for the existence of an intelligent
and conscious creator of the Cosmos, and that

"the morality of the Gospels is far higher and better than that which
shews itself in the order of Nature, and that what is objectionable in
the Christian theory, is only so when taken in connection with the
doctrine of an Omnipotent God, *at least as understood by most enlightened
Christians.* The grave error of Butler was that he shrank from admitting the hypothesis of limited powers. His appeal amounts to this.
The belief of Christians is not more absurd or immoral than that of
Deists who acknowledge an Omnipotent Creator." Mill's "Three
Essays on Religion," p. 214.

He thinks that there is strong evidence for the existence of a God of real dominion, great goodness,
and great power, and that the goodness may be held
perfect, if we admit the power to be limited. The
stumbling-block which keeps him back from accepting
the Christian faith, when he has reached its very thresh-

old, is an implicit and unreasoning adoption of current or popular impressions with regard to the true meaning of one Divine attribute. The construction of omnipotence which leaves him in a midway position, with one foot on the ground of Christian faith, and the other in a quagmire of scepticism, does not even pretend to have been derived from any direct and inductive study of the Bible itself. He takes it merely from current and popular notions, which he ascribes, in flagrant contrast to the scope of his own reasonings, to the most enlightened Christians, when he ought, to be consistent, to have said rather, the least enlightened Christians. On no better basis than this loose impression, he affirms that "the notion of a providential government by an omnipotent being, for the good of his creatures, must be entirely dismissed," and calls it "absurd and immoral." Yet Bishop Butler does virtually what he blames him for not doing, and offers thoughts which, if Mr Mill had followed them out, would have proved the rashness and utter baselessness of his own statement.

"Many instances," Butler says, "may be alleged of suppositions utterly impossible, and reducible to palpable contradictions, which not every one could perceive to be such, or perhaps any one at first sight suspect. We are unacquainted with what is in the nature of things practicable in the case before us, and our ignorance is a satisfactory answer, for some unknown impossibility may render what is objected against just and good, nay good in the highest practicable degree."

Dr Mozley, in his fourth Lecture, has developed the same thought a little further, marking the contrast between real and apparent limitations of the Divine power.

"A contradiction to necessary truth being nothing, nothing is taken away in the abstraction of the power to effect it....It is no real limitation of Omnipotence to deny the power to contradict a mathematical truth."

In the "Ways of God," I have quoted these words of
Bishop Butler, and unfolded the same important truth
still further, at some length.　I have shewn by a full
induction of Scripture, from the first to the last, that what
Mill misnames the hypothesis of limited power, is the
real doctrine of Scripture throughout—that is, a power
self-limited by the perfect wisdom and holiness of God,
so as to discern and exclude every lie, self-contradiction,
and chimera.　Thus we are taught that "God cannot
lie," that "He cannot deny Himself."　There are many
other such cases of moral contradictions, which do not
reveal themselves as such at the first glance, to ignorant
and sinful creatures.　The Bible proclaims the two doctrines side by side with equal clearness, that God is
really Almighty, in the words of the patriarch, "I know
that Thou canst do everything," Job xlii. 2; and in the
words of the angel to the Virgin, that "with God nothing
shall be impossible," Lu. ii. 37; and in the words of the
heavenly elders, "They rest not day and night, saying,
Holy, holy, holy, Lord God Almighty," Rev. iv. 8.　And
still that there is a real warfare of good and evil between
the thrice holy God, with holy angels and redeemed men
on one side, and the world, the flesh, and the devil and
his angels on the other; a warfare so real and intense,
that every warning and every promise in the word of
God is based upon the fact of its deep reality.　"To him
that overcometh will I give to eat of the tree of life
which is in the midst of the Paradise of God."　Rev. ii. 7.
"He that overcometh shall not be hurt of the second
death."　Rev. ii. 11.　"To him that overcometh will I
grant to sit with me on my throne, even as I overcame
and am set down with my Father on His throne."　Rev.
iii. 21.　Power then, not wholly vague and indefinite, but
self-limited by the eternal truth of things, by the essential nature and perfection of the Living God, and by

the essential imperfection and variability of all created being, is that glorious attribute which is brightly revealed throughout the whole of Scripture. Any other view of the Divine Omnipotence would degrade the doctrine of the Cross, and of atonement through the sufferings of the Divine and Incarnate Saviour into a gratuitous folly and act of cruelty, instead of a most glorious manifestation of the perfect love and wisdom and holiness of the Almighty.

(5) A fifth main law and principle of Redemption, and of the whole scheme of providence, is taught us in the law of God, near its close. "He is the Rock: His work is perfect; all His ways are judgment; a God of truth and without iniquity, just and right is He." The scheme of Divine providence, it is thus proclaimed, is a perfect work. It is a contrast to the vision of the prophet. "I went down to the potter's house, and behold he wrought a work upon the wheels; and the vessel that he made of clay was marred in the hand of the potter, so he made it again another vessel as it seemed good to the potter to make it." Jer. xviii. 3, 4. But the scheme of universal providence, if once marred, could never be repaired. So, if our blessed Lord had committed one sin, the perfectness of His example and His Divine atonement, as the Lamb without blemish and without spot, would have been precluded for ever. So, any mistake, error or ignorance on God's part, in His dealing with the mighty problem of the government of the universe, could never be reversed. The whole would contract a flaw that could never be repaired. But such a failure is precluded and forbidden by the perfect wisdom, the perfect goodness, and the spotless holiness of the Most High. Because "He is the Rock, a God of truth and without iniquity; just and right," therefore His "work" also is "perfect." Deut. xxxii. 4.

This Christian optimism, the faith that no man or creature can devise a better scheme of universal providence, than that which the all-wise God Himself has planned, foreseen, and appointed, and will assuredly bring to pass in the appointed season, is a direct and inseparable corollary from the revealed perfections of God. A recent Bampton Lecturer (1877) says, "It is unquestionable that the present order of the universe is not a perfect manifestation of justice. Every theist,

"it is said, will deny that the impress of perfection must of necessity be stamped on all the works of a perfect Creator. It is assumed (by Mr Mill) that if a God of infinite power, wisdom and benevolence has made the universe, He was bound to realize our highest conception of those attributes in every portion of His creative work. This we know as a matter of fact He has not done." p. 449.

In Mr Mill's statements, of which the "unsparing logic" is praised by the Lecturer, to prove the error of à priori reasoning, there is no à priori reasoning whatever. They consist of an à posteriori comparison between the actual course of providence *as a whole*, and current popular impressions of perfect goodness and Divine omnipotence, and affirm their utter inconsistency. Mr Mill fails to draw the only true conclusion, that loose popular impressions of the meaning of omnipotence are at variance with the actual facts of providence, and he might have added, contradict the consenting testimony of the whole word of God. Mr Mill's real premiss is, that perfection must be stamped, not on *all* the works of a perfect Creator, separately, one by one, but only upon creation and providence as a whole, so far at least as knowledge of them is attainable. The Lecturer affirms this premiss to be unquestionably false. It is rather a truth, expressly revealed; not of course that the moral order of the universe, so far as known to us, within the range of earthly experience, is a perfected or finished

manifestation of justice.   A small infinitesimal part
cannot have the qualities of the mighty whole.   But
those who deny that the past history of our world,
with all its solemn mysteries of prevailing rebellion,
wickedness, reigning death, wide-spread misery, wasting
and destruction, can be one part of a scheme of providence perfectly wise and good, if we could see the whole,
and fathom the mysteries of the eternal ages to come,—
flatly contradict an express statement of the word of
God, as well as the voice of sound reason.

Thus Christian optimism, or the doctrine that God's
real plan must be better than any fancied substitute, or
imaginary improvement, devised by sinful and ignorant
creatures, is a direct and sure inference from that maxim
of the Apostle, "To him that knoweth to do good, and
doeth it not, to him it is sin."   It must be sin for the
All-wise and All-good Creator to reject a greater good,
and to choose a less, out of the manifold possibilities of
being, in creation and providence, alike open to the gaze
of His immeasurable wisdom and goodness. The glorious
doctrine of Leibnitz that the actual scheme of universal
providence, is the best out of an infinite diversity of
alternatives, or of conceivable and possible universes,
however ridiculed by frivolous scoffers like Voltaire, is
a sure inference from a thorough faith in the two Divine
attributes, of perfect wisdom and perfect goodness; but
it is equally certain that to judge of this scheme as a
whole, from the limited past experience of men alone in
their earthly life for a few thousand years, would be a
prodigious folly.   The mysterious depths of evil in the
totality of created being, like the depths of the Divine
goodness, are unsearchable.   The mighty scheme of
providence as a whole, has a breadth, and length, and
depth, and height, like that love from which it flows,
which passeth all created knowledge.   And its Divine

author, out of His infinite fulness, "is able to do exceeding abundantly above all that we ask or think;" unto
Him be "glory in the Church by Christ Jesus, throughout
all ages, world without end." Eph. iii. 20, 21. The long
conflict and warfare between moral good and evil, so
dark, mysterious, and perplexing to the thoughts of men
from the beginning until now, will end, we are assured,
in a full victory of redeeming mercy, holiness, and triumphant goodness.   In that victory, the unsearchable
riches of the Divine bounty and goodness, and also the
eternal contrast between the glorious God, the Self-
existent, the Unchangeable, and the mighty universe
which He has called into being to manifest His perfections; both the depth and the height of divine holiness
and redeeming love, must and will be displayed for ever
more and more.

CHAPTER XXI.

The Perfections of the World's Redeemer.

Jesus of Nazareth is the Christ of God. What this title really implies is often overlooked and forgotten even by Christians themselves. It is virtually denied, when we are told that Christians are at liberty not to believe any miracle of the Old Testament, which has not been confirmed by direct reference to it in the Gospels. (Dr Irons, 'Supernatural Religion,' Vol. i. p. 95). The argument, it is truly said, is an amazing one. The "Christ" is a title which has a distinct and definite meaning. It means Him of whom Moses and the Prophets did write; the Redeemer, promised at first as the Seed of the woman to bruise the head of the Serpent; the Son of Abraham, the Son of David; the Person on whom there converges a whole series of predictions in the Old Testament, from the beginning of Genesis to the end of Malachi. Any attempt to get rid of the Old Testament, and retain faith in the Gospel, involves a moral and logical impossibility. If the writers of the Old Testament were not prophets commissioned by God to be messengers of His truth to men; if the Pentateuch is a forgery, the Book of Isaiah a second forgery, the Book of Daniel a third forgery, dating from the time of the Maccabees, a real Messiah could not exist; he would be a wholly imaginary person, defined by self-contradictory characters, the fulfiller of prophecies which were not real prophecies, supplying the keystone to a complete arch of forgeries composed of mistaken glosses and wicked frauds, perpetrated by unknown parties, who traded on Jewish credulity and superstition. Rejection of the Old Testament, our Lord declares, makes real faith in Himself as the Christ impossible. " Had ye believed Moses, ye would have believed me, for he wrote of me. But if ye believe not his writings, how shall ye believe my words?" Joh. v. 46, 47. And once again: " They have Moses and the prophets, let them hear them....If they hear not Moses and the prophets, neither will they be persuaded though one rose from the dead." Lu. xvi. 29, 31. This title, the " Christ" sums up and embodies the fact, that God had before announced His will to men, from the beginning of the world, by a succession of prophets, commissioned to give messages in His name. The Christ is one " of whom Moses in the law and the prophets did write." The Jews and Samaritans alike knew that such a person was to come. The Samaritan woman said to Jesus, " I know that Messias cometh, which is called Christ; when he is come, he will tell us all things. Jesus said unto her, I that speak unto thee am He." Joh. iv. 26. The message of the prophets was a first stage in that Divine husbandry which Jesus sent the Apostles to complete into a perfect harvest. " Lift up your eyes, and look on the fields, for they are white already to harvest...and he that reapeth receiveth wages, and gathereth fruit unto life eternal, that both he that soweth and he that reapeth may rejoice together.... I have sent you to reap that whereon ye bestowed no labour; other men laboured, and ye are entered into their labours." vv. 36, 38. The Christ is one who continues, completes, and fulfils a message, which had been already given in the Law and by the Prophets. Thus taught the Apostles from the first chapter of the Book of Acts to its close. The Gospel was a fulfilment of all things "which God had spoken by the mouth of all His holy prophets since the world began." Acts iii. 21. So St Paul at Rome "persuaded the Jews concerning Jesus out of the law of Moses, and out of the prophets, from morning till evening;...and some believed the things which were spoken, and some believed not; and when they agreed not among themselves they departed, after that Paul had spoken one word, Well spake the Holy Ghost by Esaias the prophet unto our fathers.". Acts xxviii. 23—25.

Thus the first message of the New Testament history is, that Jesus is the Christ, the Son of David, the Son of Abraham; the final end and consummation of the whole history of the Old Testament; also the fulfiller of distinct prophecies of Isaiah and Micah, and of implied predictions of Hosea, Jeremiah, and all the prophets. And the same history closes with the assurance by St Paul, that the words of Isaiah vi. were a voice of the Holy Spirit, by Isaiah the prophet, unto the fathers of the Jews. These testimonies are crowned by the words of the angel to St John, "The testimony of Jesus is the spirit of prophecy." Rev. xix. 10.

The Wisdom of the Lord Jesus as the Christ will be seen by reflecting on the truths implied in that title. His life from the cradle to the grave was the perfect fulfilment of a work, ordained before the foundation of the world, but revealed in part and only in part, in a series of divine predictions, ranging through 4000 years until His actual appearance. All these predictions, and the true purport of each one of them, must have successively been opened before the Son of God, from the hour of His birth at Bethlehem, to His ascension from Olivet. Their fulfilment occupied His thoughts in the hour of His extreme anguish on the cross. "Jesus knowing that all things were now accomplished, that the Scripture might be fulfilled, saith, I thirst....When He had received the vinegar, He bowed His head, and gave up the ghost." Joh. xix. 28, 30. After His Resurrection, His first message revealed to His disciples this aspect of His finished work. "These are the words which I spake unto you while I was yet with you, that all things must be fulfilled which were written in the Law, and in the Prophets, and in the Psalms, concerning me. Then opened He their understanding that they might understand the Scriptures." Lu. xxiv. 44, 45. Thus the Son of God, throughout His life, "set the Lord always before" Him, with the whole series of prophetic messages, from the first record of creation, to the announcement in Malachi of His own rising on the benighted world, as the "Sun of Righteousness, with healing in His wings." Mal. iv. 2. His task was not only to discern and fulfil all the express predictions of His life, death, and resurrection, but to satisfy and accomplish all the various types of the sacred history, or of the Divine law which really pointed to Him, and converged on Him as their common centre. How vast and unsearchable is the wisdom implied in this one aspect of the Saviour's work, as taught in His own words : "I am not come to destroy the law or the prophets, but to fulfil." Matt. v. 17. "I have glorified Thee on the earth, I have finished the work which Thou gavest me to do." Joh. xvii. 4. "I have kept my Father's commandment, and abide in His love." Joh. xv. 10. "The words that I speak unto you, I speak not of myself; but the Father which dwelleth in me, He doeth the works." Joh. xiv. 10. Thus our Lord as the Christ, was consciously fulfilling a specific work of Redeeming grace, ordained and appointed by His Father from the foundation of the world, and largely unfolded, both in express predictions, and manifold types through four thousand years. All of which lay open to

His clear and eagle gaze ; and were fulfilled in the midst of all the "contradictions of sinners," and the malice of the powers of darkness, with strict, perfect, and unswerving fidelity.

"The Scripture," He said, "cannot be broken," Joh. x. 35. "Even the things concerning Me have an end" (τέλος ἔχει, or, must be fulfilled), Lu. xxii. 37. He rejects, in the hour of His sufferings, the angelic succours which were at His command, rather than one sentence of Scripture should fail of fulfilment. "Thinkest thou that I cannot now pray to my Father, and He will presently give me more than twelve legions of angels ? But how then shall the Scriptures be fulfilled that thus it must be ?" Matt. xxvi. 53, 54. So profound is the reverence of the Incarnate Son of God for those words of the prophets, which are the "sword of the Holy Spirit," Eph. vi. 17, "the Scripture of truth," Dan. x. 21, and the "true sayings of God," Rev. xviii. 9. What an utter contrast is this to the light and flippant manner in which they are too often treated by modern Sadducees, or half disciples, who degrade them to the level of their own writings, that is, fallible sayings, mixed up of truth and falsehood in uncertain proportions. If we accept their theories they are not words of the holy Prophets, but of anonymous and unscrupulous forgers, so that their real parent would not be the God of truth, but the Father of lies. But the perfect truthfulness of Scripture shines out in the whole teaching of our blessed Lord, from His first great conflict and victory in the wilderness, to His final session at the Father's right hand in heavenly glory. There He is now "expecting," until His voice on the cross, "It is finished," Joh. xix. 30, shall be completed by that later voice of His heavenly Father, "He that sat on the throne said, Behold, I make all things new. And He said unto me write, for these words

are true and faithful, and he said unto me, " It is done."
Rev. xxi. 6.

Another aspect of the deep wisdom and love of the
Gospel of Christ will be seen, when we consider the
Kingly office of the Saviour, as specially revealed in the
first Gospel. The world in all past ages has been groan-
ing under the curse of selfish, despotic, and unrighteous
government. Oppression has made even wise men mad,
and men in the last days, recoiling from the curse of
despotic rule, have been ready to fling themselves into
a still lower gulf, of lawlessness and utter anarchy. The
promised Redeemer was predicted from the first, under
the character of a Righteous King, in whom would be
realized what sinful men had vainly longed for through
successive ages, but had never been able to attain permanently by any devices of human wisdom. He was
to be a King of the race of David, but better and greater
than David ; a King of Peace, greater and better than
Solomon, in whom the words should be fulfilled, " I will
raise unto David a righteous branch, and a King shall
reign and prosper, and execute judgment in the earth,"
Jer. xxiii. 5.

This Kingly glory of Christ is the truth specially
revealed in the first Gospel, which begins with His
line of royal descent, and with the message to the Wise
Men, "Where is He that is born King of the Jews ? for
we have seen His star in the East, and are come to
worship Him." It is continued by the solemn message of His work of judgment, " When the Son of man
shall come in His glory and all the holy angels with
Him, then shall He sit on the throne of His glory." It
is crowned and completed by His parting words, on the
mountain in·Galilee, " All power is given to me in heaven
and in earth, Go and teach all nations...teaching them
to observe all things, whatsoever I have commanded you."

The unsearchable wisdom implied in this office of Christ is shewn in three things. It is all-inclusive as to the actions on which judgment is to be passed. "God shall bring every work into judgment, with every secret thing whether it be good, or whether it be evil," Eccles. xii. 14. It is all inclusive as to the persons who are judged. "Before Him shall be gathered all nations," Matt. xxv. 32. "We must all appear before the judgment seat of Christ that every one may receive the things done in his body, according to that he hath done, whether it be good or bad," 2 Cor. v. 10. "I saw the dead, small and great, stand before God; and the books were opened... and the dead were judged out of those things which were written in the books, according to their works," Rev. xx. 12. This judgment requires in Him who executes it, unsearchable wisdom, not only because it includes all mankind and all their actions, but has respect to all the principles on which righteous judgment depends. It is a judgment without respect of persons by one "who searcheth the reins and the hearts," who "will bring to light the hidden things of darkness, and will make manifest the counsels of the hearts." It is the judgment of one who is able to weigh in scales of perfect equity, the varying opportunities, and degrees of light, which men have enjoyed or abused, and all the excuses by which they have sought to veil their guilt, from the time of the fig-leaves of Paradise, to the hour of the last judgment. And this Judge is also the great " High Priest, holy, harmless, undefiled, separated from sinners, and made higher than the heavens," Heb. vii. 26, " who can be touched with the feeling of our infirmities, and was in all points tempted like as we are, yet without sin," Heb. iv. 15. The mingled folly and blasphemy of those sinners is extreme, who charge this glorious King of Righteousness, the future Judge of all mankind, with

13—2

utter and incredible folly, in that glorious Gospel of redeeming grace and love, which is really the brightest effluence of the wisdom and grace of the "Sun of Righteousness," where it shines with a brightness above that of the sun at noonday.

A third aspect of the glorious wisdom of Christ as revealed in the Gospels is seen in His character as the Lord of all nature, the unwearied and indefatigable Worker. This is the view of our Lord's character specially revealed in the second Gospel, which ends with this solemn message. "After that the Lord had spoken unto them, He was received up into heaven and sat at the right hand of God; and they went forth and preached everywhere, the Lord working with them, and confirming the word with signs following." The fact of this unwearied working of the Son of God, is expressly stated by Himself, to justify his cure of the impotent man on the Sabbath day. "Jesus answered them, My Father worketh hitherto, and I work," Joh. v. 17. But it constitutes the main feature of the second Gospel, in which there are few discourses, but an un-wearied succession of acts of grace, swiftly following each other. "Straightway, coming up out of the water, He saw the heavens opened." "Immediately the Spirit driveth Him into the wilderness." "Straightway they forsook their nets and followed him;" and "Straight-way He called them;" and "Straightway, on the Sab-bath day, He entered into the Synagogue and taught," Mk. i. 10, 12, 18, 20, 21, 29, 43.

Along with this character of Christ, as the indefatig-able worker, answering to the symbol of the ox, there is here revealed His lordship over all nature. The double message is here given, "Is not this the carpenter? and they were offended at him." "Go into all the world, and preach the Gospel to every creature," or to the whole creation. The lordship of Christ over all nature, both material and spiritual, is further summed up in the words that follow, "These signs shall follow them that believe. In my name shall they cast out devils, they shall speak with new tongues, they shall take up serpents, and if they drink any deadly thing, it shall not hurt them; they shall lay hands on the sick, and they shall recover," Mk. xvi. 17—20.

All the acts of Him who is the Lord of nature, must in a certain sense be supernatural. The one supreme law to which they are subject is, "the counsel of His own will," or their subservience to the great ends of His universal providence. The common course of nature, as well as all that is rare and exceptional, proceeds from His supreme wisdom. The rising and setting of the sun, and the circuits of the seasons; "they continue this day according to Thine ordinances, for all are Thy servants," Ps. cxix. 90, 91; and the stedfastness of the earth itself, "Thou hast established the earth and it abideth." But so also, when He "said to the fig-tree, No man eat fruit of thee hereafter for ever, and His disciples heard it;" "in the morning as they passed by, they saw the fig-tree dried up from the roots," Mk. xi. 14, 20. For, it was the word of Him by whom all things were made at the first, and who has said, "Heaven and earth shall pass away, but my word shall not pass away." The laws of nature include not only an element of permanence, but of immense and ceaseless variation. The supreme law to which all others must ever be subordinate, is the will of the Lord God of hosts; and the nature of every seed and every plant and grain, and all the processes of human husbandry, in their profoundest wisdom, "come forth from the Lord of hosts, who is wonderful in counsel and excellent in working," Isa. xxviii. 29.

The character of Christ, as the Son of Man and as

the true High Priest is especially set before us in the third Gospel. This Gospel is especially rich in its manifestation of the human sympathies, grace, and compassion of the Saviour. He presents himself to us, as the Son of Man predicted by Daniel; the ideal man, the perfect pattern and standard, not only of grace and compassion, as in the parables of the Good Samaritan and the Prodigal Son, but also of worship, reverence, and piety towards God. When " He was praying, the heavens were opened" at His Baptism, Lu. iii. 21. When He chose the Apostles, He "went out into the mountain to pray, and continued all night in prayer to God," Lu. vi. 12. As this Gospel begins with the vision to Zacharias, while ministering in the temple, so its close sets before us the Son of Man, ascending to the throne of God, in the very act of priestly benediction. "While He blessed them, He was parted from them and carried up into heaven, and they worshipped Him, and returned to Jerusalem with great joy," Lu. xxiv. 51, 52. In all these passages is implied the full and perfect wisdom of Christ as the Son of Man.

In the "old Serpent," one name of the great adversary, is implied the greatness of that perverse and unprincipled cunning, which forms the treasury of delusion and falsehood, on which the kingdom of darkness is founded. He is set before us in the word of God, as combining angelic and superhuman intelligence, the utmost tortuosity, fertility in inventing ever varying delusions and falsehoods; the utmost conceivable blindness to the superior wisdom of God; an intense power of self-delusion, and along with all this the consciousness of power to wage a warfare against God and His truth, and a temper wholly devoid of fear and alarm, so as to harden himself against the Most High. Such are the characters in which he was revealed to that Patriarch who was especially exposed to his temptations. He is the "king over all the children of pride, and beholdeth all high things : on earth there is not his like, who is made without fear .... his heart is as firm as a stone, yea, hard as a piece of the nether mill-stone : the sword of him that layeth at him cannot hold," Job xli. 24, 33, 34. As he is the foremost and chief of rebels against God, so he seems to be pronounced, in natural gifts, the foremost of created intelligences. "He is the chief of the ways of God, but He that made him, can make His sword to approach unto him," Job xl. 19. The great day of Christ's judgment is that in which "the Lord with his sore, and great, and strong sword, shall punish Leviathan the piercing and crooked serpent," Isa. xxvii. 1.

As in this enemy we have set before us, the sum and climax of all perverse cunning as figured in the serpent tribes, employed for the dishonour of God and the injury of man; so this perfect cunning, perversity and malice of "the spirit who worketh in the children of disobedience," Eph. ii. 2, can only be overcome by the all-perfect wisdom of the God-man. "For this purpose was the Son of God manifested that He might destroy the works of the Devil," 1 Jo. iii. 8. "Christ is the power of God and the wisdom of God," 1 Cor. i. 24. "The cross is that mystery of godliness and of redeeming grace, wherein Christ, the Son of Man, "spoiled principalities and made a show of them openly, triumphing over them in it," Col. ii. 15. The adversary is the "strong man armed" with seemingly interminable resources of delusion, which constitute the armoury of the kingdom of darkness. As human nature in its perfection is higher and nobler than the nature of the serpent, the Redeemer is that "stronger than he," who can overcome him, "take from him all the armour wherein he trusted, and divide his spoils;" because He is the Incarnate

Wisdom, the Word, "in whom are hid all the treasures of wisdom and knowledge," ver. 3.

Inexpressibly mournful and solemn are charges of folly, falsehood, and delusion, brought by guilty mortals against that glorious Gospel, in which omniscient Wisdom, and inexpressible grace, and spotless holiness have conspired to reveal the choicest treasures of Divine goodness, so as to rescue all but the more stubborn and perverse of the human race, from the ruin of that fall in which they were involved at first, by the malice of the great ringleader of evil.

CHAPTER XXII.

The Increase of Knowledge in the Last Days, a Scripture Prophecy.

The present century has witnessed the solution of a great problem, which awakened the curiosity, and baffled the researches of the ancients, from Herodotus onward through more than two thousand years, till it passed into a proverb. The sources of the Nile have been detected and explored, by the laborious researches of Livingstone, Krapf, Grant, Speke, Stanley, Cameron, and other travellers. They have been found to lie in a series of Lakes in the South of Africa, fed by the copious and abundant rains of the Tropics.

From these hidden sources, for thousands of years, has flowed the fertilizing stream which formed the pride and glory of Egypt, the main source of its wealth, fertility, and greatness, through successive ages, when the land of the Pharaohs was the foremost of the world's empires. That stream of the Nile received on its bosom, almost four thousand years ago, in an ark of papyrus the infant Moses, the first and noblest in the series of those messengers by whom it has pleased God to give written messages of His will to mankind. On the side of this stream in later years, were built those pyramids, which are the most conspicuous and enduring products of man's skill and labour to be found on the face of the whole

earth.   Both these, and their contents, are the record of
his vain and earnest efforts to resist the reign of corruption, to baffle death and the grave.

There is another flood which in these days is pouring
its broad and fertilizing stream, not over the valley of
the Nile alone, but over the far wider range of all the
civilized regions of the earth.   That flood is the wide,
and still widening stream of physical science, growing
in depth and breadth from year to year, with its manifold
contributions to the arts of life, and to the supply of
human wants.   Very wonderful and various are its discoveries of the secrets of nature, with its microscope, its
telescope, steam engines, steam boats, locomotives, rail-
ways, electric telegraphs, spectroscope, in the strata of
the earth below, and throughout the starry universe to
the farthest depths of space.   This wide and fertilizing
flood has changed the whole face of modern society, and
by its mighty operation has introduced a new era in the
history of our world.   It has laid bare a thousand secrets
in nature, long veiled in darkness, to the contemplation of
the human reason, and made them minister to the supply
of human wants, and to the development of the secret
and mysterious faculties of the mind of man.   Now it
is a natural inquiry, Is there any lake on a mountain
side near some mighty watershed, to which we can
trace the secret origin of this fertilizing flood of modern
scientific discovery?   There is such a source.   We find
it in one sentence of the inspired word of God ; one
verse near the close of the visions of the prophet Daniel,
which Christ has given His disciples a special charge to
read with understanding ; given to him in vision 2,400
years ago.   It is the prediction that in the time of the
end, and in the near approach of a time of great politi-
cal and national trouble, "many shall run to and fro, and
knowledge shall be increased."   Dan. xii. 4.

This verse was singled out by Lord Bacon as the motto of his immortal work, which gave the first great impulse to that revived energy of inductive search into nature which has gone on increasing ever since. The increase of travelling, or running to and fro in the earth, is here described as the first step in this predicted growth of knowledge. The knowledge of every child of man, has both its pedestal, and its commencement, in his familiar knowledge of a few persons, things, plants, animals, and material objects in that small spot of earth where he lives ; on his intimate knowledge of this small and narrow circle of the objects immediately around him, he founds the whole fabric and structure of his later knowledge. Thus an age of increased facilities for travelling and running to and fro in the earth, increases at once for every individual, the range of that circle of persons, things, spots, local relations, and material objects, which is the intellectual foundation upon which all his wider knowledge of the material universe, and his further speculations, or philosophical conjectures on the system of the universe, and on the nature of all his fellow creatures must be founded. Thus facilities for travelling, and a general habit of running to and fro in the earth, are a natural preparation for any further increase and development of man's knowledge of natural things. They provide a wider and broader basis than can exist, when each person is tied down, and limited, to the range of one day's foot journey on the face of the earth, and remains almost wholly ignorant, except by report, of all that lies beyond.

It has been estimated, by statistical inquirers, that the amount of locomotion, or travelling to and fro upon the earth, has increased more than a hundredfold in the course of the present century. The Roman Empire in this respect had made à great advance on all earlier ages. The Romans paid special attention to the construction of roads, the building of bridges, and the formation of regular pathways between Rome itself, and every part of her widely extended empire. It is probable that the amount and ease of travelling was increased tenfold under the Roman Empire, as compared with all previous ages of the world. It is plain that running to and fro in the earth, and the increase of natural knowledge, and a development of zeal in the study of the works of God, have been marked features in the whole history of the world, from the date of Bacon's work, down to the present hour.

What view did Lord Bacon himself take of his own work? Plainly, he believed that he was one selected instrument, for the fulfilment of an express promise and prophecy, which God had already given so long before by His holy Prophet, to the children of men. Hence arose his strong faith in the success of his great effort, to open a clearer pathway into the fields of science. Hence also his warning against the deceptive shortcuts which human impatience is ever prone to make, when it substitutes mere guess-work of a pretentious kind, for a patient induction of particular facts, and that careful testing of hypotheses at every step, on which the whole efficacy and value of induction, in his opinion, depended. He had a firm and sublime faith in the success of his own labours, even when all past experience, from the slow and scanty increase of knowledge for nearly 2000 years, might have seemed most discouraging. Because as man, he truly says, is the minister and interpreter of nature, so he felt himself in this great work, of laying the foundations for a theory of the inductive study of nature, to be only a servant, an interpreter of a promise already given to men, by the Lord God of the holy prophets. This promise assured the arrival in the time of the end, (which he referred with good reason to the times after the Reformation, and the fall of the Eastern empire of Rome), of an age when travelling and running to and fro in the earth should be greatly multiplied. And when along with this increase in the stimulus and materials of science, science itself should also be increased.

That increase he might well expect, would be twofold, like that of a river, spreading over a wider surface, and including a greater number of individuals; and also piercing further into the secrets of nature than had ever been done before; so as not only to increase the intellectual wealth of the race, but to furnish human life with a large variety of inventions, ministering to the hourly comfort of mankind. It was probably a deep, secret conviction of the true fountain from which his work derived its inspiration, that led Bacon, in the confidence of expected success, to append to his work the following prayer:—

The Student's Prayer.

"To God the Father, God the Word, God the Spirit, we pour forth most humble and hearty supplications; that he remembering the calamities of mankind, and the pilgrimage of this our life, in which we wear out days few and evil, would please to open to us new refreshments out of the fountains of his goodness, for the alleviating of our miseries. This also we humbly and earnestly beg, that human things may not prejudice such as are divine; neither that from the unlocking of the gates of sense, and the kindling of a greater natural light, any thing of incredulity, or intellectual night, may arise in our minds towards divine mysteries. But rather, that by our mind thoroughly cleansed and purged from fancy and vanities, and yet subject and perfectly given up to the divine oracles, there may be given unto faith the things that are faith's." Amen.

The rash and ambitious hypotheses of many modern speculators in science, while they depart very widely from the strict and exact laws of Bacon's Inductive Philosophy, at the same time suggest the duty to all the friends of real science, as well as to every sincere disciple of Christ, to offer up once more, with renewed earnestness, both for themselves, and for all their fellow students, this simple and striking prayer of Bacon, and to follow it by adopting his prayer as a writer.

THE WRITER'S PRAYER.

" Thou, O Father, who gavest the visible light as the first-born of thy creatures, and didst pour into man the intellectual light as the top and consummation of thy workmanship, be pleased to protect and govern this work, which coming from thy goodness, returneth to thy glory. Thou, after thou hadst reviewed the works which thy hands had made, beheldest that every thing was very good, and thou didst rest with complacency in them. But man, reflecting on the works which he had made, saw that all was vanity and vexation of spirit, and could by no means acquiesce in them. Wherefore if we labour in thy works with the sweat of our brows, thou wilt make us partakers of thy vision and thy sabbath. We humbly beg that this mind may be steadfastly in us ; and that thou, by our hands, and also by the hands of others, on whom thou shalt bestow the same spirit, wilt please to convey a largess of new alms to thy family of mankind. These things we commend to thy everlasting love, by our Jesus, thy Christ, God with us."

The true relation between Christian faith and genuine science, so often distorted or denied by sceptics or sciolists, is well defined by the same great philosopher in " Filum Labyrinthi," and in the Essay on Truth.

"There cannot be a greater and more evident truth than this, that all knowledge, specially that of natural philosophy, tendeth highly to the magnifying of the glory of God, in his power, providence and benefits;...as engraven in his works, which, without this knowledge, are beheld but as through a veil. ·If the heavens in the body of them, do declare the glory of God to the eye, much more do they in the rule and decrees of them, declare it to the understanding. And another reason (for its culture) not inferior to this, is that the same natural philosophy principally among all human knowledge, doth give an excellent defence against both extremes in religion, superstition and infidelity; for both it freeth the mind from a number of weak fancies and imaginations, and raiseth it to acknowledge that to God 'all things are possible.' To this purpose speaketh our Saviour in that first

Canon against heresies ... 'Ye do err, not knowing the Scriptures, nor the power of God'... So He saw well that natural philosophy was of excellent use to the exaltation of the Divine Majesty. And what is admirable, being a remedy for superstitions, it is nevertheless a help to faith... 'What is truth?' asked Pilate. Certainly there are that delight in giddiness, and count it a bondage to fix a belief, affecting free-will in thinking as well as in acting. It is not only the difficulty and labour which men have in finding out of truth that doth bring lies into favour, but a natural though corrupt love of the lie itself ... This same truth is a naked and open daylight, which doth not shew the masks and mummeries of the world half so stately and daintily as candle-light. A mixture of a lie doth ever add pleasure. Doth any doubt that if there were taken out of men's minds vain opinions, flattering hopes, and false imaginations, it would leave the minds of a number of men poor shrunken things, full of melancholy and unpleasing to themselves? But howsoever these things are in men's depraved judgments and affections, yet truth, which only doth judge itself, teacheth that inquiry for truth, which is the wooing of it, the knowledge of truth, which is the presence of it, and the belief of truth, which is the enjoying of it, is the sovereign good ·of human nature.

"The first creature of God, in the works of the days, was the light of the sense: the last was the light of reason, and His Sabbath work ever since is the illumination of His Spirit. First, he breathed light on the face of the matter, or chaos; then he breathed light into the face of man, and still he breatheth and inspireth light into the face of His chosen. The poet (Lucretius), that beautified the sect that otherwise was inferior to the rest, saith yet excellently well, 'It is a pleasure to stand upon the shore and to see ships tossed upon the sea; a pleasure to stand in the window of a castle, and to see a battle and the adventures thereof below: but no pleasure is comparable to the standing on the vantage-ground of truth, a hill not to be commanded, and where the air is always clear and serene: and to see the errors and wanderings, and mists and tempests in the vale below.' But so always that this prospect be with pity and not with swelling or pride. Certainly it is heaven upon earth to have a man's mind move in charity, rest in providence, and turn upon the poles of truth. To pass from theological and philosophical truth to the truth of civil business; it will be acknowledged even by those who practise it not, that clear and round dealing is the honour of man's nature, and the mixture of falsehood is like alloy that embaseth it."

CHAPTER XXIII.

The Antagonism between Christian Faith and Science "falsely so called," in the Last Days.

The "Gospel of the Resurrection" by Dr Westcott contains two hundred pages developing the truths involved in, and growing out of, the Resurrection of Christ, which seem to me mainly true and beautiful. Still there are two drawbacks which do much to obscure the whole, and deprive it of practical power. The first is, the mistaken transfer to the Son, God Incarnate, of the transcendental conception of God, as a Being above time and space, with whom there is no past, present, or future, but simply an ETERNAL NOW. It is one main feature of the great mystery of godliness, that God has condescended, in the person of His Son, not only to be tempted like as we are, but subject, like His creatures, to the conditions of time and place. This is the very central truth of the Christian creed, that God the Son became incarnate at Bethlehem, a specific place, in the reign of Herod and Augustus, and during the government of Pilate, a specific time, in "the last days." To forget and overlook this great truth, instead of helping us to see deeper into sacred mysteries, spreads a veil of mist and confusion over the whole. The other drawback is the entire omission of the doctrine of a Judgment to come, and of the fundamental contrast between the church and the world; and the double character of Christ as the "head of every man," and as the head of the body, the church.   This is the truth which forms the woof of the whole message of Scripture, from the history of Cain and Abel to the last chapter of the Apocalypse. The entire pretermission of this great and fundamental truth, turns the whole discussion into a kind of luminous haze, where every part produces an effect, like that of the nebulous spaces in the milky way, instead of shedding a definite light, like that of the pole star or the southern cross.

The Appendix of thirty pages, is an attempt to proclaim a peace and friendship between Christian faith and the Positivism of M. Comte ; an attempt as hopeless as it is suicidal, in a Professor of Divinity.   I have read it with intense surprise and regret, but it would require a book to unfold fully the reasons of my entire dissent from that Appendix.

Positivism, in its fundamental law of progress, combines a fearful blasphemy, with a complete reversal of the very first principle of genuine philosophy.   For that principle is the transition in our thoughts from momentary phenomena, to the causes, things, and persons, the real existences, mental or material, on which phenomena depend.   The creed which denies the living God, and consigns Him to the 'moles and bats,' as a dream of the infancy of science, that must disappear with the daybreak, and then be replaced by M. Comte's NEW SUPREME BEING, COLLECTIVE HUMANITY, is exactly the creed of the last Antichrist, in that final stage in which he will have dropped every veil, or theological disguise, aud when openly, and no longer in a mystery, he "opposes and exalts himself against all that is called God, or that is worshipped, so that he as God sitteth in the temple of God, shewing himself that he is God," 2 Thess. ii. 4.

It is refreshing to escape from the mephitic neighbourhood of this Satanic religion without a God, which, when they approach it incautiously, seems able to confuse and dazzle the senses and instincts even of some Christian men. Let us listen to the clear and manly testimony of that Christian philosopher, who is the second great glory of Cambridge. What a contrast to the blasphemy of M. Comte, with his " new Supreme Being," collective humanity, or a total including all the sinners of mankind, who have murdered and tortured one another, from Cain and Abel to the orgies of the Commune of Paris, and the last Turkish or Bulgarian atrocities. Let us turn from this " new God " of Positivism which has " lately come up," to the words of that noble Scholium which closes the " Principia " of Newton. That work is the greatest single step of advance in the knowledge of nature which man has been permitted to attain; and the Scholium is its fitting close.

" This most beautiful system of the sun, planets and comets could only proceed from the counsel and dominion of an intelligent and powerful being. If the fixed stars are the centres of other like systems, these being formed by the like wise counsel, must all be subject to the dominion of One. From every system light passes into all the others, and lest the systems of the fixed stars should fall on each other, He hath placed them at immense distances one from another. This being governs all things, not as a soul of the world, but as Lord over all, and on account of His dominion he is wont to be called the Lord God, παντοκράτωρ, or universal ruler ...

" The supreme God is a being, eternal, infinite, absolutely perfect. But a being however perfect, without dominion, cannot be said to be the Lord God. It is the dominion of a spiritual being which constitutes a God. A true, supreme or imaginary dominion makes a true, supreme or imaginary God; and from His true dominion it follows that the true God is a living, intelligent and powerful being; and from His other perfections that He is supreme or most perfect. He is eternal, infinite, omnipotent and omniscient. That is, His duration reaches from eternity to eternity, His presence from infinity to infinity. He governs all things, and knows all things that are or can be done.   God is the same God, always and everywhere.   In Him are all things contained and moved, yet neither affects the other.   God suffers nothing from the motion of bodies, and bodies find no resistance from the omnipresence of God ...

" We know Him only by His most wise and excellent contrivances of things and final causes; but we admire Him for His perfections, but we reverence and adore Him on account of His dominion ; for we adore Him as His servants; and a God without dominion, providence and final causes, is nothing else but fate and nature.   Blind metaphysical necessity, which is certainly the same always and everywhere, could produce no variety of things; and that diversity of natural things which we find suited to different times and places, could arise from nothing but the ideas and will of a being necessarily existing.   Thus much concerning God, to discourse of whom from the appearances of things, does certainly belong to natural philosophy."

The Agnosticism of the nineteenth century differs in two respects from the Gnosticism of the first century, and its "oppositions of science falsely so called," to the truth of God and the glorious message of the everlasting Gospel, while it agrees with it in most of its other features.   First, it strives to incorporate with itself the materials, provided by the progress of real science, in man's knowledge of the works of God, or the divine fulfilment of the gracious promise of God made by the prophet Daniel so long before, that in the time of the end knowledge should be increased.   It seeks to interweave all these discoveries of science into the web of its own unbelieving speculations, and it uses them to form fresh weapons of assault against the true sayings of God, as well as to point afresh the blunted shafts that have recoiled, and aim them at the shield of truth again.   It thus fulfils a real law of progress announced by the great Apostle of the Gentiles, in his parting message to the church of Christ ; there is a law of moral development in the case of wilful and open opposers of the truth, no less real, than that progress of real science which had been earlier assured to mankind by the Divine promise. "Evil men and seducers shall wax worse and worse, deceiving and being deceived." But this downward progress is to receive a sudden arrest and reversal in the last times, when the blasphemous presumption of those who have succeeded to the task of Jannes and Jambres shall have reached its height. "As Jannes and Jambres withstood Moses, so do these also resist the truth, men of perverted understanding, devoid of discernment as to the faith. They shall proceed no further, for their folly shall be manifest unto all men, as theirs also was." This climax seems almost reached in Positivism, and its Satanic religion, if religion it is to be called, which consigns the true and living God to eternal oblivion and contempt, as one of the dreams of a childish and outworn superstition, and would place upon His throne, for the worship of a coming and more enlightened generation, the "new Supreme Being" of M. Comte, "collective humanity."

Along with this downward moral progress of Agnosticism it has a second feature, in the reversal of the simple and noble prayer of Bacon, that "from the kindling of greater natural light, nothing of incredulity or intellectual night may arise toward the Divine mysteries." The warning prophecy of the Psalmist with regard to Judas has been fulfilled in its disciples, with regard to the higher intellectual food of the soul. "Their table is turned into a snare, a trap, a recompense, a stumblingblock to them." The words of the Psalmist do not refer mainly to the food of the body, but to the higher and richer food in the Divine discourses of Christ, and His multiplied acts of grace, the gift of working miracles, and the high privilege of the call to be an Apostle of Christ, all which the traitor abused and perverted to his own loss and shame. The celebrated saying of M. Comte, that to

the eyes of an enlightened philosopher, the heavens reveal no glory but that of the astronomers by whom their
laws are discovered, fulfils perfectly the description of
Milton, the third great light and glory of Cambridge:

> " For swinish gluttony
> Ne'er looks to Heav'n amidst its gorgeous feast,
> But with besotted base ingratitude
> Crams and blasphemes its feeder."

The words of Milton apply with still greater emphasis
to the rich and abundant intellectual feast which science,
by its manifold discoveries, has provided for all its disciples and students in these last days, than to abuse and
excess in the indulgence of the bodily appetites alone.

CHAPTER XXIV.

The Revelation in the Old and New Testaments one Harmonious Whole.

RATIONALISM may be defined as the abuse and perversion of human reason, in dealing with the claims of Divine Revelation. Its source is an undue confidence in man's unaided faculties, and an excessive estimate of his religious instincts and reasoning powers. Its effect is to set aside all the truths of Christianity, or else to choose out such as suit individual taste or fancy, and to depreciate or deny the supernatural evidence by which they are all invested with Divine authority, and claim the reverence and submission of mankind. It ranges through many degrees of error, from the broad assertion that Christianity is a fraud, and supernatural revelation impossible, to the rejection of some secondary truths, or books of an inferior importance, or of particular passages or texts, on insufficient evidence, from their rightful place in the volume of inspired truth.

If God has made a supernatural revelation of His will to mankind, it is plain that the gift may be perverted in two opposite ways. Men may add to it, or take away from it. They may corrupt it by spurious additions, or mutilate it by either a partial or a total rejection. They may confound false interpretations, and human traditions or additions, with the message itself, so as to invest them with a like authority; or they may pare down and extenuate its meaning till only a scanty residuum is left, which few people would think worth the trouble, of being conveyed to men by a special revelation.

The Pharisees and Sadducees in the time of our Lord are striking instances of these opposite evils. We have a warning against both, alike in the opening of Deuteronomy, iv. 2, and at the close of the Apocalypse, Rev. xxii. 18, 19. The same charge was given by Christ Himself to his disciples. We are thus taught that under the Law and the Gospel these are two lasting sources of danger to the Church of God. Such is the natural relation of these two errors, that every faithful Christian is likely to be charged in turn with each of them. Some will condemn him for believing too little, others for believing too much. He will seem a Rationalist or semi-Sadducee to superstitious devotees; or again, a superstitious bigot to the disciples of human reason. The best, wisest, and holiest Christians have only a partial and incomplete understanding of divine truth. The void left by an immature faith will either be filled up with opinions and misinterpretations which men mistake in their haste for parts of the divine message; or else they may accept a maimed and imperfect creed, instead of including within the circle of their faith the full scope and compass of the whole word of God. In one case they will add to its teaching, in the other they will take away from it. We ought never to suppose that we ourselves are free from all participation in one or other of these evils, against both of which it is our duty to contend. Renouncing rationalism we may fall easily into the arms of superstition; in condemning formalism and a mere traditional creed, we may contract a captious and sceptical habit of thought, which must betray us into partial unbelief. In dealing with slighter departures, on either side, from the line of truth, we need to be very guarded in our censures, lest the fault after all should prove to be our own. We may think that we have detected rationalism in others, when the real fault is some mixture of superstition in our own faith ; or, in other cases, we may charge men wrongfully with superstition, through a false and diseased estimate of our own powers of spiritual discernment. The arrows from both camps, that of the Sadducee and of the Pharisee, will be aimed, not less frequently against the truth which lies between them, than against each other. As Caiaphas and Pilate conspired together against the Lord of glory, a double reproach, both from the Pharisee and the Sadducee, is the natural consequence and usual price of a faithful adherence to the inspired word of God.

The stage of Rationalism farthest removed from Christianity, is that which denies even the possibility of a supernatural revelation, either in an oral or written form. In Atheists of the French school, such as Helvetius, Condillac and Volney, in the last century, and M. Comte and the Positivists of our own day, this doctrine is only the natural consequence of their dreary creed. The " fool" who says in his heart " There is no God," must naturally infer, there can be no Divine Revelation. With such men, nature is an immense lumber-room of effects without a cause, and of laws without any lawgiver. Their barren theory makes every star in the firmament re-echo the boast ascribed by Milton to the arch-fiend in the hour of his rebellion :

> " We know no time when we were not as now,
> Know none before us, self-begot, self-rais'd,
> By our own quick'ning power, when fatal course
> Had circled its full orb, the birth mature
> Of this our native Heav'n, ethereal sons."

But the paradox that all revelation is impossible, is not confined to Atheists, whose one great falsehood incorporates into itself a thousand lesser follies. It is held more or less fully by some who profess to be Theists, and even Christians of a high order, ardent lovers of "the absolute religion." It appears in F. Newman's works on "the Soul;" T. Parker's "Discourses on Religion;" and Strauss's "Mythical Theory of the Gospels." In the first, religion is a sentiment, not a conclusion of the intellect, and therefore can never be embodied in a creed, or conveyed by a "Book revelation." In the second, the perfections of God imply the certainty of a *universal* revelation of pure and absolute religion, and exclude any other of an historical, limited, and partial kind. In the last, the alleged proofs of Supernatural revelation are said to be proved impossible by the progress of sound metaphysics, and their inconsistency with the discoveries of modern science.

The doctrine that miracles are impossible in their own nature, is itself a moral miracle, a marvellous extreme of presumptuous folly, veiled under a thin mantle of metaphysical subtleties. From the fact that God has richly displayed His wisdom in the universe, as the great architect and mechanician, it draws the inference that He can never manifest any nobler attributes as the Father of mercies, the supreme Judge and moral Governor of all reasonable beings. Creation, and the silent quiet course of daily providence, as man now experiences it here on earth, can never exhaust all the conceivable or probable modes of His operation, who is "wonderful in counsel and excellent in working." Man is able easily to convince his fellow-man of his own presence. And shall the Almighty God, who upholds all things by His power, and fills Heaven and earth by His presence, be unable to manifest Himself by means more decisive and effectual than those which, at the present hour, leave Atheists at full liberty to deride the superstition of His worshippers, and to boast of their own superior wisdom, in their strenuous efforts to banish the Creator from His own universe? How much wiser to say with the ancient patriarch, after all our fancied advances in metaphysics and real progress in natural science, "Lo! these are a part of His ways; but how faint a whisper is heard of Him; the thunder of His power who can understand?"

But Supernatural religion, though not impossible, may perhaps be superfluous. Natural reason may be sufficient without the feeble help of historical records like those of the Gospels. The traditional saying of Omar has been applied to this subject by some modern writers.

"If the doctrine of Scripture agree with the conclusions of sound reason, they are superfluous; if opposed to it they are untrue and ought to be thrown away. To ascertain what is absolute religion," (Mr Parker affirms) "is not difficult. It is perfect obedience to the law of God; perfect love towards God and man exhibited in a life allowing the harmonious action of all the faculties. Christianity is either absolute religion and morality, or it is less; greater it cannot be. Jesus of Nazareth may either have taught absolute religion, or an imperfect form; he may have omitted what was essential, or have added what was national, temporal and personal. But if His religion has none of these faults, then it is the absolute religion, eternally true before revelation." Parker's 'Discourses,' pp. 180—182.

One would suppose that a single glance at the present state or past history of the world, would dispose at once of this strange wild fancy, that a supernatural revelation is entirely needless. A few jackdaws in Christian countries may strut about in borrowed feathers, and may boast of an "absolute religion" which they have stolen from the Bible, and then carved and mangled, till it is no better than a bleeding corpse. This residuum is a law without any sanction, a morality without life; the worship of a Being wholly unknown, without any remedy for conscious guilt, or any clear hope of life beyond the grave, or of any deliverance from the dark despotism of death. There is in fact no myth so purely mythical, as this dream of some philosophers in their dotage, that the light of man's reason has made all supernatural revelation superfluous.

If the sun of Christianity were once blotted out of the firmament, the dim feeble moonlight which these pretentious deists call "the absolute religion," a mere reflection lighted by that sun, on the sterile plains and volcanic caverns of the human heart, in its ceaseless lunations, would also disappear and pass away for ever. Wherever the true sunlight from heaven has not dawned, the words of the prophet have been verified, "Darkness has covered the earth, and gross darkness the people." Amidst all these declamations on the virtue and clearness of the absolute religion, the words of the Apostle remain still as true as ever, "after that in the wisdom of God, the world by wisdom knew not God, it pleased God by the foolishness (τοῦ κηρύγματος) of the preached word to save them that believe."

Though a divine revelation be admitted to be both possible and desirable, it may still be maintained that it has never been actually given. When the evidences of the Gospel are pleaded in the court of reason, the verdict may be returned, 'It is either an imposture or a mere dream of excited imagination.' Rationalism, in its third form, admits that a divine message might be given to men, and be in some respects desirable, and affirms only, that the proof of the fact, in the case of the Gospel, and still more of other religions, is insufficient and defective. This view is common to the earlier rationalism of Germany, and to the mythical theory which has widely displaced it. In reality it is seldom found to be maintained on its own merits. In those who maintain it, there is commonly a secret conviction that the laws of Nature have, in some way or other, tied up the hands of the supreme lawgiver. Or else there is an evident desire to whitewash the religious history of the world, and to make it out that fetichism and devil-worship, human sacrifices and widow-burning, infanticide, the crocodile gods of Egypt, and the monster gods of India, are very fair and respectable varieties of the one universal religion. Once let the double truth be frankly admitted, that the living God *can* make a revelation of His own will, character and purposes, and that mankind greatly need it, and nine-tenths of the cavils brought against Christianity and its evidences will die away of themselves.

The elder form of German rationalism, beginning with Semler, aimed its attacks solely against the miraculous elements in the Scripture history. These were got rid of, by any expedients, however violent. According to Bahrdt, the angel who appeared to Zacharias was a flash of lightning; Paulus explains it as the light of lamps falling upon a cloud of incense, and followed by an apoplectic stroke; his solution of the later history of the miraculous conception is too revolting to be repeated. The magi were common merchant travellers, and the star of Bethlehem either a comet, or a conjunction of planets; and the dreams were the accidental reflections of Joseph's own waking meditations. The opening of the heavens at our Lord's baptism was a parting of the clouds, or a flash of lightning, while Paulus gravely adduces examples of the tameness of birds, to shew that a real dove might have alighted on the head of Jesus. The angel who appeared to the shepherds, in one writer is a Jewish messenger, carrying a torch; and the song, the merry notes of a party who were with him. In a second, it was an *ignis fatuus*, or a flash of lightning; and again, in a third a swoon, or mental vision. These examples, which weary us by their monotony of dull absurdity, shew the desperate efforts made by the elder rationalists to pare down the Gospel narratives to the level of common history.

The features of the other system are equally strange. It admits that there was a person called John the Baptist, and a Jewish peasant called Jesus, who lived for some time at Nazareth, but all beyond these two facts is mythical invention, the result of a creative and legendary habit of thought in the early Christians. No miracles were wrought by this Jewish peasant, and no prophecy was fulfilled in him. He was perhaps condemned to death, but was either taken down from the cross while still alive, or never appeared again after his burial. But a small company of disciples resolved to treat him as the promised Messiah, in the teeth of all their deepest prejudices as Jews, without one grain of real evidence, and yet without the least purpose of fraud. Through the vividness of their fancy, and their faith in prophecies which they wholly misunderstood and misapplied, they ascribed to him cures he never wrought, and a resurrection which never occurred; parables and discourses, rich with treasures of divine wisdom, which he never spoke; and a character both in word and in deed, which was due to their own creative imagination alone. The very inventors of these fictions, according to the theory, mistook them for facts, and spent their lives in persuading others that they were facts, while the woof of the fiction was only half complete.

The case is just the same as if Bunyan, when he had written one half of the Pilgrim's Progress, had founded a society to preach these doctrines; that Christian, Obstinate, and Pliable, were three villagers of Bedfordshire; that the City of Destruction was Bedford, the county town; that the Slough of Despond was one of the fens of Cambridgeshire; and the castle of Giant Despair, the county jail; and that while he and his friends were fined, imprisoned, and hunted out of society for teaching these strange doctrines, he calmly employed his intervals of leisure in completing the allegory; and enriched his creed with the further dogma, that the Delectable mountains were a district somewhere in Wales. In short, on this mythical hypothesis, the Apostles turned the world upside down by proclaiming with the utmost zeal, self-sacrifice, and apparent conviction, the truth and immense importance of legends, which they were gradually weaving, at the very time, out of their own diseased and fertile imagination.

It is some comfort to the plain Christian, that these two schools of rationalism flatly contradict each other, and thereby lend an indirect confirmation to the truth of the Gospel. From the school of Semler and Paulus we learn that the Gospel narrative is so deeply rooted in the history of the times, and in the whole course of the known events of that age, that a thousand grossly absurd criticisms must be ventured on, rather than attempt the Herculean task of uprooting the whole from its historical context by denying its reality. From the mythical school of Bauer, Gabler, and Strauss, we learn that the supernatural element is so closely interwoven in the whole texture of the New Testament, that its exclusion is quite hopeless. When we combine these reluctant admissions, the evidence for the Gospel, as a revelation from heaven, is complete. The countless and absurd glosses of the naturalists bear witness that the substratum is true and real history; the late invented and laboured hypotheses of their rivals prove that this real history is indisputably miraculous. Thus, unless we revive the old blasphemy of the Pharisees, we must also own that it is truly and properly divine. We are thus landed, concerning our blessed Lord, in the confession of Nicodemus, which may ripen afterwards into fuller and clearer faith: " Rabbi, we know that thou art a teacher come from God, for no man can do these miracles that thou doest, except God be with him." The mythical theorists have thus, indirectly, done some service to truth, by sweeping away without compunction many cobwebs of criticism, which had been spun with much labour and perverse ingenuity by Rationalists of the earlier school. But the scheme which they would substitute, from its very nature, must be still more ephemeral than its predecessor. No intelligent Englishman can read the "Horæ Paulinæ" with care, the Epistles of St Paul, and the Book of Acts, and not feel sure that the letters are genuine documents of the first century, and the narrative a contemporary history, true and faithful, at least in its main outlines. Let him read them again, comparing the letters with the narrative, and striving honestly to realize the course of actual history thus implied, both on the part of the apostle himself, and of the early churches; and he will discover clear evidence of a state of things, which, both in its moral features, its historical freshness, and the sparing, but yet inseparable admixture of a supernatural and miraculous element with the whole current of the history, involves, requires, and presupposes all the main facts, whether miraculous or not, which compose the substance of the four Gospels.

The New Testament, which is a mine and treasury of truth to simple Christians, when it has to encounter the subtle theories of modern unbelief, will be found to possess a further character. It is a golden chain of evidence, where every link is firm as the foundations of heaven and earth; from the known history of the early church after the close of the Gospels to the twenty-one Epistles; from these again to the later portion of the Book of Acts; and from the facts, doctrines, and allusions in all these, to the contents of the early chapters from the day of Pentecost; and further, from all these combined, to the great fundamental facts of the Baptism, the moral

teaching, and the miracles of the Lord Jesus; His transfiguration, agony, crucifixion, burial, resurrection and
ascension, as they are recorded in all the four evangelists.
There is no crevice in this panoply of divine truth given
to the church by the Spirit of God. "Without controversy great is the mystery of godliness; God was manifested in the flesh, justified in the spirit, seen of angels,
preached unto the Gentiles, believed on in the world,
received up into glory."

The history then is real, the facts are miraculous, the
message is both divine and unspeakably glorious.

Doctrinal Rationalism has three varieties. The first
accounts Christ a mere fallible man, however good and
wise; it pretends to separate his mistakes and those of
his followers from that "absolute religion" which was the
sum of his teaching. The second teaches that Christianity is a sentiment, and not a set of dogmas, so that
if only we entertain a feeling of religious reverence towards Christ, all questions of doctrine are superfluous.
The third sets aside particular doctrines, commonly held
to be main parts of the Gospel, as due to Jewish prejudices and misconceptions of the apostles and evangelists,
which our more advanced and enlightened reason is
bound to cast away.

The first of these views is held by those pietists of
unbelief who pretend to glorify the essence of Christianity, and borrow largely from its phrases, while they
discard its authority. In Parker's Discourses, we have
such monstrous statements as these :—

"Did Jesus lay any stress on this watery baptism, then we must
drop a tear for the weakness. If it came from him, we can only say,
there is no perfect guide but the Father. It is apparent that he shared the
erroneous notion of the times respecting devils and possessions. He
never set up for a teacher of physiology. The acceptance of this error
is no impeachment of his moral and religious excellence, more than his

ignorance of the steam engine. The errors of great men are the glory of dunces alone. He was mistaken in his interpretation of the Old Testament, if we may believe the Gospels. If he supposed those earlier writers spoke of him, it is but a trifling mistake, affecting a man's head, not his heart (!). He is said to be an enthusiast, who hoped to found a visible kingdom, and to return in the clouds, and certainly a strong case may be made out to favour the charge (!). What then? If the dull evangelists have not thrust their fancies into his mouth, it does not militate against his morality and religion. How many a saint has been mistaken in such matters."

How kind and generous are these half-believers, or demi-semi-believers, to extend their patronage to the Son of God, in spite of all these serious errors, with which " if the dull evangelists " are to be credited, He has disfigured the beauty of their "absolute religion." Such statements, however offensive, are quite natural, in those who reject the idea of any direct and supernatural revelation of God to man. The Gospel, in their view, is a surprising windfall of "absolute religion," covered with rotten twigs and branches of Jewish ignorance and prejudice, which, by some strange chance or other, found its way into a world where it was much needed, through a Galilean peasant. On any other view, such statements are not more offensive than absurd. If God has indeed spoken to man, what can be more unreasonable than to maintain that the message is filled up with Jewish prejudices, scientific errors, scraps of unmeaning ritual, and enthusiastic mistakes and follies? If the truth is allowed, that our Lord, at the least, is a teacher sent from God, without which the claim to be a Christian is a direct fraud, what a folly it must be to claim the right of instructing our teacher. What an extreme folly to pretend to enlighten Him, whose name and office has been revealed by His own lips, and sealed by signs and wonders, as the " Light of the world." We cannot be at once both patrons and disciples of the Lord. We cannot claim to be possessors

of an "absolute religion," pure, perfect, and undefiled, and
praise him for teaching so much of it, and profess piously
to "drop a tear" of pity over his mistakes, and still pretend
to believe even the first and lowest of his claims, that he
is the prophet of God, commissioned to guide our feet
into the way of peace.   This mongrel Christianity, amidst
all its spiritual phrases and pretences, is really less honest,
and much more revolting to every sincere disciple, than
open and avowed unbelief.

Others admit vaguely the claim of Christ to be the
Son of God, but they are possessed with the notion
that dogmas have been the chief bane of true religion.
Spiritual Christianity consists simply, in their view, in
an undefined and mysterious reverence for the person and
character of Christ.   This view has its source in the
recoil from a dry orthodoxy, and the critical follies of
rationalism within the Lutheran church.   This is the
school of Schleiermacher, and in a less degree of the
lamented Neander.   However useful its protest against
two great evils, and whatever the beauty with which it may
have sometimes been clothed, its principle is fatally opposite to the truth of the Gospel.   There can be no deep
reverence for Christ, without submission to the truth and
authority of His own repeated sayings.   He does insist
strongly on the acceptance and belief of certain distinct
and definite truths.   He calls Himself "the way, the
truth, and the life."   Truth takes precedence even of life
itself.   We must first climb this steep hill-side, and gaze
from this mountain-top on the glorious landscape, before
the joy of spiritual life can take possession of our souls.
The promise is express, "Ye shall know the truth, and
the truth shall make you free."   Eternal life is solemnly
declared to consist in the knowledge of God the Father
and of Jesus Christ.   In many sayings of our Lord we
find the clear and distinct assertion of great religious

truths, which every disciple is bound to receive on His authority. All professions of reverence must be insincere, while we evade this simple test of a genuine disciple, and try to steal away, under a mist of our own raising, from hearty submission to these true sayings of God.

The view which denies all doctrine in Christianity is equally untenable on the ground of reason. The words of Solomon are true of the palace of the soul, and all its hidden chambers of emotion, sympathy, and affection: "Through wisdom a house is builded, and by understanding it is established, and by knowledge shall the chambers be filled with all precious and pleasant riches." It is knowledge of the truth which makes the Christian free, knowledge of sin which makes him humble, knowledge of the love of God which inspires him with love. To be "saved," and "to come to the knowledge of the truth," in the language of Christ and His Apostles, are equivalent expressions. It is foolish to suppose that a vague, misty sentiment, which dare not clothe itself in words, lest it should become a dogma, can serve for the basis of a new moral being. Light must precede life, both in the old and the new creation.

The fact that a revelation from heaven is needed, implies that the conscience of man has been darkened by sin, and his reason greatly obscured in its perceptions of moral truth. This must also make him liable to èrr in his interpretation of the message. What then is his duty, when the first impressions of his reason, and his first notions as to the meaning of the revelation, are found to diverge? Both alike must be re-examined. He must search more deeply both into the Bible and his own heart, till he discovers the real source of this seeming opposition. When we screen our conscience from this purifying process, and throw the blame at once on the

message, or at least on the divinely appointed vehicle of
that message, we commit a double error; we indulge
both our pride and our unbelief; we defeat one main
purpose for which the revelation is given, which is to
purify and elevate the faculties of the soul, and we
strike directly at the root of its authority as a message
of God to man.

Our present life is really a childhood, to prepare us
for a life to come; the law of childhood, under which
alone its training can be carried on, is to receive many
truths on authority, and to wait till riper years for more
direct and full evidence. This is an imperfect state,
when compared with the wisdom and insight of a later
age; but it is wisdom itself, when contrasted with the
perverseness of the child who refuses to believe anything,
of which the proof is not plain at once to his childish
understanding. This mimicry of manly reason only
shuts up the rebel of the nursery in hopeless ignorance.
The price which has to be paid, for affecting to be wise
before the time, is never to grow wise at all. The acceptance of honest and well-informed testimony, in daily
life as in religion, is the only bridge that can lead us
from childish ignorance, across impassable perplexities,
to a clear and full discernment, and firm possession, of
heavenly truth.

The love of God is deeper, sterner, and higher than
what sentimentalists pass off under its name. It includes
three distinct forms of goodness, answering to three main
facts or principles of the moral universe. There is benevolence to being as being; there is righteousness, or
holiness, discriminating goodness to creatures as morally
good or evil; there is mercy and grace to creatures, as
guilty, but still recoverable to goodness and holiness again.
The maxim "God is Love," would seem simple, if it had
to be applied only to a sinless world. But it is the pro-

blem of problems, to know in what forms it will reveal itself in a world, where sin and rebellion have ploughed their deepest furrows. We need to learn how sinners may be translated from the outer court of simple benevolence, as shewn in the sunlight and fruitful seasons, into the highest and innermost region of triumphant mercy. Who shall span and bridge over for us the region of infinite justice which lies between, and severs as with an impassable gulf, the fallen, the proud, the impure, and the profligate, from the bright land of purity and unspotted holiness? The religions of fear and superstition cannot solve the problem. They lead man within the edge of that sphere of justice by their penances and macerations and bloody or unbloody sacrifices, but they leave him only on the brink of this vast gulf, which the conscience feels it can never fathom or cross over by its own efforts. A voice is heard from beyond the abyss: "No man can by any means redeem his brother, or give to God a ransom for him: the redemption of their soul is precious, and it ceaseth for ever." The doctrine of the atonement, revealed in the Gospel of Christ, can alone carry us across this dreary wilderness, in which reason is lost, and where remorse wanders up and down, seeking in vain for rest, with deep outcries and sorrowful wailings. There alone the three glorious elements are harmonized which compose the heavenly light of God's love. A benevolence wide as creation; a righteousness and justice deep as hell; and a mercy and grace reaching far above those clouds where reason is lost, vast and infinite as heaven.

The form of Rationalism most prevalent among real Christians is that which denies, or greatly depreciates, the authority of the Old Testament. Its extreme is found in writers of the infidel school, who think no terms too strong to express their dislike of the Divine character, as pourtrayed in the Old Testament, and speak of the "wrathful Jehovah of the Jews." Thus Theodore Parker gives this judgment on Num. xiv.:

" If an unprejudiced Christian were to read this in a heathen author, related of Kronos or Moloch, he would say, 'What foul ideas these heathen had of God! Thank heaven, we cannot believe in a Deity so terrible.' There are some things which may be true, but must be rejected for lack of evidence, but this story no amount of evidence could render possible."

The moral darkness is indeed prodigious, which can utter such railings against the Bible history, in one of the most solemn, tender, noble, pathetic, and profoundly spiritual of its messages. But there are many Christians who would recoil from them with utter abhorrence, who yet betray a secret wish to sever Christianity from its connection with the Law and the Prophets, as if these, not only in particular passages, but in their general tone and character, were unworthy to be associated on a footing of equal authority with the Christian revelation. It is very common, even with earnest and devout men, to speak of the New Testament alone, as the Christian Scriptures, binding on our faith. Coleridge says in the "Confessions of an inquiring spirit" that

"it is the imagined contrast and diversity of spirit which many have believed themselves to find in the Old Testament and in the Gospel which has given occasion to the doubt, and in the heart of thousands supplies fuel to a fearful wish, that it were permitted to make a distinction."

So far as this feeling of a general dislike to the Old Testament extends, it is clear that it cannot be relieved by the sacrifice of one or another obnoxious passage. The questions whether the books are genuine, and the canon free from spurious additions, are subordinate to one still higher and larger, whether the whole is defective in its general tone, opposed to the spirit of the Gospel, and the instincts of universal morality. The forms and degrees of rejection, dislike, and partial approval, may vary widely. Parker, whose blasphemy we have just quoted, speaks also of

"the sweet notes of David's prayers; his mystic hymn, full of rippling life; his lofty Psalm, which unites the warbling music of the wind, the sun's glance, and the rush of the lightning; and the stalwart character and masculine piety of the old prophets, that puts to shame our puny littleness."

Coleridge writes vaguely of these same Scriptures, that we see in them

"the first ferment of the great affections, the protoplastic waves of the microcosmic chaos, swelling up against the outspreadings of the Dove that lies brooding on the troubled waters."

In this gentle and somewhat misty and poetic disclaimer, the language of men's hearts may be thus expounded. 'The New Testament, at least in the main, is a revelation worthy of God, which approves itself to our inmost conscience. We cannot deny the fact that it is closely linked with the Old Testament, and seems to recognise in it an origin and authority as Divine as its own. We can also admire and enjoy the greater part of the Psalms, and many passages of the Prophets; but still the book, as a whole, jars greatly against our moral instincts. We could wish from our heart that Christianity stood alone. We should love it more, and count it more worthy of a Divine author, if it were encumbered by no connection with the Jewish law, and the trivial ceremonies, or stern and harsh features, of the Mosaic economy.'

The two features of the Old Testament which bring down upon it the dislike of sentimental dreamers, are its minute ceremonial details and barren genealogies, and the severe, awful, and alarming tone of its messages. What can be wider apart than Kant's Treatise on the Pure Reason, Schelling's Theory of the Absolute, or

Hegel's Scheme for the evolution of the Universe out of the possible, and the first chapters of the Chronicles, or the offerings of the Princes in the Book of Numbers? What can be more opposite to that amiable, gentle, passive benevolence, which appears to sentimentalists the proper conception of Divine goodness, than the account of the plagues of Egypt, or the overthrow of Sodom and Gomorrah by fire from heaven?

These very features of the Old Testament, by which it is contrasted with the Gospel, have not been left for modern objectors to discover, but are stated prominently in the Gospels themselves. The mention of them, in reality, forms the preface to the most gracious and tender, the most spiritual and heavenly, of the discourses of our Lord, in the gospel of the beloved disciple, who was chosen to announce the sublime doctrine, that God is Love: "The law was given by Moses, but grace and truth came by Jesus Christ." Grace in contrast with the law's judicial severity; and truth in equal contrast with its copious historical details, and its multitude of outward rites and ceremonies. The difficulty is not eluded; nay, rather, the contrast is stated in such a manner, as to imply that no difficulty was felt by the Apostle. For we find in the same gospel those striking words of the Saviour: "Had ye believed Moses, ye would have believed me: for he wrote of me. But if ye believe not his writings, how shall ye believe my words?" Joh. v. 46. And a similar statement meets us in that gospel which of the three others is fullest of human gentleness and grace. Our Lord there puts the evidence of truth in the Old Testament on a level with the approaching miracle of His own resurrection. "If they hear not Moses and the prophets, neither will they be persuaded though one rose from the dead," Lu. xvi. 31. The difficulty then is no sunken rock, on which our faith may be

stranded, because its first discovery is due to the ingenuity of unbelievers. It is rather a landmark on the
wide sea of Divine revelation, which the New Testament itself holds up prominently to our view.

Again, the ceremonial features of the Old Testament,
when we view it as an earlier revelation preparing for a
later, are in full agreement with the favourite theories of
these philosophical objectors themselves. They delight to
represent mankind as self-educated, without any need for
Divine interference. In their theory of progress, the race
ascends through Fetichism of the most barbarous kind to
Polytheism, then to Dualism and Pantheism, and finally
to Monotheism. The history of all nations is carved
into shape, to suit this fancied law of human development.
The interval to be traversed, then, is immense; whether
man is left to the hopeful task of raising himself from the
worship of rags, flies, and monkeys, to the pure "absolute
religion"; or whether, as Christians believe, it has pleased
God to carry on the great work, by Supernatural revelations of His will. The change is like the upheaving of
a deep ocean-bed to form a Himalayan range, that may
pierce far into the blue vault of heaven. Now if the
All-Wise God undertakes this work, may we not expect
that He will do it wisely? In His messages to mankind,
must He not begin by stooping to their actual state, that
He may raise them above it? Will not the degree of
light which He sees fit to impart depend, more or less, on
the capacity of vision, which has been the result of previous steps in the course of Divine revelation? If the
Word of God be food, must not the milk be supplied
earlier than the strong meat? if light, must not the twilight come before the day-break, and the day-break before
the brilliance of noon-day? In short, are not the words
of our great poet the sketch of a truer and juster philosophy of revelation, than that monotony of spiritual efful-

gence which these objectors would impose as a law to
the messages of the Almighty ?

> "So law appears imperfect, and but given
> With purpose to resign them, in full time,
> Up to a better covenant, disciplined
> From shadowy types to truth, from flesh to spirit,
> From imposition of strict laws, to free
> Acceptance of large grace, from servile fear
> To filial, works of law to works of faith."
>
> "Par. Lost," Bk. XII.

Nor will we refuse, however fanciful in the eye of dim-
sighted theorists, the typical fore-shadowing of the same
truth, by which the angel is made to confirm his own
explanation.

> "And therefore shall not Moses, though of God
> Greatly beloved, being but the minister
> Of law, His people into Canaan lead :
> But Joshua, whom the Gentiles Jesus call ;
> His name and office bearing, who shall quell
> The Adversary Serpent, and bring back
> Thro' this world's wilderness, long-wandered man,
> Safe, to eternal Paradise of rest." *Ib.*

The other feature in the Old Testament, which repels or
perplexes many, is its sternness and severity. And this,
too, admits of a full explanation, when we gaze with reverence on the perfections of the Most High, or look
thoughtfully into the hidden depths of our own being.

Benevolence, justice, and mercy, it has been remarked
already, are the three contrasted, yet harmonious elements
of the Divine goodness. They answer to three possibilities affecting the rational creation, happiness, guilt, and
recovery. Benevolence alone could be fully manifested
to unfallen creatures, and it shone clearly upon man in
the days of Paradise. Since the Fall, even this light has
been obscured from his view. True, there is still a voice
in the shower and the sunshine, in the beauty and fra-
grance of the flowers, and in the quiet glory of the stars,

which whispers to him—"The Lord is good to all; his tender mercies are over all his works."   But it reaches his ears, mingled with sterner sounds which awaken forebodings of evil in the guilty conscience, the voice of the hurricane and the thunderstorm, and the deep sad howling of wintry winds.   Meanwhile there are fears and hopes within his heart, which utter confusedly the double and seemingly contradictory message, that God is terrible in justice, and also wonderful in mercy.   But who can solve and reconcile these solemn and mysterious truths by the light of fallen reason alone?   Who shall quiet the fears of a darkened self-accusing conscience, or reduce the blind flatteries of hope into concord with the voice of righteousness?   Man alone never has done and never can do it.   Many dim imperfect guesses he has made, and commonly with light borrowed from a higher source. But these dim guesses have had no sanction to assure him of their truth, and the little power they might else have gained has been lost by their inconsistency and contradiction.   When the thought of God's justice has flashed out upon him, he has framed a creed of terror and darkness, like the dark rites of Egypt, or the Hindoo worship of Siva the Destroyer.   When this sterner voice has slumbered within him, he has resigned himself to the sportive illusions of childhood, and framed an airy creed, like the Grecian Polytheism; though even here conscience has claimed its rights, and spoken to the soul of Nemesis and Tartarus, of awful Fates and avenging Furies.   The problem of life remained still unsolved.   The mystery was too complex and too deep to be fathomed.   The facts of Providence, even in this life, were confused and chequered, and there mingled with them strange and uncertain forebodings of a life to come.   The soul of man could only utter its sorrowful complaint: "Behold I go forward, but he is not there, and backward, but I cannot perceive him; on the left hand where he doth work, but I cannot behold him: he hideth himself on the right hand, that I cannot see him."

What man was unable to do for himself, it has pleased God, in His love and wisdom, to do for him, by a supernatural revelation of His will. The fact of the Divine benevolence had already abundant voices to proclaim it, in the course of Providence, and the instincts of the heart, if only these were cleared from the pains and dissonant notes of care and sorrow, which sin had introduced in the world. It was justice and mercy which needed to be revealed, and all the more, because of their seeming contradiction, which the wisdom of men could never resolve into their true and hidden harmony. In the instincts of the heart, each seemed to interfere with the other, till no impression was left on the conscience, but a vague uncertainty, as when twilight and moonlight struggle with each other. Amidst the anomalies of Providence, justice ceased to be just; and amidst the sorrows of life, mercy itself, it might seem, had forgotten to be merciful. To disentangle the web, and bring out in full relief once more the Divine character which sin had entirely shrouded, each voice required to find a separate utterance. It was needful that God should, first of all, reveal His justice, and then crown this by a further revelation of His grace. Revelation, to fulfil its great end, thus required to be parted into two main portions, of which the respective voices should be, severity to the sinner in his rebellion, and mercy to the prodigal, returning to seek rest in a Father's love. It is true that the separation could not be complete. For since these three perfections all unite in the mind of God, they must all coexist in every part of His revelation, though one of them may form its predominant feature. The main feature of the old covenant is the voice of Law, denouncing death to the sinner, and "revealing the wrath of God from heaven, against all ungodliness, and unrighteousness of men." But even here, there will be found a memory of Paradise, and a hope of Paradise to be restored, and undertones that speak of God's universal benevolence, wherever the dark clouds of sin come not in the way.   And deeper notes resound first in types from the mercy-seat, and more plainly from the harp of prophecy, which tell of rich mercy, still in reserve, and shortly to be revealed to the sons of men. And thus we are brought to the conclusion, that the feature of the Old Testament which revolts the proud heart, and staggers the sentimental and the timorous, is the secret pledge of its Divine wisdom.   The law with all its severity, as given by Moses, as well as the grace and truth which have come by Jesus Christ, are alike from the Lord of hosts, and the Father of mercies; they are varied but harmonious exhibitions of His character "who is wonderful in counsel, and excellent in working."

The first step towards a cure of Rationalism is to recognise, at the outset, the just claims and real dignity of human reason. No error can be effectually overcome, till we have made an ally of that truth, of which it is the parody. The superstition of the Romans, who began their wars or sieges by public ceremonies, inviting the gods of their enemies to a new and lasting home in the Capitol, conveys a deep lesson in every moral conflict.   Truth, perverted and held down in unrighteousness, is the guardian-power in every citadel of error.   This Palladium once removed, the walls will crumble to pieces.   Now the truth on which Rationalism builds its strength, is that dignity of human reason, by which man is distinguished from the beasts that perish. We cannot advance the cause of Christianity by a blind attempt to depreciate this gift of God to mankind.   To found the claims of the Gospel on an utter denial of man's moral faculties, by whomsoever it may be attempted, is a suicidal course, and resigns us to the mercy of every superstition, which comes pretending to be a voice from heaven.   The power of moral discern-

ment is not wholly lost, though grievously obscured.
The Bible does not speak to us as stocks and stones, or
brute creatures without reason, else its message would be
in vain; but simply as to children, whose reason is
unripe, and whose ignorance is aggravated by moral perverseness.   But the faculty itself is recognised on every
page.   Its admitted presence gives keenness to every
rebuke, and emphasis to every warning. "Yea, and why
even of your own selves judge ye not what is right?"
Lu. xii. 57. "I speak as to wise men, judge ye what I
say." 1 Cor. x. 15. "O inhabitants of Jerusalem, and
men of Judah, judge, I pray you, between me and my
vineyard." Isa. v. 3. Revelation never attempts to silence the voice of reason. It simply recalls it from
heights and depths of speculation, where it loses all sure
footing, that it may give its verdict on truths within its
reach, and where the answer must be plain, unless pride
falsifies it—the two truths of the righteousness of God,
and the guiltiness of man.

But when the presence and excellence of this Divine
faculty of the soul has been clearly recognised, we
need, further, to have a just and clear perception of its
actual weakness, when employed in the search for religious truth. And for this we have only to review
the history of the heathen world, or to consider the
ignorance and spiritual darkness, which prevails everywhere even in countries nominally Christian. Wherever
the light of the Word of God is unknown, or criminally
withheld by a priesthood who love darkness, what dense
and deadly ignorance meets us on every side! We
have the worship of flies, of apes and crocodiles, of monkeys and wafers of bread, of hideous images, or of bones
and rags, to which superstition ascribes some magical
virtue. A darkness that may be felt, like the plague of
Egypt, settles down upon the nations. History in all
ages has the same lesson, and tells us that reason, without

external revelation, and without Divine teaching to apply that revelation to the heart, is too feeble to restore mankind to the knowledge of God, and to the practice of true and solid piety.   The result is uniform, from the philosophers of Greece and Rome, down to the savages of South Africa and the Fiji Islands.

Another main help, in resisting the inroads of Rationalism, and the pretences of that mock spiritual religion which disowns the authority of the Bible, consists in a familiar acquaintance with the historical aspect of Christianity.   There are many who treat the New Testament as a mere string of texts and mottoes, and lose sight of the connection of the parts, the object of each separate book, and the countless links by which it is connected with the history of the times, and the actual state and practical wants of the early churches.   It stands midway, between a dry narrative of facts without soul or purpose, and speculative theories, which look in vain for any fact whatever to confirm their reality.   In the New Testament we have a real message, addressed by real messengers to living men.

The historical study of the New Testament is the practical remedy for every form of loose and floating unbelief, if it be honest.   "If any man will do His will" (i.e. of the Father) "he shall know of the doctrine whether it be of God." Joh. vii. 17.   Let the Christian, who feels perplexity, and has clouds on some part of the wide horizon of his faith, practise what he feels to be duty, and meditate on the truths he clearly sees to be Divine, and then use a wise suspense, waiting for clearer light whereever shadows are still round him.   Then the promise will be fulfilled: "At the eventide there shall be light."   Clouds will, by degrees, be rolled away; difficulties, that once seemed formidable, will disappear.   What once was mistaken for a spectre of darkness, will prove to be a signpost for the pilgrim on his homeward journey.   If the father of the faithful had listened to the voice of the tempter, the God of love might have seemed to him, in the hour of his trial, a Moloch of cruelty; and the blasphemies of modern disciples of the "absolute religion" would have been anticipated four thousand years ago. But obedience, and faith in the Divine goodness proved by long experience, had their full reward. "In the mountain, the Lord was seen." That trial of his faith, so dark and stern in prospect, became a window, through which he could see the day of Christ afar off; "and he saw it and was glad." Joh. viii. 56. His words of simple trust became a glorious prophecy, "My son, God will provide a lamb for a burnt-offering." Gen. xxii. 8.

Mere unassisted reason, in its search for religious truth, is like a blear-eyed observer, gazing on a landscape veiled in mist or twilight shadow. He sees enough to convince him that there is a reality before him, but not enough to guide his footsteps aright. We need the revelation in the word of God, to roll away the mist from the landscape; and the secret power of the Holy Spirit, to anoint our eyes, in order that we may see it clearly. Then, and not till then, doubt after doubt will vanish, and mystery after mystery be explained. We shall see the hills and valleys of a glorious land of promise, standing out in full relief before us, clothed in heavenly beauty. And our spirits will be prepared, even in this vale of sorrow and twilight darkness, for that holier and happier world, where they "need no candle" of human reason, nor even the brighter sunshine of written revelation, "for the Lord God giveth them light, and they shall reign for ever and ever." Rev. xxii. 5.

CAMBRIDGE: PRINTED BY C. J. CLAY, M.A. AT THE UNIVERSITY PRESS.

A Catalogue of Theological Books,

with a Short Account of their

Character and Aim,

Published by

MACMILLAN AND CO.

Bedford Street, Strand, London, W.C.

Abbott (Rev. E. A.)—Works by the Rev. E. A. ABBOTT, D.D., Head Master of the City of London School :

BIBLE LESSONS. Second Edition. Crown 8vo. 4s. 6d.

"*Wise, suggestive, and really profound initiation into religious thought.*"
—Guardian. *The Bishop of St. David's, in his speech at the Education Conference at Abergwilly, says he thinks "nobody could read them without being the better for them himself, and being also able to see how this difficult duty of imparting a sound religious education may be effected.*"

THE GOOD VOICES: A Child's Guide to the Bible. With upwards of 50 Illustrations. Crown 8vo. cloth gilt. 5s.

"*It would not be easy to combine simplicity with fulness and depth of meaning more successfully than Mr. Abbott has done.*"—Spectator. *The Times says—"Mr. Abbott writes with clearness, simplicity, and the deepest religious feeling.*"

CAMBRIDGE SERMONS PREACHED BEFORE THE UNIVERSITY. Second Edition. 8vo. 6s.

3,000 : 5 : 79.

ABBOTT (Rev. E. A.)—*continued.*

THROUGH NATURE TO CHRIST ; or, The Ascent of Worship through Illusion to the Truth.   8vo.   12*s.* 6*d.*

" The beauty of its style, its tender feeling, and its perfect sympathy, the originality and suggestiveness of many of its thoughts, would of themselves go far to recommend it. But far besides these, it has a certain value in its bold, comprehensive, trenchant method of apology, and in the adroitness with which it turns the flank of the many modern fallacies that caricature in order to condemn Christianity."—Church Quarterly Review.

Ainger (Rev. Alfred).—SERMONS PREACHED IN THE TEMPLE CHURCH.   By the Rev. ALFRED AINGER, M.A. of Trinity Hall, Cambridge, Reader at the Temple Church.   Extra fcap. 8vo.   6*s.*

" It is," the British Quarterly *says, "the fresh unconventional talk of a clear independent thinker, addressed to a congregation of thinkers . . . . Thoughtful men will be greatly charmed by this little volume."*

Alexander.—THE LEADING IDEAS of the GOSPELS. Five Sermons preached before the University of Oxford in 1870—71.   By WILLIAM ALEXANDER, D.D., Brasenose College ; Lord Bishop of Derry and Raphoe ; Select Preacher.   Cr. 8vo.   4*s.* 6*d.*

"Eloquence and force of language, clearness of statement, and a hearty appreciation of the grandeur and importance of the topics upon which he writes, characterize his sermons."—Record.

Arnold.—Works by MATTHEW ARNOLD :

A BIBLE READING FOR SCHOOLS.   THE GREAT PROPHECY OF ISRAEL'S RESTORATION (Isaiah, Chapters 40—66).   Arranged and Edited for Young Learners.   By MATTHEW ARNOLD, D.C.L., formerly Professor of Poetry in the University of Oxford, and Fellow of Oriel.   Third Edition.   18mo. cloth.   1*s.*

The Times *says—" Whatever may be the fate of this little book in Government Schools, there can be no doubt that it will be found excellently calculated to further instruction in Biblical literature in any school into which it may be introduced. . . . We can safely say that whatever school uses this book, it will enable its pupils to understand Isaiah, a great advantage compared with other establishments which do not avail themselves of it."*

ISAIAH XL.—LXVI., with the Shorter Prophecies allied to it.   Arranged and Edited with Notes.   Crown 8vo.   5*s.*

Bather.—ON SOME MINISTERIAL DUTIES, CATECHISING, PREACHING, &c.   Charges by the late Archdeacon BATHER.   Edited, with Preface, by Dr. C. J. VAUGHAN.   Extra fcap. 8vo.   4*s.* 6*d.*

Benham.—A COMPANION TO THE LECTIONARY, being a Commentary on the Proper Lessons for Sundays and Holydays. By the Rev. W. BENHAM, B.D., Vicar of Margate. Cheaper Edition. Crown 8vo. 6s.

"*A very useful book. Mr. Benham has produced a good and welcome companion to our revised Lectionary. Its contents will, if not very original or profound, prove to be sensible and practical, and often suggestive to the preacher and the Sunday School teacher. They will also furnish some excellent Sunday reading for private hours.*"—Guardian.

Bernard.—THE PROGRESS OF DOCTRINE IN THE NEW TESTAMENT. By THOMAS D. BERNARD, M.A., Rector of Walcot and Canon of Wells. Third and Cheaper Edition. Crown 8vo. 5s. (Bampton Lectures for 1864.)

"*We lay down these lectures with a sense not only of being edified by sound teaching and careful thought, but also of being gratified by conciseness and clearness of expression and elegance of style.*"—Churchman.

Binney.—SERMONS PREACHED IN THE KING'S WEIGH HOUSE CHAPEL, 1829—69. By THOMAS BINNEY, D.D. New and Cheaper Edition. Extra fcap. 8vo. 4s. 6d. :

"*Full of robust intelligence, of reverent but independent thinking on the most profound and holy themes, and of earnest practical purpose.*"— London Quarterly Review.

A SECOND SERIES OF SERMONS. Edited, with Biographical and Critical Sketch, by the Rev. HENRY ALLON, D.D. With Portrait of Dr. Binney engraved by JEENS. 8vo. 12s.

Birks.—Works by T. R. BIRKS, M.A., Professor of Moral Philosophy, Cambridge :

THE DIFFICULTIES OF BELIEF in connection with the Creation and the Fall, Redemption and Judgment. Second Edition, enlarged. Crown 8vo. 5s.

AN ESSAY ON THE RIGHT ESTIMATION OF MSS. EVIDENCE IN THE TEXT OF THE NEW TESTAMENT. Crown 8vo. 3s. 6d.

COMMENTARY ON THE BOOK OF ISAIAH, Critical, Historical and Prophetical; including a Revised English Translation. With Introduction and Appendices on the Nature of Scripture Prophecy, the Life and Times of Isaiah, the Genuineness of the Later Prophecies, the Structure and History of the whole Book, the Assyrian History in Isaiah's Days, and various Difficult Passages. Second Edition, revised. 8vo. 12s. 6d.

SUPERNATURAL REVELATION, or First Principles of Moral Theology. 8vo. 8s.

Bradby.—SERMONS PREACHED AT HAILEYBURY. By E. H. BRADBY, M.A., Master. 8vo. 10s. 6d.

"*He who claims a public hearing now, speaks to an audience accustomed to Cotton, Temple, Vaughan, Bradley, Butler, Farrar, and others......Each has given us good work, several, work of rare beauty, force, or originality; but we doubt whether any one of them has touched deeper chords, or brought more freshness and strength into his sermons, than the last of their number, the present Head Master of Haileybury.*"—Spectator.

Butcher.—THE ECCLESIASTICAL CALENDAR; its Theory and Construction. By SAMUEL BUTCHER, D.D., late Bishop of Meath. 4to. 14s.

Butler (G.)—Works by the Rev. GEORGE BUTLER, M.A., Principal of Liverpool College :

FAMILY PRAYERS. Crown 8vo. 5s.

The prayers in this volume are all based on passages of Scripture—the morning prayers on Select Psalms, those for the evening on portions of the New Testament.

SERMONS PREACHED in CHELTENHAM COLLEGE CHAPEL. Crown 8vo. 7s. 6d.

Butler (Rev. H. M.)—SERMONS PREACHED in the CHAPEL OF HARROW SCHOOL. By H. MONTAGU BUTLER, Head Master. Crown 8vo. 7s. 6d.

"*These sermons are adapted for every household. There is nothing more striking than the excellent good sense with which they are imbued.*" —Spectator.

A SECOND SERIES. Crown 8vo. 7s. 6d.

"*Excellent specimens of what sermons should be—plain, direct, practical, pervaded by the true spirit of the Gospel, and holding up lofty aims before the minds of the young.*"—Athenæum.

Butler (Rev. W. Archer).—Works by the Rev. WILLIAM ARCHER BUTLER, M.A., late Professor of Moral Philosophy in the University of Dublin :

SERMONS, DOCTRINAL AND PRACTICAL. Edited, with a Memoir of the Author's Life, by THOMAS WOODWARD, Dean of Down. With Portrait. Ninth Edition. 8vo. 8s.

The Introductory Memoir narrates in considerable detail and with much interest, the events of Butler's brief life; and contains a few specimens of his poetry, and a few extracts from his addresses and essays, including a long and eloquent passage on the Province and Duty of the Preacher.

BUTLER (Rev. W. Archer)—*continued.*

A SECOND SERIES OF SERMONS. Edited by J. A. JEREMIE, D.D., Dean of Lincoln. Seventh Edition. 8vo. 7s.

The North British Review *says, " Few sermons in our language exhibit the same rare combination of excellencies; imagery almost as rich as Taylor's; oratory as vigorous often as South's; judgment as sound as Barrow's; a style as attractive but more copious, original, and forcible than Atterbury's; piety as elevated as Howe's, and a fervour as intense at times as Baxter's. Mr. Butler's are the sermons of a true poet."*

LETTERS ON ROMANISM, in reply to Dr. Newman's Essay on Development. Edited by the Dean of Down. Second Edition, revised by Archdeacon HARDWICK. 8vo. 10s. 6d.

These Letters contain an exhaustive criticism of Dr. Newman's famous "Essay on the Development of Christian Doctrine." "A work which ought to be in the Library of every student of Divinity."—BP. ST. DAVID'S.

Campbell.—Works by JOHN M'LEOD CAMPBELL:

THE NATURE OF THE ATONEMENT AND ITS RELATION TO REMISSION OF SINS AND ETERNAL LIFE. Fourth and Cheaper Edition, crown 8vo. 6s.

"Among the first theological treatises of this generation."—Guardian.
"One of the most remarkable theological books ever written."—Times.

CHRIST THE BREAD OF LIFE. An Attempt to give a profitable direction to the present occupation of Thought with Romanism. Second Edition, greatly enlarged. Crown 8vo. 4s. 6d.

" Deserves the most attentive study by all who interest themselves in the predominant religious controversy of the day."—Spectator.

REMINISCENCES AND REFLECTIONS, referring to his Early Ministry in the Parish of Row, 1825—31. Edited with an Introductory Narrative by his Son, DONALD CAMPBELL, M.A., Chaplain of King's College, London. Crown 8vo. 7s. 6d.

These 'Reminiscences and Reflections,' written during the last year of his life, were mainly intended to place on record thoughts which might prove helpful to others. " We recommend this book cordially to all who are interested in the great cause of religious reformation."—Times.
" There is a thoroughness and depth, as well as a practical earnestness, in his grasp of each truth on which he dilates, which make his reflections very valuable."—Literary Churchman.

THOUGHTS ON REVELATION, with Special Reference to the Present Time. Second Edition. Crown 8vo. 5s.

CAMPBELL (J. M'Leod)—*continued.*

RESPONSIBILITY FOR THE GIFT OF ETERNAL LIFE. Compiled by permission of the late J. M'LEOD CAMPBELL, D.D., from Sermons preached chiefly at Row in 1829—31. Crown 8vo. 5*s.*

"*There is a healthy tone as well as a deep pathos not often seen in sermons. His words are weighty and the ideas they express tend to perfection of life.*"—Westminster Review.

Campbell (Lewis).—SOME ASPECTS OF THE CHRISTIAN IDEAL. Sermons by the Rev. L. CAMPBELL, M.A., LL.D., Professor of Greek in the University of Glasgow. Crown 8vo. 6*s.*

Canterbury.—Works by ARCHIBALD CAMPBELL, Archbishop of Canterbury :

THE PRESENT POSITION OF THE CHURCH OF ENGLAND. Seven Addresses delivered to the Clergy and Church-wardens of his Diocese, as his Charge, at his Primary Visitation, 1872. Third Edition. 8vo. cloth. 3*s.* 6*d.*

SOME THOUGHTS ON THE DUTIES OF THE ESTABLISHED CHURCH OF ENGLAND AS A NATIONAL CHURCH. Seven Addresses delivered at his Second Visitation. 8vo. 4*s.* 6*d.*

Cheyne.—Works by T. K. CHEYNE, M.A., Fellow of Balliol College, Oxford :

THE BOOK OF ISAIAH CHRONOLOGICALLY ARRANGED. An Amended Version, with Historical and Critical Introductions and Explanatory Notes. Crown 8vo. 7*s.* 6*d.*

The Westminster Review *speaks of it as "a piece of scholarly work, very carefully and considerately done." The* Academy *calls it "a successful attempt to extend a right understanding of this important Old Testament writing."*

NOTES AND CRITICISMS on the HEBREW TEXT OF ISAIAH. Crown 8vo. 2*s.* 6*d.*

Choice Notes on the Four Gospels, drawn from Old and New Sources. Crown 8vo. 4*s.* 6*d.* each Vol. (St. Matthew and St. Mark in one Vol. price 9*s.*)

Church.—Works by the Very Rev. R. W. CHURCH, M.A., D.C.L., Dean of St. Paul's :

ON SOME INFLUENCES OF CHRISTIANITY UPON NATIONAL CHARACTER. Three Lectures delivered in St. Paul's Cathedral, Feb. 1873. Crown 8vo. 4*s.* 6*d.*

CHURCH (Very Rev. R. W.)—*continued.*

"Few books that we have met with have given us keener pleasure than this. . . . . . It would be a real pleasure to quote extensively, so wise and so true, so tender and so discriminating are Dean Church's judgments, but the limits of our space are inexorable. We hope the book will be bought." —Literary Churchman.

THE SACRED POETRY OF EARLY RELIGIONS. Two Lectures in St. Paul's Cathedral. 18mo. 1s. I. The Vedas. II. The Psalms.

ST. ANSELM. Second Edition. Crown 8vo. 6s.

"It is a sketch by the hand of a master, with every line marked by taste, learning, and real apprehension of the subject."—Pall Mall Gazette.

HUMAN LIFE AND ITS CONDITIONS. Sermons preached before the University of Oxford, 1876—78, with Three Ordination Sermons. Crown 8vo. 6s.

Clergyman's Self-Examination concerning the APOSTLES' CREED. Extra fcap. 8vo. 1s. 6d.

Colenso.—THE COMMUNION SERVICE FROM THE BOOK OF COMMON PRAYER; with Select Readings from the Writings of the Rev. F. D. MAURICE, M.A. Edited by the Right Rev. J. W. COLENSO, D.D., Lord Bishop of Natal. New Edition. 16mo. 2s. 6d.

Collects of the Church of England. With a beautifully Coloured Floral Design to each Collect, and Illuminated Cover. Crown 8vo. 12s. Also kept in various styles of morocco.

The distinctive characteristic of this edition is the coloured floral design which accompanies each Collect, and which is generally emblematical of the character of the day or saint to which it is assigned; the flowers which have been selected are such as are likely to be in bloom on the day to which the Collect belongs. The Guardian *thinks it "a successful attempt to associate in a natural and unforced manner the flowers of our fields and gardens with the course of the Christian year."*

Congreve.—HIGH HOPES, AND PLEADINGS FOR A REASONABLE FAITH, NOBLER THOUGHTS, LARGER CHARITY. Sermons preached in the Parish Church of Tooting Graveney, Surrey. By J. CONGREVE, M.A., Rector. Cheaper Issue. Crown 8vo. 5s.

Cotton.—Works by the late GEORGE EDWARD LYNCH COTTON, D.D., Bishop of Calcutta :

COTTON (Bishop)—*continued.*

SERMONS PREACHED TO ENGLISH CONGREGA-
TIONS IN INDIA. Crown 8vo. 7s. 6d.

EXPOSITORY SERMONS ON THE EPISTLES FOR
THE SUNDAYS OF THE CHRISTIAN YEAR. Two
Vols. Crown 8vo. 15s.

Curteis.—DISSENT in its RELATION to the CHURCH
OF ENGLAND. Eight Lectures preached before the University
of Oxford, in the year 1871, on the foundation of the late Rev.
John Bampton, M.A., Canon of Salisbury. By GEORGE HERBERT
CURTEIS, M.A., late Fellow and Sub-Rector of Exeter College;
Principal of the Lichfield Theological College, and Prebendary of
Lichfield Cathedral; Rector of Turweston, Bucks. New Edition.
Crown 8vo. 7s. 6d.

"*Mr. Curteis has done good service by maintaining in an eloquent,
temperate, and practical manner, that discussion among Christians is
really an evil, and that an intelligent basis can be found for at least a
proximate union.*"—Saturday Review. "*A well timed, learned, and
thoughtful book.*"

Davies.—Works by the Rev. J. LLEWELYN DAVIES, M.A.,
Rector of Christ Church, St. Marylebone, etc. :

THE GOSPEL AND MODERN LIFE; with a Preface
on a Recent Phase of Deism. Second Edition. To which is
added Morality according to the Sacrament of the Lord's Supper,
or Three Discourses on the Names, Eucharist, Sacrifice, and Communion. Extra fcap. 8vo. 6s.

WARNINGS AGAINST SUPERSTITION, IN FOUR
SERMONS FOR THE DAY. Extra fcap. 8vo. 2s. 6d.

"*We have seldom read a wiser little book. The Sermons are short,
terse, and full of true spiritual wisdom, expressed with a lucidity and a
moderation that must give them weight even with those who agree least
with their author....... Of the volume as a whole it is hardly possible to
speak with too cordial an appreciation.*"—Spectator.

THE CHRISTIAN CALLING. Sermons. Extra fcap.
8vo. 6s.

Donaldson.—THE APOSTOLICAL FATHERS: a Critical
Account of their Genuine Writings and of their Doctrines. By
JAMES DONALDSON, LL.D. Crown 8vo. 7s. 6d.

DONALDSON (J., LL.D.)—*continued.*

This book was published in 1864 as the first volume of a 'Critical History of Christian Literature and Doctrine from the death of the Apostles to the Nicene Council.' The intention was to carry down the history continuously to the time of Eusebius, and this intention has not been abandoned. But as the writers can be sometimes grouped more easily according to subject or locality than according to time, it is deemed advisable to publish the history of each group separately. The Introduction to the present volume serves as an introduction to the whole period.

Drake.—THE TEACHING OF THE CHURCH DURING THE FIRST THREE CENTURIES ON THE DOCTRINES OF THE CHRISTIAN PRIESTHOOD AND SACRIFICE. By the Rev. C. B. DRAKE, M.A., Warden of the Church of England Hall, Manchester. Crown 8vo. 4s. 6d.

Eadie.—Works by JOHN EADIE, D.D., LL.D., Professor of Biblical Literature and Exegesis, United Presbyterian Church :

THE ENGLISH BIBLE. An External and Critical History of the various English Translations of Scripture, with Remarks on the Need of Revising the English New Testament. Two vols. 8vo. 28s.

"Accurate, scholarly, full of completest sympathy with the translators and their work, and marvellously interesting."—Literary Churchman.

" The work is a very valuable one. It is the result of vast labour, sound scholarship, and large erudition."—British Quarterly Review.

ST. PAUL'S EPISTLES TO THE THESSALONIANS. A Commentary on the Greek Text. Edited by the Rev. W. YOUNG, M.A., with a Preface by the Rev. Professor CAIRNS, D.D. 8vo. 12s.

Ecce Homo. A SURVEY OF THE LIFE AND WORK OF JESUS CHRIST. Fourteenth Edition. Crown 8vo. 6s.

"A very original and remarkable book, full of striking thought and delicate perception; a book which has realised with wonderful vigour and freshness the historical magnitude of Christ's work, and which here and there gives us readings of the finest kind of the probable motive of His individual words and actions."—Spectator. *" The best and most established believer will find it adding some fresh buttresses to his faith."*—Literary Churchman. *"If we have not misunderstood him, we have before us a writer who has a right to claim deference from those who think deepest and know most."*—Guardian.

Faber.—SERMONS AT A NEW SCHOOL. By the Rev.
ARTHUR FABER, M.A., Head Master of Malvern College. Cr.
8vo. 6s.

*"These are high-toned, earnest Sermons, orthodox and scholarlike, and
laden with encouragement and warning, wisely adapted to the needs of
school-life."*—Literary Churchman.

Farrar.—Works by the Rev. F. W. FARRAR, D.D., F.R.S.,
Canon of Westminster, late Head Master of Marlborough College:

THE FALL OF MAN, AND OTHER SERMONS.
Third Edition. Crown 8vo. 6s.

The Nonconformist *says of these Sermons,* "Mr. Farrar's Sermons
are almost perfect specimens of one type of Sermons, which we may con-
cisely call beautiful. The style of expression is beautiful—there is beauty
in the thoughts, the illustrations, the allusions—they are expressive of
genuinely beautiful perceptions and feelings." *The* British Quarterly *says,*
"Ability, eloquence, scholarship, and practical usefulness, are in these
Sermons combined in a very unusual degree."

THE WITNESS OF HISTORY TO CHRIST. Being
the Hulsean Lectures for 1870. Fourth Edition. Crown 8vo. 5s.

*The following are the subjects of the Five Lectures:—I. " The Ante-
cedent Credibility of the Miraculous." II. "The Adequacy of the Gospel
Records." III. "The Victories of Christianity." IV. "Christianity and
the Individual." V. "Christianity and the Race." The subjects of the
four Appendices are:—A. " The Diversity of Christian Evidences."
B. "Confucius." C. "Buddha." D. " Comte."*

SEEKERS AFTER GOD. The Lives of Seneca, Epictetus,
and Marcus Aurelius. New Edition. Crown 8vo. 6s.

"A very interesting and valuable book."—Saturday Review.

THE SILENCE AND VOICES OF GOD : University
and other Sermons. Third Edition. Crown 8vo. 6s.

*"We can most cordially recommend Dr. Farrar's singularly beautiful
volume of Sermons. . . . . . For beauty of diction, felicity of style, aptness of
illustration and earnest loving exhortation, the volume is without its
parallel."*—John Bull. *" They are marked by great ability, by an honesty
which does not hesitate to acknowledge difficulties and by an earnestness
which commands respect."*—Pall Mall Gazette.

"IN THE DAYS OF THY YOUTH." Sermons on Practical Subjects, preached at Marlborough College from 1871—76.
Third Edition. Crown 8vo. 9s.

FARRAR (Rev. F. W.)—*continued.*

"All Dr. Farrar's peculiar charm of style is apparent here, all that care and subtleness of analysis, and an even-added distinctness and clearness of moral teaching, which is what every kind of sermon wants, and especially a sermon to boys."—Literary Churchman.

ETERNAL HOPE. Five Sermons preached in Westminster Abbey, in 1876. With Preface, Notes, etc. Contents : What Heaven is.—Is Life Worth Living?—'Hell,' What it is not.— Are there few that be saved?—Earthly and Future Consequences of Sin. Sixteenth Thousand. Crown 8vo. 6s.

SAINTLY WORKERS. Lenten Lectures delivered in St. Andrew's, Holborn, March and April, 1878. Crown 8vo. 6s.

Fellowship: LETTERS ADDRESSED TO MY SISTER MOURNERS. Fcap. 8vo. cloth gilt. 3s. 6d.

Ferrar.—A COLLECTION OF FOUR IMPORTANT MSS. OF THE GOSPELS, viz., 13, 69, 124, 346, with a view to prove their common origin, and to restore the Text of their Archetype. By the late W. H. FERRAR, M.A., Professor of Latin in the University of Dublin. Edited by T. K. ABBOTT, M.A., Professor of Biblical Greek, Dublin. 4to., half morocco. 10s. 6d.

Forbes.—Works by GRANVILLE H. FORBES, Rector of Broughton :

THE VOICE OF GOD IN THE PSALMS. Cr. 8vo. 6s. 6d.

VILLAGE SERMONS. By a Northamptonshire Rector. Crown 8vo. 6s.

"Such a volume as the present . . . is as great an accession to the cause of a deep theology as the most refined exposition of its fundamental principles . . . We heartily accept his actual teaching as a true picture of what revelation teaches us, and thank him for it as one of the most profound that was ever made perfectly simple and popular . . . . It is part of the beauty of these sermons that while they apply the old truth to the new modes of feeling they seem to preserve the whiteness of its simplicity . . . . There will be plenty of critics to accuse this volume of inadequacy of doctrine because it says no more than Scripture about vicarious suffering and external retribution. For ourselves we welcome it most cordially as expressing adequately what we believe to be the true burden of the Gospel in a manner which may take hold either of the least or the most cultivated intellect."—Spectator.

Hardwick.—Works by the Ven. ARCHDEACON HARDWICK :
CHRIST AND OTHER MASTERS. A Historical Inquiry
into some of the Chief Parallelisms and Contrasts between Christ-
ianity and the Religious Systems of the Ancient World. New
Edition, revised, and a Prefatory Memoir by the Rev. FRANCIS
PROCTER, M.A. New Edition. Cr. 8vo. 10s. 6d.

*The plan of the work is boldly and almost nobly conceived. . . . We com-
mend it to the perusal of all those who take interest in the study of ancient
mythology, without losing their reverence for the supreme authority of the
oracles of the living God."*—Christian Observer.

A HISTORY OF THE CHRISTIAN CHURCH. Middle
Age. From Gregory the Great to the Excommunication of Luther,
Edited by WILLIAM STUBBS, M.A., Regius Professor of Modern
History in the University of Oxford. With Four Maps constructed
for this work by A. KEITH JOHNSTON. New Edition. Crown
8vo. 10s. 6d.

*"As a Manual for the student of ecclesiastical history in the Middle
Ages, we know no English work which can be compared to Mr. Hardwick's
book."*—Guardian.

A HISTORY of the CHRISTIAN CHURCH DURING
THE REFORMATION. New Edition, revised by Professor
STUBBS. Crown 8vo. 10s. 6d.

*This volume is intended as a sequel and companion to the "History
of the Christian Church during the Middle Age."*

Hare.—Works by the late ARCHDEACON HARE :
THE VICTORY OF FAITH. By JULIUS CHARLES
HARE, M.A., Archdeacon of Lewes. Edited by Prof. PLUMPTRE.
With Introductory Notices by the late Prof. MAURICE and Dean
STANLEY. Third Edition. Crown 8vo. 6s. 6d.

THE MISSION OF THE COMFORTER. With Notes.
New Edition, edited by Prof. E. H. PLUMPTRE. Crn. 8vo. 7s. 6d.

Harris.—SERMONS. By the late GEORGE COLLYER
HARRIS, Prebendary of Exeter, and Vicar of St. Luke's, Torquay.
With Memoir by CHARLOTTE M. YONGE, and Portrait. Extra
fcap. 8vo. 6s.

Hervey.—THE GENEALOGIES OF OUR LORD AND
SAVIOUR JESUS CHRIST, as contained in the Gospels of
St. Matthew and St. Luke, reconciled with each other, and shown
to be in harmony with the true Chronology of the Times. By Lord
ARTHUR HERVEY, Bishop of Bath and Wells. 8vo. 10s. 6d.

Hort.—TWO DISSERTATIONS. I. On ΜΟΝΟΓΕΝΗΣ ΘΕΟΣ in Scripture and Tradition. II. On the "Constantinopolitan" Creed and other Eastern Creeds of the Fourth Century. By F. J. A. HORT, D.D., Fellow and Divinity Lecturer of Emmanuel College, Cambridge. 8vo. 7s. 6d.

Howson (Dean)—Works by :

BEFORE THE TABLE. An Inquiry, Historical and Theological, into the True Meaning of the Consecration Rubric in the Communion Service of the Church of England. By the Very Rev. J. S. HOWSON, D.D., Dean of Chester. With an Appendix and Supplement containing Papers by the Right Rev. the Bishop of St. Andrew's and the Rev. R. W. KENNION, M.A. 8vo. 7s. 6d.

THE POSITION OF THE PRIEST DURING CONSECRATION IN THE ENGLISH COMMUNION SERVICE. A Supplement and a Reply. Crown 8vo. 2s. 6d.

Hymni Ecclesiæ.—Fcap. 8vo. 7s. 6d.

This collection was edited by Dr. Newman while he lived at Oxford.

Hyacinthe.—CATHOLIC REFORM. By FATHER HYACINTHE. Letters, Fragments, Discourses. Translated by Madame HYACINTHE-LOYSON. With a Preface by the Very Rev. A. P. STANLEY, D.D., Dean of Westminster. Cr. 8vo. 7s. 6d.

"A valuable contribution to the religious literature of the day, and is especially opportune at a time when a controversy of no ordinary importance upon the very subject it deals with is engaged in all over Europe."— Daily Telegraph.

Imitation of Christ.—FOUR BOOKS. Translated from the Latin, with Preface by the Rev. W. BENHAM, B.D., Vicar of Margate. Printed with Borders in the Ancient Style after Holbein, Dürer, and other Old Masters. Containing Dances of Death, Acts of Mercy, Emblems, and a variety of curious ornamentation. Cr. 8vo. gilt edges. 7s. 6d.

Jacob.—BUILDING IN SCIENCE, AND OTHER SERMONS. By J. A. JACOB, M.A., Minister of St. Thomas's, Paddington. Extra fcap. 8vo. 6s.

Jellett.—THE EFFICACY OF PRAYER : being the Donnellan Lectures for 1877. By J. H. JELLETT, B.D., Senior Fellow of Trinity College, Dublin, formerly President of the Royal Irish Academy. Second Edition. 8vo. 5s.

Jennings and Lowe.—THE PSALMS, with Introductions and Critical Notes. By A. C. JENNINGS, B.A., Jesus College, Cambridge, Tyrwhitt Scholar, Crosse Scholar, Hebrew University Scholar, and Fry Scholar of St. John's College; helped in parts by W. H. LOWE, M.A., Hebrew Lecturer and late Scholar of Christ's College, Cambridge, and Tyrwhitt Scholar. Complete in two vols. crown 8vo. 10s. 6d. each. Vol. 1, Psalms i.—lxxii., with Prolegomena; Vol. 2, Psalms lxxiii.—cl.

Killen.—THE ECCLESIASTICAL HISTORY OF IRELAND from the Earliest Period to the Present Time. By W. D. KILLEN, D.D., President of Assembly's College, Belfast, and Professor of Ecclesiastical History. Two vols. 8vo. 25s.

" *Those who have the leisure will do well to read these two volumes. They are full of interest, and are the result of great research.*"—Spectator.

Kingsley.—Works by the late Rev. CHARLES KINGSLEY, M.A., Rector of Eversley, and Canon of Westminster :

THE WATER OF LIFE, AND OTHER SERMONS. New Edition. Crown 8vo. 6s.

THE GOSPEL OF THE PENTATEUCH ; AND DAVID. New Edition. Crown. 8vo. 6s.

GOOD NEWS OF GOD. Eighth Edition. Crown 8vo. 6s.

SERMONS FOR THE TIMES. New Edition. Crown 8vo. 6s.

VILLAGE AND TOWN AND COUNTRY SERMONS. New Edition. Crown 8vo. 6s.

SERMONS on NATIONAL SUBJECTS. Second Edition. Fcap. 8vo. 3s. 6d.

THE KING OF THE EARTH, and other Sermons, a Second Series of Sermons on National Subjects. Second Edition. Fcap. 8vo. 3s. 6d.

DISCIPLINE, AND OTHER SERMONS. Second Edition. Fcap. 8vo. 3s. 6d.

WESTMINSTER SERMONS. With Preface. New Edition. Crown 8vo. 6s.

Kynaston.—SERMONS PREACHED IN THE COL-
LEGE CHAPEL, CHELTENHAM, during the First Year
of his Office. By the Rev. HERBERT KYNASTON, M.A., Principal of Cheltenham College. Crown 8vo. 6s.

Lightfoot.—Works by J. B. LIGHTFOOT, D.D., Bishop of
Durham.

S. PAUL'S EPISTLE TO THE GALATIANS. A Re-
vised Text, with Introduction, Notes, and Dissertations. Fifth
Edition, revised. 8vo. cloth. 12s.

*While the Author's object has been to make this commentary generally
complete, he has paid special attention to everything relating to St. Paul's
personal history and his intercourse with the Apostles and Church of the
Circumcision, as it is this feature in the Epistle to the Galatians which
has given it an overwhelming interest in recent theological controversy.
The* Spectator *says, " There is no commentator at once of sounder judgment and more liberal than Dr. Lightfoot."*

ST. PAUL'S EPISTLE TO THE PHILIPPIANS. A
Revised Text, with Introduction, Notes, and Dissertations. Fourth
Edition, revised. 8vo. 12s.

*"No commentary in the English language can be compared with it in
regard to fulness of information, exact scholarship, and laboured attempts
to settle everything about the epistle on a solid foundation."*—Athenæum.

ST. PAUL'S EPISTLES TO THE COLOSSIANS AND
TO PHILEMON. A Revised Text with Introduction, Notes, etc.
Third Edition, revised. 8vo. 12s.

*" It bears marks of continued and extended reading and research, and
of ampler materials at command. Indeed, it leaves nothing to be desired
by those who seek to study thoroughly the epistles contained in it, and to do
so with all known advantages presented in sufficient detail and in convenient form."*—Guardian.

S. CLEMENT OF ROME. An Appendix containing the
newly discovered portions of the two Epistles to the Corinthians
with Introductions and Notes, and a Translation of the whole.
8vo. 8s. 6d.

ON A FRESH REVISION OF THE ENGLISH NEW
TESTAMENT. Second Edition. Crown 8vo. 6s.

*The Author shews in detail the necessity for a fresh revision of the
authorized version on the following grounds:—*1. False Readings. 2.
Artificial distinctions created. 3. Real distinctions obliterated. 4. Faults

of Grammar.   5. *Faults of Lexicography.*   6. *Treatment of Proper Names, official titles, etc.*   7. *Archaisms, defects in the English, errors of the press, etc.   "The book is marked by careful scholarship, familiarity with the subject, sobriety, and circumspection."*—Athenæum.

Lorne.—THE PSALMS LITERALLY RENDERED IN VERSE.   By the MARQUIS OF LORNE.   With three Illustrations.   New Edition.   Crown 8vo.   7s. 6d.

Luckock.—THE TABLES OF STONE.   A Course of Sermons preached in All Saints' Church, Cambridge, by H. M. LUCKOCK, M.A., Canon of Ely.   Fcap. 8vo.   3s. 6d.

Maclaren.—SERMONS PREACHED at MANCHESTER. By ALEXANDER MACLAREN.   Sixth Edition.   Fcap. 8vo.   4s. 6d.

These Sermons represent no special school, but deal with the broad principles of Christian truth, especially in their bearing on practical, every day life.   A few of the titles are:—"The Stone of Stumbling," "Love and Forgiveness," "The Living Dead," "Memory in Another World," Faith in Christ," "Love and Fear," "The Choice of Wisdom," "The Food of the World."

A SECOND SERIES OF SERMONS.   Fourth Edition. Fcap. 8vo.   4s. 6d.

The Spectator *characterises them as "vigorous in style, full of thought, rich in illustration, and in an unusual degree interesting."*

A THIRD SERIES OF SERMONS.   Third Edition. Fcap. 8vo.   4s. 6d.

"Sermons more sober and yet more forcible, and with a certain wise and practical spirituality about them it would not be easy to find."—Spectator.

WEEK-DAY EVENING ADDRESSES.   Delivered in Manchester.   Extra Fcap. 8vo.   2s. 6d.

Maclear.—Works by the Rev. G. F. MACLEAR, D.D., Head Master of King's College School:

A CLASS-BOOK OF OLD TESTAMENT HISTORY. With Four Maps.   New Edition.   18mo.   4s. 6d.

"The present volume," says the Preface, "forms a Class-Book of Old Testament History from the Earliest Times to those of Ezra and Nehemiah.   In its preparation the most recent authorities have been consulted, and wherever it has appeared useful, Notes have been subjoined illustrative of the Text, and, for the sake of more advanced students, references

MACLEAR (Dr. G. F.)—*continued.*

added to larger works. The Index has been so arranged as to form a concise Dictionary of the Persons and Places mentioned in the course of the Narrative." The Maps, prepared by Stanford, materially add to the value and usefulness of the book. The British Quarterly Review *calls it " A careful and elaborate, though brief compendium of all that modern research has done for the illustration of the Old Testament. We know of no work which contains so much important information in so small a compass."*

A CLASS-BOOK OF NEW TESTAMENT HISTORY.
Including the Connexion of the Old and New Testament. New Edition. 18mo. 5s. 6d.

The present volume forms a sequel to the Author's Class-Book of Old Testament History, and continues the narrative to the close of S. Paul's second imprisonment at Rome. The work is divided into three Books— I. The Connection between the Old and New Testament. II. The Gospel History. III. The Apostolic History. In the Appendix are given Chronological Tables. The Clerical Journal *says, " It is not often that such an amount of useful and interesting matter on biblical subjects, is found in so convenient and small a compass, as in this well-arranged volume."*

A CLASS-BOOK OF THE CATECHISM OF THE CHURCH OF ENGLAND. New and Cheaper Edition. 18mo. 1s. 6d.

The present work is intended as a sequel to the two preceding books. " Like them, it is furnished with notes and references to larger works, and it is hoped that it may be found, especially in the higher forms of our Public Schools, to supply a suitable manual of instruction in the chief doctrines of our Church, and a useful help in the preparation of Candidates for Confirmation." The Literary Churchman *says, " It is indeed the work of a scholar and divine, and as such, though extremely simple, it is also extremely instructive. There are few clergy who would not find it useful in preparing Candidates for Confirmation; and there are not a few who would find it useful to themselves as well."*

A FIRST CLASS-BOOK OF THE CATECHISM OF THE CHURCH OF ENGLAND, with Scripture Proofs for Junior Classes and Schools. New Edition. 18mo. 6d.

This is an epitome of the larger Class-book, meant for junior students and elementary classes. The book has been carefully condensed, so as to contain clearly and fully, the most important part of the contents of the larger book.

MACLEAR (Dr. G. F.)—*continued.*

A SHILLING-BOOK of OLD TESTAMENT HISTORY.
New Edition. 18mo. cloth limp. 1s.

This Manual bears the same relation to the larger Old Testament History, that the book just mentioned does to the larger work on the Catechism. It consists of Ten Books, divided into short chapters, and subdivided into sections, each section treating of a single episode in the history, the title of which is given in bold type.

A SHILLING-BOOK of NEW TESTAMENT HISTORY.
New Edition. 18mo. cloth limp. 1s.

A MANUAL OF INSTRUCTION FOR CONFIRMATION AND FIRST COMMUNION, with Prayers and Devotions. 32mo. cloth extra, red edges. 2s.

This is an enlarged and improved edition of 'The Order of Confirmation.' To it have been added the Communion Office, with Notes and Explanations, together with a brief form of Self Examination and Devotions selected from the works of Cosin, Ken, Wilson, and others.

THE ORDER OF CONFIRMATION, with Prayers and Devotions. 32mo. cloth. 6d.

THE FIRST COMMUNION, with Prayers and Devotions for the Newly Confirmed. 32mo. 6d.

THE HOUR OF SORROW ; or, The Order for the Burial of the Dead. With Prayers and Hymns. 32mo. cloth extra. 2s.

APOSTLES OF MEDIÆVAL EUROPE. Cr. 8vo. 4s. 6d.

In two Introductory Chapters the author notices some of the chief characteristics of the mediæval period itself; gives a graphic sketch of the devastated state of Europe at the beginning of that period, and an interesting account of the religions of the three great groups of vigorous barbarians—the Celts, the Teutons, and the Sclaves—who had, wave after wave, overflowed its surface. He then proceeds to sketch the lives and work of the chief of the courageous men who devoted themselves to the stupendous task of their conversion and civilization, during a period extending from the 5th to the 13th century; such as St. Patrick, St. Columba, St. Columbanus, St. Augustine of Canterbury, St. Boniface, St. Olaf, St. Cyril, Raymond Sull, and others. "Mr. Maclear will have done a great work if his admirable little volume shall help to break up the dense ignorance which is still prevailing among people at large."—Literary Churchman.

Macmillan.—Works by the Rev. HUGH MACMILLAN, LL.D. F.R.S.E. (For other Works by the same Author, see CATALOGUE OF TRAVELS and SCIENTIFIC CATALOGUE).

MACMILLAN (Rev. H., LL.D.)——*continued.*

THE TRUE VINE; or, the Analogies of our Lord's
Allegory. Third Edition. Globe 8vo. 6s.

The Nonconformist *says, " It abounds in exquisite bits of description,
and in striking facts clearly stated." The* British Quarterly *says, " Readers
and preachers who are unscientific will find many of his illustrations as
valuable as they are beautiful."*

BIBLE TEACHINGS IN NATURE. Twelfth Edition.
Globe 8vo. 6s.

*In this volume the author has endeavoured to shew that the teaching of
Nature and the teaching of the Bible are directed to the same great end ;
that the Bible contains the spiritual truths which are necessary to make us
wise unto salvation, and the objects and scenes of Nature are the pictures
by which these truths are illustrated. " He has made the world more
beautiful to us, and unsealed our ears to voices of praise and messages of
love that might otherwise have been unheard."*—British Quarterly Review.
*" Dr. Macmillan has produced a book which may be fitly described as one
of the happiest efforts for enlisting physical science in the direct service of
religion."*—Guardian.

THE SABBATH OF THE FIELDS. A Sequel to " Bible
Teachings in Nature." Second Edition. Globe 8vo. 6s.

*" This volume, like all Dr. Macmillan's productions, is very delight-
ful reading, and of a special kind. Imagination, natural science, and
religious instruction are blended together in a very charming way."*—
British Quarterly Review.

THE MINISTRY OF NATURE. Fourth Edition. Globe
8vo. 6s.

*" Whether the reader agree or not with his conclusions, he will ac-
knowledge he is in the presence of an original and thoughtful writer."*—
Pall Mall Gazette. *" There is no class of educated men and women that
will not profit by these essays."*—Standard.

OUR LORD'S THREE RAISINGS FROM THE DEAD.
Globe 8vo. 6s.

M'Clellan.—THE NEW TESTAMENT. A New Trans-
lation on the Basis of the Authorised Version, from a Critically revised Greek Text, with Analyses, copious References and Illustrations from original authorities, New Chronological and Analytical Harmony of the Four Gospels, Notes and Dissertations.
A contribution to Christian Evidence. By JOHN BROWN M'CLEL-
LAN, M.A., late Fellow of Trinity College, Cambridge. In Two

M'CLELLAN (J. B.)—*continued.*

Vols.   Vol. I.—The Four Gospels with the Chronological and
Analytical Harmony. 8vo. 30s.

"*One of the most remarkable productions of recent times,*" *says the*
Theological Review, "*in this department of sacred literature;*" *and the*
British . Quarterly Review *terms it* "*a thesaurus of first-hand investiga-
tions.*" "*Of singular excellence, and sure to make its mark on the
criticism of the New Testament.*"—John Bull.

Maurice.—Works by the late Rev. F. DENISON MAURICE,
M.A., Professor of Moral Philosophy in the University of Cambridge :

The Spectator *says,*—"*Few of those of our own generation whose names
will live in English history or literature have exerted so profound and so
permanent an influence as Mr. Maurice.*"

**THE PATRIARCHS AND LAWGIVERS OF THE
OLD TESTAMENT.** Third and Cheaper Edition. Crown
8vo. 5s.

*The Nineteen Discourses contained in this volume were preached in the
chapel of Lincoln's Inn during the year 1851. The texts are taken from
the books of Genesis, Exodus, Numbers, Deuteronomy, Joshua, Judges,
and Samuel, and involve some of the most interesting biblical topics discussed in recent times.*

**THE PROPHETS AND KINGS OF THE OLD TES-
TAMENT.** Third Edition, with new Preface. Crown 8vo.
10s. 6d.

*Mr. Maurice, in the spirit which animated the compilers of the Church
Lessons, has in these Sermons regarded the Prophets more as preachers of
righteousness than as mere predictors—an aspect of their lives which, he
thinks, has been greatly overlooked in our day, and than which, there is
none we have more need to contemplate. He has found that the Old
Testament Prophets, taken in their simple natural sense, clear up many
of the difficulties which beset us in the daily work of life; make the past
intelligible, the present endurable, and the future real and hopeful.*

THE GOSPEL OF THE KINGDOM OF HEAVEN.
A Series of Lectures on the Gospel of St. Luke. Crown 8vo. 9s.

Mr. Maurice, in his Preface to these Twenty-eight Lectures, says,—
"*In these Lectures I have endeavoured to ascertain what is told us respecting the life of Jesus by one of those Evangelists who proclaim Him to be
the Christ, who says that He did come from a Father, that He did baptize
with the Holy Spirit, that He did rise from the dead. I have chosen the*

MAURICE (Rev. F. D.)—*continued.*

one who is most directly connected with the later history of the Church, who was not an Apostle, who professedly wrote for the use of a man already instructed in the faith of the Apostles. I have followed the course of the writer's narrative, not changing it under any pretext. I have adhered to his phraseology, striving to avoid the substitution of any other for his."

THE GOSPEL OF ST. JOHN. A Series of Discourses. Third and Cheaper Edition. Crown 8vo. 6*s.*

The Literary Churchman *thus speaks of this volume: "Thorough honesty, reverence, and deep thought pervade the work, which is every way solid and philosophical, as well as theological, and abounding with suggestions which the patient student may draw out more at length for himself."*

THE EPISTLES OF ST. JOHN. A Series of Lectures on Christian Ethics. Second and Cheaper Edition. Cr. 8vo. 6*s.*

These Lectures on Christian Ethics were delivered to the students of the Working Men's College, Great Ormond Street, London, on a series of Sunday mornings. Mr. Maurice believes that the question in which we are most interested, the question which most affects our studies and our daily lives, is the question, whether there is a foundation for human morality, or whether it is dependent upon the opinions and fashions of different ages and countries. This important question will be found amply and fairly discussed in this volume, which the National Review *calls "Mr. Maurice's most effective and instructive work. He is peculiarly fitted by the constitution of his mind, to throw light on St. John's writings." Appended is a note on "Positivism and its Teacher."*

EXPOSITORY SERMONS ON THE PRAYER-BOOK. The Prayer-book considered especially in reference to the Romish System. Second Edition. Fcap. 8vo. 5*s.* 6*d.*

After an Introductory Sermon, Mr. Maurice goes over the various parts of the Church Service, expounds in eighteen Sermons, their intention and significance, and shews how appropriate they are as expressions of the deepest longings and wants of all classes of men.

WHAT IS REVELATION? A Series of Sermons on the Epiphany; to which are added, Letters to a Theological Student on the Bampton Lectures of Mr. Mansel. Crown 8vo. 10*s.* 6*d.*

Both Sermons and Letters were called forth by the doctrine maintained by Mr. Mansel in his Bampton Lectures, that Revelation cannot be a direct Manifestation of the Infinite Nature of God. Mr. Maurice maintains

MAURICE (Rev. F. D.)—*continued.*

the opposite doctrine, and in his Sermons explains why, in spite of the high authorities on the other side, he must still assert the principle which he discovers in the Services of the Church and throughout the Bible.

SEQUEL TO THE INQUIRY, "WHAT IS REVELA- TION?" Letters in Reply to Mr. Mansel's Examination of "Strictures on the Bampton Lectures." Crown 8vo. 6*s.*

This, as the title indicates, was called forth by Mr. Mansel's examina- tion of Mr. Maurice's Strictures on his doctrine of the Infinite.

THEOLOGICAL ESSAYS. Third Edition. Crown 8vo. 10*s.* 6*d.*

"The book," says Mr. Maurice, "expresses thoughts which have been working in my mind for years; the method of it has not been adopted carelessly; even the composition has undergone frequent revision." There are seventeen Essays in all, and although meant primarily for Unitarians, to quote the words of the Clerical Journal, *"it leaves untouched scarcely any topic which is in agitation in the religious world; scarcely a moot point between our various sects; scarcely a plot of debateable ground be- tween Christians and Infidels, between Romanists and Protestants, between Socinians and other Christians, between English Churchmen and Dis- senters on both sides. Scarce is there a misgiving, a difficulty, an aspira- tion stirring amongst us now—now, when men seem in earnest as hardly ever before about religion, and ask and demand satisfaction with a fear- lessness which seems almost awful when one thinks what is at stake—which is not recognised and grappled with by Mr. Maurice."*

THE DOCTRINE OF SACRIFICE DEDUCED FROM THE SCRIPTURES. Crown 8vo. 7*s.* 6*d.*

THE RELIGIONS OF THE WORLD, AND THEIR RELATIONS TO CHRISTIANITY. Fifth Edition. Crown 8vo. 5*s.*

ON THE LORD'S PRAYER. Fourth Edition. Fcap. 8vo. 2*s.* 6*d.*

ON THE SABBATH DAY; the Character of the Warrior, and on the Interpretation of History. Fcap. 8vo. 2*s.* 6*d.*

THE LORD'S PRAYER, THE CREED, AND THE COMMANDMENTS. A Manual for Parents and Schoolmasters. To which is added the Order of the Scriptures. 18mo. cloth limp. 1*s.*

DIALOGUES ON FAMILY WORSHIP. Crown 8vo. 6*s.*

MAURICE (Rev. F. D.)—*continued.*

SOCIAL MORALITY. Twenty-one Lectures delivered in the University of Cambridge. New and Cheaper Edition. Cr. 8vo. 10s. 6d.

"Whilst reading it we are charmed by the freedom from exclusiveness and prejudice, the large charity, the loftiness of thought, the eagerness to recognise and appreciate whatever there is of real worth extant in the world, which animates it from one end to the other. We gain new thoughts and new ways of viewing things, even more, perhaps, from being brought for a time under the influence of so noble and spiritual a mind." —Athenæum.

THE CONSCIENCE: Lectures on Casuistry, delivered in the University of Cambridge. Second and Cheaper Edition. Crown 8vo. 5s.

The Saturday Review *says: "We rise from the perusal of these lectures with a detestation of all that is selfish and mean, and with a living impression that there is such a thing as goodness after all."*

LECTURES ON THE ECCLESIASTICAL HISTORY OF THE FIRST AND SECOND CENTURIES. 8vo. 10s. 6d.

LEARNING AND WORKING. Six Lectures delivered in Willis's Rooms, London, in June and July, 1854.—THE RELIGION OF ROME, and its Influence on Modern Civilisation. Four Lectures delivered in the Philosophical Institution of Edinburgh, in December, 1854. Crown 8vo. 5s.

SERMONS PREACHED IN COUNTRY CHURCHES. Crown 8vo. 10s. 6d.

"Earnest, practical, and extremely simple."—Literary Churchman. *"Good specimens of his simple and earnest eloquence. The Gospel incidents are realized with a vividness which we can well believe made the common people hear him gladly. Moreover they are sermons which must have done the hearers good."*—John Bull.

Moorhouse.—Works by JAMES MOORHOUSE, M.A., Bishop of Melbourne:

SOME MODERN DIFFICULTIES RESPECTING the FACTS OF NATURE AND REVELATION. Fcap. 8vo. 2s. 6d.

JACOB. Three Sermons preached before the University of Cambridge in Lent 1870. Extra fcap. 8vo. 3s. 6d.

O'Brien.—PRAYER. Five Sermons preached in the Chapel of Trinity College, Dublin. By JAMES THOMAS O'BRIEN, D.D., Bishop of Ossory and Ferns. 8vo. 6s.

"It is with much pleasure and satisfaction that we render our humble tribute to the value of a publication whose author deserves to be remembered with such deep respect."—Church Quarterly Review.

Palgrave.—HYMNS. By FRANCIS TURNER PALGRAVE. Third Edition, enlarged. 18mo. 1s. 6d.

This is a collection of twenty original Hymns, which the Literary Churchman *speaks of as "so choice, so perfect, and so refined,—so tender in feeling, and so scholarly in expression."*

Paul of Tarsus. An Inquiry into the Times and the Gospel of the Apostle of the Gentiles. By a GRADUATE. 8vo. 10s. 6d.

"Turn where we will throughout the volume, we find the best fruit of patient inquiry, sound scholarship, logical argument, and fairness of conclusion. No thoughtful reader will rise from its perusal without a real and lasting profit to himself, and a sense of permanent addition to the cause of truth."—Standard.

Philochristus.—MEMOIRS OF A DISCIPLE OF THE LORD. Second Edition. 8vo. 12s.

"The winning beauty of this book and the fascinating power with which the subject of it appeals to all English minds will secure for it many readers."—Contemporary Review.

Picton.—THE MYSTERY OF MATTER; and other Essays. By J. ALLANSON PICTON, Author of "New Theories and the Old Faith." Cheaper Edition. With New Preface. Crown 8vo. 6s.

Contents—*The Mystery of Matter: The Philosophy of Ignorance: The Antithesis of Faith and Sight: The Essential Nature of Religion: Christian Pantheism.*

Plumptre.—MOVEMENTS IN RELIGIOUS THOUGHT. Sermons preached before the University of Cambridge, Lent Term, 1879. By E. H. PLUMPTRE, D.D., Professor of Divinity, King's College, London, Prebendary of St. Paul's, etc. Fcap. 8vo. 3s. 6d.

Prescott.—THE THREEFOLD CORD. Sermons preached before the University of Cambridge. By J. E. PRESCOTT, B.D. Fcap. 8vo. 3s. 6d.

Procter.—A HISTORY OF THE BOOK OF COMMON PRAYER: With a Rationale of its Offices. By FRANCIS PROCTER, M.A. Thirteenth Edition, revised and enlarged. Cr. 8vo. 10s. 6d.

The Athenæum *says:*—*"The origin of every part of the Prayer-book has been diligently investigated,—and there are few questions or facts connected with it which are not either sufficiently explained, or so referred to that persons interested may work out the truth for themselves."*

Procter and Maclear.—AN ELEMENTARY INTRO-
DUCTION TO THE BOOK OF COMMON PRAYER.
Re-arranged and Supplemented by an Explanation of the Morning
and Evening Prayer and the Litany. By F. PROCTER, M.A., and
G. F. MACLEAR, D.D. New Edition. Enlarged by the addition
of the Communion Service and the Baptismal and Confirmation
Offices. 18mo. 2s. 6d.

The Literary Churchman *characterizes it as " by far the completest
and most satisfactory book of its kind we know. We wish it were in
the hands of every schoolboy and every schoolmaster in the kingdom."*

Psalms of David CHRONOLOGICALLY ARRANGED.
An Amended Version, with Historical Introductions and Ex-
planatory Notes. By FOUR FRIENDS. Second and Cheaper
Edition, much enlarged. Crown 8vo. 8s. 6d.

*One of the chief designs of the Editors, in preparing this volume, was
to restore the Psalter as far as possible to the order in which the Psalms
were written. They give the division of each Psalm into strophes, and
of each strophe into the lines which composed it, and amend the errors of
translation. The* Spectator *calls it "one of the most instructive and
valuable books that have been published for many years."*

Psalter (Golden Treasury).—THE STUDENT'S EDITION.
Being an Edition of the above with briefer Notes. 18mo. 3s. 6d.

*The aim of this edition is simply to put the reader as far as possible in
possession of the plain meaning of the writer. " It is a gem," the* Nonconformist *says.*

Pulsford.—SERMONS PREACHED IN TRINITY
CHURCH, GLASGOW. By WILLIAM PULSFORD, D.D.
Cheaper Edition. Crown 8vo. 4s. 6d.

Ramsay.—THE CATECHISER'S MANUAL; or, the
Church Catechism Illustrated and Explained, for the Use of
Clergymen, Schoolmasters, and Teachers. By ARTHUR RAMSAY,
M.A. Second Edition. 18mo. 1s. 6d.

Rays of Sunlight for Dark Days. A Book of Selections for the Suffering. With a Preface by C. J. VAUGHAN, D.D.
18mo. Eighth Edition. 3s. 6d. Also in morocco, old style.

*Dr. Vaughan says in the Preface, after speaking of the general run of
Books of Comfort for Mourners, "It is because I think that the little
volume now offered to the Christian sufferer is one of greater wisdom and*

of deeper experience, that I have readily consented to the request that I would introduce it by a few words of Preface." The book consists of a series of very brief extracts from a great variety of authors, in prose and poetry, suited to the many moods of a mourning or suffering mind. "Mostly gems of the first water."—Clerical Journal.

Reynolds.—NOTES OF THE CHRISTIAN LIFE. A Selection of Sermons by HENRY ROBERT REYNOLDS, B.A., President of Cheshunt College, and Fellow of University College, London. Crown 8vo. 7s. 6d.

Roberts.—DISCUSSIONS ON THE GOSPELS. By the Rev. ALEXANDER ROBERTS, D.D. Second Edition, revised and enlarged. 8vo. 16s.

Robinson.—MAN IN THE IMAGE OF GOD; and other Sermons preached in the Chapel of the Magdalen, Streatham, 1874—76. By H. G. ROBINSON, M.A., Prebendary of York. Crown 8vo. 7s. 6d.

Romanes.—CHRISTIAN PRAYER AND GENERAL LAWS, being the Burney Prize Essay for 1873. With an Appendix, examining the views of Messrs. Knight, Robertson, Brooke, Tyndall, and Galton. By GEORGE J. ROMANES, M.A. Crown 8vo. 5s.

Salmon.—THE REIGN OF LAW, and other Sermons, preached in the Chapel of Trinity College, Dublin. By the Rev. GEORGE SALMON, D.D., Regius Professor of Divinity in the University of Dublin. Crown 8vo. 6s.

"Well considered, learned, and powerful discourses."—Spectator.

Sanday.—THE GOSPELS IN THE SECOND CEN-TURY. An Examination of the Critical part of a Work entitled "Supernatural Religion." By WILLIAM SANDAY, M.A., late Fellow of Trinity College, Oxford. Crown 8vo. 8s. 6d.

"A very important book for the critical side of the question as to the authenticity of the New Testament, and it is hardly possible to conceive a writer of greater fairness, candour, and scrupulousness."—Spectator.

Selborne.—THE BOOK OF PRAISE: From the Best English Hymn Writers. Selected and arranged by Lord SELBORNE. With Vignette by WOOLNER. 18mo. 4s. 6d.

SELBORNE (Lord)—*continued.*

It has been the Editor's desire and aim to adhere strictly, in all cases in which it could be ascertained, to the genuine uncorrupted text of the authors themselves. The names of the authors and date of composition of the hymns, when known, are affixed, while notes are added to the volume, giving further details. The Hymns are arranged according to subjects. " There is not room for two opinions as to the value of the 'Book of Praise.'" —Guardian. *"Approaches as nearly as one can conceive to perfection."* —Nonconformist.

BOOK OF PRAISE HYMNAL. *See* end of this Catalogue.

Service.—SALVATION HERE AND HEREAFTER. Sermons and Essays. By the Rev. JOHN SERVICE, D.D., Minister of Inch. Fourth Edition. Crown 8vo. 6s.

"We have enjoyed to-day a rare pleasure, having just closed a volume of sermons which rings true metal from title page to finis, and proves that another and very powerful recruit has been added to that small band of ministers of the Gospel who are not only abreast of the religious thought of their time, but have faith enough and courage enough to handle the questions which are the most critical, and stir men's minds most deeply, with frankness and thoroughness."—Spectator.

Shipley.—A THEORY ABOUT SIN, in relation to some Facts of Daily Life. Lent Lectures on the Seven Deadly Sins. By the Rev. ORBY SHIPLEY, M.A. Crown 8vo. 7s. 6d.

"Two things Mr. Shipley has done, and each of them is of considerable worth. He has grouped these sins afresh on a philosophic principle..... and he has applied the touchstone to the facts of our moral life...so wisely and so searchingly as to constitute his treatise a powerful antidote to self-deception."—Literary Churchman.

Smith.—PROPHECY A PREPARATION FOR CHRIST. Eight Lectures preached before the University of Oxford, being the Bampton Lectures for 1869. By R. PAYNE SMITH, D.D., Dean of Canterbury. Second and Cheaper Edition. Crown 8vo. 6s.

The author's object in these Lectures is to shew that there exists in the Old Testament an element, which no criticism on naturalistic principles can either account for or explain away: that element is Prophecy. The author endeavours to prove that its force does not consist merely in its predictions. "These Lectures overflow with solid learning."—Record.

Smith.—CHRISTIAN FAITH. Sermons preached before the University of Cambridge. By W. SAUMAREZ SMITH, M.A., Principal of St. Aidan's College, Birkenhead. Fcap. 8vo. 3s. 6d.

Stanley.—Works by the Very Rev. A. P. STANLEY, D.D., Dean of Westminster :

THE ATHANASIAN CREED, with a Preface on the General Recommendations of the RITUAL COMMISSION. Cr. 8vo. 2s.

"Dr. Stanley puts with admirable force the objections which may be made to the Creed ; equally admirable, we think, in his statement of its advantages."—Spectator.

THE NATIONAL THANKSGIVING. Sermons preached in Westminster Abbey. Second Edition. Crown 8vo. 2s. 6d.

ADDRESSES AND SERMONS AT ST. ANDREW'S in 1872, 1875 and 1876. Crown 8vo. 5s.

Stewart and Tait.—THE UNSEEN UNIVERSE ; or, Physical Speculations on a Future State. By Professors BALFOUR STEWART and P. G. TAIT. Sixth Edition, Revised and Enlarged. Crown 8vo. 6s.

"A most remarkable and most interesting volume, which, probably more than any that has appeared in modern times, will affect religious thought on many momentous questions—insensibly it may be, but very largely and very beneficially."—Church Quarterly. *" This book is one which well deserves the attention of thoughtful and religious readers...... It is a perfectly safe enquiry, on scientific grounds, into the possibilities of a future existence."*—Guardian.

Swainson.—Works by C. A. SWAINSON, D.D., Canon of Chichester :

THE CREEDS OF THE CHURCH in their Relations to Holy Scripture and the Conscience of the Christian 8vo. cloth. 9s.

THE AUTHORITY OF THE NEW TESTAMENT, and other LECTURES, delivered before the University of Cambridge. 8vo. cloth. 12s.

Taylor.—THE RESTORATION OF BELIEF. New and Revised Edition. By ISAAC TAYLOR, Esq. Crown 8vo. 8s. 6d.

Temple.—SERMONS PREACHED IN THE CHAPEL of RUGBY SCHOOL. By F. TEMPLE, D.D., Bishop of Exeter. New and Cheaper Edition. Extra fcap. 8vo. 4s. 6d.

This volume contains Thirty-five Sermons on topics more or less intimately connected with every-day life. The following are a few of the subjects discoursed upon:—"Love and Duty;" "Coming to Christ;"

TEMPLE (Dr.)—*continued.*

"Great Men;" "Faith;" "Doubts;" "Scruples;" "Original Sin;"
"Friendship;" "Helping Others;" "The Discipline of Temptation;"
"Strength a Duty;" "Worldliness;" "Ill Temper;" "The Burial of
the Past."

A SECOND SERIES OF SERMONS PREACHED IN
THE CHAPEL OF RUGBY SCHOOL. Second Edition.
Extra fcap. 8vo. 6s.

This Second Series of Forty-two brief, pointed, practical Sermons, on
topics intimately connected with the every-day life of young and old, will be
acceptable to all who are acquainted with the First Series. The following
are a few of the subjects treated of:—"Disobedience," "Almsgiving,"
"The Unknown Guidance of God," "Apathy one of our Trials," "High
Aims in Leaders," "Doing our Best," "The Use of Knowledge," "Use
of Observances," "Martha and Mary," "John the Baptist," "Severity
before Mercy," "Even Mistakes Punished," "Morality and Religion,"
"Children," "Action the Test of Spiritual Life," "Self-Respect," "Too
Late," "The Tercentenary."

A THIRD SERIES OF SERMONS PREACHED IN
RUGBY SCHOOL CHAPEL IN 1867—1869. Extra fcap.
8vo. 6s.

This Third Series of Bishop Temple's Rugby Sermons, contains thirty-six
brief discourses, including the "Good-bye" sermon preached on his leaving
Rugby to enter on the office he now holds.

Thring.—Works by Rev. EDWARD THRING, M.A.:

SERMONS DELIVERED AT UPPINGHAM SCHOOL.
Crown 8vo. 5s.

THOUGHTS ON LIFE-SCIENCE. New Edition, enlarged and revised. Crown 8vo. 7s. 6d.

Trench.—Works by R. CHENEVIX TRENCH, D.D., Archbishop of Dublin:

NOTES ON THE PARABLES OF OUR LORD.
Thirteenth Edition. 8vo. 12s.

This work has taken its place as a standard exposition and interpreta-
tion of Christ's Parables. The book is prefaced by an Introductory Essay
in four chapters:—I. On the definition of the Parable. II. On Teach-
ing by Parables. III. On the Interpretation of the Parables. IV. On
other Parables besides those in the Scriptures. The author then proceeds
to take up the Parables one by one, and by the aid of philology, history,
antiquities, and the researches of travellers, shews forth the significance,

TRENCH (Archbishop)—*continued.*

beauty, and applicability of each, concluding with what he deems its true moral interpretation. In the numerous Notes are many valuable references, illustrative quotations, critical and philological annotations, etc., and appended to the volume is a classified list of fifty-six works on the Parables.

NOTES ON THE MIRACLES OF OUR LORD.
Eleventh Edition, revised. 8vo. 12s.

In the 'Preliminary Essay' to this work, all the momentous and interesting questions that have been raised in connection with Miracles, are discussed with considerable fulness. The Essay consists of six chapters:—I. On the Names of Miracles, i.e. the Greek words by which they are designated in the New Testament. II. The Miracles and Nature—What is the difference between a Miracle and any event in the ordinary course of Nature? III. The Authority of Miracles—Is the Miracle to command absolute obedience? IV. The Evangelical, compared with the other cycles of Miracles. V. The Assaults on the Miracles—1. The Jewish. 2. The Heathen (Celsus etc.). 3. The Pantheistic (Spinosa etc.). 4. The Sceptical (Hume). 5. The Miracles only relatively miraculous (Schleiermacher). 6. The Rationalistic (Paulus). 7. The Historico-Critical (Woolston, Strauss). VI. The Apologetic Worth of the Miracles. The author then treats the separate Miracles as he does the Parables.

SYNONYMS OF THE NEW TESTAMENT. Eighth
Edition, enlarged. 8vo. cloth. 12s.

This Edition has been carefully revised, and a considerable number of new Synonyms added. Appended is an Index to the Synonyms, and an Index to many other words alluded to or explained throughout the work. "He is," the Athenæum says, "a guide in this department of knowledge to whom his readers may intrust themselves with confidence. His sober judgment and sound sense are barriers against the misleading influence of arbitrary hypotheses."

ON THE AUTHORIZED VERSION OF THE NEW
TESTAMENT. Second Edition. 8vo. 7s.

After some Introductory Remarks, in which the propriety of a revision is briefly discussed, the whole question of the merits of the present version is gone into in detail, in eleven chapters. Appended is a chronological list of works bearing on the subject, an Index of the principal Texts considered, an Index of Greek Words, and an Index of other Words referred to throughout the book.

STUDIES IN THE GOSPELS. Fourth Edition, revised.
8vo. 10s. 6d.

This book is published under the conviction that the assertion often made is untrue,—viz. that the Gospels are in the main plain and easy,

TRENCH (Archbishop)—*continued.*

and that all the chief difficulties of the New Testament are to be found in the Epistles. These "Studies," sixteen in number, are the fruit of a much larger scheme, and each Study deals with some important episode mentioned in the Gospels, in a critical, philosophical, and practical manner. Many references and quotations are added to the Notes. Among the subjects treated are:—The Temptation; Christ and the Samaritan Woman; The Three Aspirants; The Transfiguration; Zacchæus; The True Vine; The Penitent Malefactor; Christ and the Two Disciples on the way to Emmaus.

COMMENTARY ON THE EPISTLES to the SEVEN CHURCHES IN ASIA. Third Edition, revised. 8vo. 8s. 6d.

The present work consists of an Introduction, being a commentary on Rev. i. 4—20, a detailed examination of each of the Seven Epistles, in all its bearings, and an Excursus on the Historico-Prophetical Interpretation of the Epistles.

THE SERMON ON THE MOUNT. An Exposition drawn from the writings of St. Augustine, with an Essay on his merits as an Interpreter of Holy Scripture. Third Edition, enlarged. 8vo. 10s. 6d.

The first half of the present work consists of a dissertation in eight chapters on "Augustine as an Interpreter of Scripture," the titles of the several chapters being as follow:—I. Augustine's General Views of Scripture and its Interpretation. II. The External Helps for the Interpretation of Scripture possessed by Augustine. III. Augustine's Principles and Canons of Interpretation. IV. Augustine's Allegorical Interpretation of Scripture. V. Illustrations of Augustine's Skill as an Interpreter of Scripture. VI. Augustine on John the Baptist and on St. Stephen. VII. Augustine on the Epistle to the Romans. VIII. Miscellaneous Examples of Augustine's Interpretation of Scripture. The latter half of the work consists of Augustine's Exposition of the Sermon on the Mount, not however a mere series of quotations from Augustine, but a connected account of his sentiments on the various passages of that Sermon, interspersed with criticisms by Archbishop Trench.

SHIPWRECKS OF FAITH. Three Sermons preached before the University of Cambridge in May, 1867. Fcap. 8vo. 2s. 6d.

These Sermons are especially addressed to young men. The subjects are "Balaam," "Saul," and "Judas Iscariot," These lives are set forth as beacon-lights, " to warn us off from perilous reefs and quicksands, which have been the destruction of many, and which might only too easily be ours." The John Bull *says, "they are, like all he writes, affectionate and earnest discourses."*

TRENCH (Archbishop)—*continued.*

SERMONS Preached for the most part in Ireland. 8vo.
10s. 6d.

*This volume consists of Thirty-two Sermons, the greater part of which
were preached in Ireland; the subjects are as follow:—Jacob, a Prince
with God and with Men—Agrippa—The Woman that was a Sinner—
Secret Faults—The Seven Worse Spirits—Freedom in the Truth—Joseph
and his Brethren—Bearing one another's Burdens—Christ's Challenge to
the World—The Love of Money—The Salt of the Earth—The Armour of
God—Light in the Lord—The Jailer of Philippi—The Thorn in the Flesh
—Isaiah's Vision—Selfishness—Abraham interceding for Sodom—Vain
Thoughts—Pontius Pilate—The Brazen Serpent—The Death and Burial
of Moses—A Word from the Cross—The Church's Worship in the
Beauty of Holiness—Every Good Gift from Above—On the Hearing of
Prayer—The Kingdom which cometh not with Observation—Pressing
towards the Mark—Saul—The Good Shepherd—The Valley of Dry Bones
—All Saints.*

LECTURES ON MEDIEVAL CHURCH HISTORY.
Being the Substance of Lectures delivered in Queen's College,
London. Second Edition, revised. 8vo. 12s.

*Contents:—The Middle Ages Beginning—The Conversion of Eng-
land—Islam—The Conversion of Germany—The Iconoclasts—The
Crusades—The Papacy at its Height—The Sects of the Middle Ages—
The Mendicant Orders—The Waldenses—The Revival of Learning—
Christian Art in the Middle Ages, &c., &c.*

Tulloch.—THE CHRIST OF THE GOSPELS AND
THE CHRIST OF MODERN CRITICISM. Lectures on
M. RENAN's "Vie de Jésus." By JOHN TULLOCH, D.D.,
Principal of the College of St. Mary, in the University of St.
Andrew's. Extra fcap. 8vo. 4s. 6d.

Vaughan.—Works by the very Rev. CHARLES JOHN VAUGHAN,
D.D., Dean of Llandaff and Master of the Temple:

CHRIST SATISFYING THE INSTINCTS OF HU-
MANITY. Eight Lectures delivered in the Temple Church.
Second Edition. Extra fcap. 8vo. 3s. 6d.

*"We are convinced that there are congregations, in number unmistakably
increasing, to whom such Essays as these, full of thought and learning,
are infinitely more beneficial, for they are more acceptable, than the recognised type of sermons."*—John Bull.

THE BOOK AND THE LIFE, and other Sermons,
preached before the University of Cambridge. Third Edition.
Fcap. 8vo. 4s. 6d.

VAUGHAN (Dr. C. J.)—*continued.*

TWELVE DISCOURSES on SUBJECTS CONNECTED WITH THE LITURGY and WORSHIP of the CHURCH OF ENGLAND. Fcap. 8vo. 6s.

LESSONS OF LIFE AND GODLINESS. A Selection of Sermons preached in the Parish Church of Doncaster. Fourth and Cheaper Edition. Fcap. 8vo. 3s. 6d.

This volume consists of Nineteen Sermons, mostly on subjects connected with the every-day walk and conversation of Christians. The Spectator *styles them "earnest and human. They are adapted to every class and order in the social system, and will be read with wakeful interest by all who seek to amend whatever may be amiss in their natural disposition or in their acquired habits."*

WORDS FROM THE GOSPELS. A Second Selection of Sermons preached in the Parish Church of Doncaster. Third Edition. Fcap. 8vo. 4s. 6d.

The Nonconformist *characterises these Sermons as "of practical earnestness, of a thoughtfulness that penetrates the common conditions and experiences of life, and brings the truths and examples of Scripture to bear on them with singular force, and of a style that owes its real elegance to the simplicity and directness which have fine culture for their roots."*

LIFE'S WORK AND GOD'S DISCIPLINE. Three Sermons. Third Edition. Fcap. 8vo. 2s. 6d.

THE WHOLESOME WORDS OF JESUS CHRIST. Four Sermons preached before the University of Cambridge in November 1866. Second Edition. Fcap. 8vo. 3s. 6d.

Dr. Vaughan uses the word "Wholesome" here in its literal and original sense, the sense in which St. Paul uses it, as meaning healthy, sound, conducing to right living; and in these Sermons he points out and illustrates several of the "wholesome" characteristics of the Gospel, —the Words of Christ. The John Bull *says this volume is "replete with all the author's well-known vigour of thought and richness of expression."*

FOES OF FAITH. Sermons preached before the University of Cambridge in November 1868. Second Edition. Fcap. 8vo. 3s. 6d.

The "Foes of Faith" preached against in these Four Sermons are:—I. "Unreality." II. "Indolence." III. "Irreverence." IV. "Inconsistency."

LECTURES ON THE EPISTLE to the PHILIPPIANS. Third and Cheaper Edition. Extra fcap. 8vo. 5s.

Each Lecture is prefaced by a literal translation from the Greek of the paragraph which forms its subject, contains first a minute explanation

VAUGHAN (Dr. C. J.)—*continued.*

of the passage on which it is based, and then a practical application of the verse or clause selected as its text.

LECTURES ON THE REVELATION OF ST. JOHN.
Fourth Edition. Two Vols. Extra fcap. 8vo. 9s.

In this Edition of these Lectures, the literal translations of the passages expounded will be found interwoven in the body of the Lectures themselves. "Dr. Vaughan's Sermons," the Spectator *says, "are the most practical discourses on the Apocalypse with which we are acquainted." Prefixed is a Synopsis of the Book of Revelation, and appended is an Index of passages illustrating the language of the Book.*

EPIPHANY, LENT, AND EASTER. A Selection of
Expository Sermons.   Third Edition.   Crown 8vo.   10s. 6d.

THE EPISTLES OF ST. PAUL.   For English Readers.
PART I., containing the FIRST EPISTLE TO THE THESSALONIANS.
Second Edition.   8vo.   1s. 6d.

It is the object of this work to enable English readers, unacquainted with Greek, to enter with intelligence into the meaning, connexion, and phraseology of the writings of the great Apostle.

ST. PAUL'S EPISTLE TO THE ROMANS. The Greek
Text, with English Notes.   Fourth Edition.   Crown 8vo.   7s. 6d.

The Guardian *says of the work,—"For educated young men his commentary seems to fill a gap hitherto unfilled. . . . As a whole, Dr. Vaughan appears to us to have given to the world a valuable book of original and careful and earnest thought bestowed on the accomplishment of a work which will be of much service and which is much needed."*

THE CHURCH OF THE FIRST DAYS.
Series I. ⸱ The Church of Jerusalem.   Third Edition.
  "   II.   The Church of the Gentiles.   Third Edition.
  " III.   The Church of the World.   Third Edition.
Fcap. 8vo.   4s. 6d. each.

The British Quarterly *says, "These Sermons are worthy of all praise, and are models of pulpit teaching."*

COUNSELS for YOUNG STUDENTS.   Three Sermons
preached before the University of Cambridge at the Opening of the Academical Year 1870-71.   Fcap. 8vo.   2s. 6d.

The titles of the Three Sermons contained in this volume are:—I. "The Great Decision." II. "The House and the Builder." III. "The Prayer and the Counter-Prayer." They all bear pointedly, earnestly, and sympathisingly upon the conduct and pursuits of young students and young men generally.

VAUGHAN (Dr. C. J.)—*continued.*

NOTES FOR LECTURES ON CONFIRMATION, with suitable Prayers. Tenth Edition. Fcap. 8vo. 1s. 6d.

THE TWO GREAT TEMPTATIONS. The Temptation of Man, and the Temptation of Christ. Lectures delivered in the Temple Church, Lent 1872. Second Edition. Extra fcap. 8vo. 3s. 6d.

WORDS FROM THE CROSS: Lent Lectures, 1875; and Thoughts for these Times: University Sermons, 1874. Extra fcap. 8vo. 4s. 6d.

ADDRESSES TO YOUNG CLERGYMEN, delivered at Salisbury in September and October, 1875. Extra fcap. 8vo. 4s. 6d.

HEROES OF FAITH: Lectures on Hebrews xi. Extra fcap. 8vo. 6s.

THE YOUNG LIFE EQUIPPING ITSELF FOR GOD'S SERVICE: Sermons before the University of Cambridge. Sixth Edition. Extra fcap. 8vo. 3s. 6d.

THE SOLIDITY OF TRUE RELIGION; and other Sermons. Second Edition. Extra fcap. 8vo. 3s. 6d.

SERMONS IN HARROW SCHOOL CHAPEL (1847). 8vo. 10s. 6d.

NINE SERMONS IN HARROW SCHOOL CHAPEL (1849). Fcap. 8vo. 5s.

"MY SON, GIVE ME THINE HEART," SERMONS Preached before the Universities of Oxford and Cambridge, 1876—78. Fcap. 8vo. 5s.

Vaughan (E. T.)—SOME REASONS OF OUR CHRISTIAN HOPE. Hulsean Lectures for 1875. By E. T. VAUGHAN, M.A., Rector of Harpenden. Crown 8vo. 6s. 6d.

" His words are those of a well-tried scholar and a sound theologian, and they will be read widely and valued deeply by an audience far beyond the range of that which listened to their masterly pleading at Cambridge." —Standard.

Vaughan (D. J.)—Works by CANON VAUGHAN, of Leicester:

SERMONS PREACHED IN ST. JOHN'S CHURCH, LEICESTER, during the Years 1855 and 1856. Cr. 8vo. 5s. 6d.

VAUGHAN (D. J.)—*continued.*

CHRISTIAN EVIDENCES AND THE BIBLE. New Edition, revised and enlarged. Fcap. 8vo. cloth. 5*s.* 6*d.*

THE PRESENT TRIAL OF FAITH. Sermons preached in St. Martin's Church, Leicester. Crown 8vo. 9*s.*

Venn.—ON SOME OF THE CHARACTERISTICS OF BELIEF, Scientific and Religious. Being the Hulsean Lectures for 1869. By the Rev. J. VENN, M.A. 8vo. 6*s.* 6*d.*

These discourses are intended to illustrate, explain, and work out into some of their consequences, certain characteristics by which the attainment of religious belief is prominently distinguished from the attainment of belief upon most other subjects.

Warington.—THE WEEK OF CREATION; or, The Cosmogony of Genesis considered in its Relation to Modern Science. By GEORGE WARINGTON, Author of "The Historic Character of the Pentateuch vindicated." Crown 8vo. 4*s.* 6*d.*

"A very able vindication of the Mosaic Cosmogony by a writer who unites the advantages of a critical knowledge of the Hebrew text and of distinguished scientific attainments."—Spectator.

Westcott.—Works by BROOKE FOSS WESTCOTT, D.D., Regius Professor of Divinity in the University of Cambridge; Canon of Peterborough :

The London Quarterly, speaking of Mr. Westcott, says, "To a learning and accuracy which command respect and confidence, he unites what are not always to be found in union with these qualities, the no less valuable faculties of lucid arrangement and graceful and facile expression."

AN INTRODUCTION TO THE STUDY OF THE GOSPELS. Fifth Edition. Crown 8vo. 10*s.* 6*d.*

The author's chief object in this work has been to shew that there is a true mean between the idea of a formal harmonization of the Gospels and the abandonment of their absolute truth. After an Introduction on the General Effects of the course of Modern Philosophy on the popular views of Christianity, he proceeds to determine in what way the principles therein indicated may be applied to the study of the Gospels.

A GENERAL SURVEY OF THE HISTORY OF THE CANON OF THE NEW TESTAMENT during the First Four Centuries. Fourth Edition, revised, with a Preface on "Supernatural Religion." Crown 8vo. 10*s.* 6*d.*

The object of this treatise is to deal with the New Testament as a whole, and that on purely historical grounds. The separate books of which it is

WESTCOTT (Dr.)—*continued.*

composed are considered not individually, but as claiming to be parts of the apostolic heritage of Christians. The Author has thus endeavoured to connect the history of the New Testament Canon with the growth and consolidation of the Catholic Church, and to point out the relation existing between the amount of evidence for the authenticity of its component parts and the whole mass of Christian literature. "The treatise," says the British Quarterly, "is a scholarly performance, learned, dispassionate, discriminating, worthy of his subject and of the present state of Christian literature in relation to it."

THE BIBLE IN THE CHURCH. A Popular Account of the Collection and Reception of the Holy Scriptures in the Christian Churches. Sixth Edition. 18mo. 4s. 6d.

A GENERAL VIEW OF THE HISTORY OF THE ENGLISH BIBLE. Second Edition. Crown 8vo. 10s. 6d.

The Pall Mall Gazette *calls the work "A brief, scholarly, and, to a great extent, an original contribution to theological literature."*

THE CHRISTIAN LIFE, MANIFOLD AND ONE. Six Sermons preached in Peterborough Cathedral. Crown 8vo. 2s. 6d.

The Six Sermons contained in this volume are the first preached by the author as a Canon of Peterborough Cathedral. The subjects are:— I. "Life consecrated by the Ascension." II. "Many Gifts, One Spirit." III. "The Gospel of the Resurrection." IV. "Sufficiency of God." V. "Action the Test of Faith." VI. "Progress from the Confession of God."

THE GOSPEL OF THE RESURRECTION. Thoughts on its Relation to Reason and History. Third Edition, enlarged. Crown 8vo. 6s.

The present Essay is an endeavour to consider some of the elementary truths of Christianity, as a miraculous Revelation, from the side of History and Reason. The author endeavours to shew that a devout belief in the Life of Christ is quite compatible with a broad view of the course of human progress and a frank trust in the laws of our own minds. In the third edition the author has carefully reconsidered the whole argument, and by the help of several kind critics has been enabled to correct some faults and to remove some ambiguities, which had been overlooked before.

ON THE RELIGIOUS OFFICE OF THE UNIVERSITIES. Crown 8vo. 4s. 6d.

"There is certainly no man of our time—no man at least who has obtained the command of the public ear—whose utterances can compare with those of Professor Westcott for largeness of views and comprehensiveness of

grasp. . . . . . There is wisdom, and truth, and thought enough, and a harmony and mutual connection running through them all, which makes the collection of more real value than many an ambitious treatise."— Literary Churchman.

Wilkins.—THE LIGHT OF THE WORLD. An Essay, by A. S. WILKINS, M.A., Professor of Latin in Owens College, Manchester. Second Edition. Crown 8vo. 3*s.* 6*d.*

" *It would be difficult to praise too highly the spirit, the burden, the conclusions, or the scholarly finish of this beautiful Essay.*"—British Quarterly Review.

Wilson.—THE BIBLE STUDENT'S GUIDE TO THE MORE CORRECT UNDERSTANDING of the ENGLISH TRANSLATION OF THE OLD TESTAMENT, by Reference to the Original Hebrew. By WILLIAM WILSON, D.D., Canon of Winchester. Second Edition, carefully revised. 4to. 25*s.*

" *The author believes that the present work is the nearest approach to a complete Concordance of every word in the original that has yet been made: and as a Concordance, it may be found of great use to the Bible student, while at the same time it serves the important object of furnishing the means of comparing synonymous words, and of eliciting their precise and distinctive meaning. The knowledge of the Hebrew language is not absolutely necessary to the profitable use of the work. The plan of the work is simple: every word occurring in the English Version is arranged alphabetically, and under it is given the Hebrew word or words, with a full explanation of their meaning, of which it is meant to be a translation, and a complete list of the passages where it occurs. Following the general work is a complete Hebrew and English Index, which is, in effect, a Hebrew-English Dictionary.*

Worship (The) of God and Fellowship among Men. Sermons on Public Worship. By Professor MAURICE, and others. Fcap. 8vo. 3*s.* 6*d.*

Yonge (Charlotte M.)—Works by CHARLOTTE M. YONGE, Author of "The Heir of Redclyffe :"

SCRIPTURE READINGS FOR SCHOOLS AND FA-MILIES. 5 vols. Globe 8vo. 1*s.* 6*d.* With Comments, 3*s.* 6*d.* each.

FIRST SERIES. Genesis to Deuteronomy.

SECOND SERIES. From Joshua to Solomon.

THIRD SERIES. The Kings and Prophets.

FOURTH SERIES. The Gospel Times.

FIFTH SERIES. Apostolic Times.

YONGE (Charlotte M.)—*continued.*

Actual need has led the author to endeavour to prepare a reading book convenient for study with children, containing the very words of the Bible, with only a few expedient omissions, and arranged in Lessons of such length as by experience she has found to suit with children's ordinary power of accurate attentive interest. The verse form has been retained because of its convenience for children reading in class, and as more resembling their Bibles; but the poetical portions have been given in their lines. Professor Huxley at a meeting of the London School-board, particularly mentioned the Selection made by Miss Yonge, as an example of how selections might be made for School reading. "Her Comments are models of their kind."—Literary Churchman.

THE PUPILS OF ST. JOHN THE DIVINE. New Edition. Crown 8vo. 6s.

"Young and old will be equally refreshed and taught by these pages, in which nothing is dull, and nothing is far-fetched."—Churchman.

PIONEERS AND FOUNDERS; or, Recent Workers in the Mission Field. With Frontispiece and Vignette Portrait of Bishop HEBER. Crown 8vo. 6s.

The missionaries whose biographies are here given, are—John Eliot, the Apostle of the Red Indians; David Brainerd, the Enthusiast; Christian F. Schwartz, the Councillor of Tanjore; Henry Martyn, the Scholar-Missionary; William Carey and Joshua Marshman, the Serampore Missionaries; the Judson Family; the Bishops of Calcutta—Thomas Middleton, Reginald Heber, Daniel Wilson; Samuel Marsden, the Australian Chaplain and Friend of the Maori; John Williams, the Martyr of Erromango; Allen Gardener, the Sailor Martyr; Charles Frederick Mackenzie, the Martyr of Zambesi.

THE "BOOK OF PRAISE" HYMNAL,

COMPILED AND ARRANGED BY

LORD SELBORNE.

In the following four forms:—

A. Beautifully printed in Royal 32mo., limp cloth, price 6d.

B.   ,,   ,,   Small 18mo., larger type, cloth limp, 1s.

C. Same edition on fine paper, cloth, 1s. 6d.

Also an edition with Music, selected, harmonized, and composed by JOHN HULLAH, in square 18mo., cloth, 3s. 6d.

The large acceptance which has been given to "The Book of Praise" by all classes of Christian people encourages the Publishers in entertaining the hope that this Hymnal, which is mainly selected from it, may be extensively used in Congregations, and in some degree at least meet the desires of those who seek uniformity in common worship as a means towards that unity which pious souls yearn after, and which our Lord prayed for in behalf of his Church. "The office of a hymn is not to teach controversial Theology, but to give the voice of song to practical religion. No doubt, to do this, it must embody sound doctrine; but it ought to do so, not after the manner of the schools, but with the breadth, freedom, and simplicity of the Fountain-head." On this principle has Sir R. Palmer proceeded in the preparation of this book.

The arrangement adopted is the following:—

PART I. *consists of Hymns arranged according to the subjects of the Creed—"God the Creator," "Christ Incarnate," "Christ Crucified," "Christ Risen," "Christ Ascended," "Christ's Kingdom and Judgment," etc.*

PART II. *comprises Hymns arranged according to the subjects of the Lord's Prayer.*

PART III. *Hymns for natural and sacred seasons.*

There are 320 Hymns in all.

CAMBRIDGE:—PRINTED BY J. PALMER.

www.ingramcontent.com/pod-product-compliance
Lightning Source LLC
Chambersburg PA
CBHW020850020726
47497CB00005B/1341